Australian & New Zealand Edition

Success as a Real Estate Agent

FOR
DUMMIES
A Wiley Brand

by Terri M. Cooper
Dirk Zeller

Success as a Real Estate Agent For Dummies®

Australian and New Zealand Edition published by
Wiley Publishing Australia Pty Ltd
42 McDougall Street
Milton, Qld 4064
www.dummies.com

National Library of Australia
Cataloguing-in-Publication data:

Author:	Cooper, Terri Mary.
Title:	Success as a Real Estate Agent For Dummies / Terri M. Cooper, Dirk Zeller.
ISBN:	9780730309116 (pbk.)
	9780730309123 (ebook)
Series:	For Dummies.
Notes:	Includes index.
Subjects:	Real estate agents — Australia. Real estate agents — New Zealand. Real property — Australia. Real property — New Zealand. House buying — Australia. House buying — New Zealand. House selling — Australia. House selling — New Zealand.
Other authors/ contributors:	Zeller, Dirk.
Dewey Number:	333.330994

Typeset by diacriTech, Chennai, India

10 9 8 7 6 5 4 3 2 1

Contents at a Glance

Table of Contents

Part IV: Running a Successful Real Estate Business... 257

Introduction

Welcome! You're about to move into the league of the most successful real estate agents.

Real estate sales is the greatest business in the world. Together, we have more than 35 years in the industry as business owners and entrepreneurs, and we've yet to find a business equal to real estate sales when it comes to income potential versus capital investment. In any marketplace, a real estate agent has the opportunity to create hundreds of thousands of dollars in income. (We coach many agents and teams who earn more than $3 million per year.) An agent's income is especially significant when viewed against the capital investment required by the business. Most agents need as little as $2,000 to start up their practices. Compare that to any other business and you'll find that most involve sizeable investments and burdensome loans to buy equipment, lease space, create marketing pieces, develop business strategies and hire employees — all to achieve what is usually a smaller net profit than what a real estate agent can achieve in the first few years. It's almost too good to be true!

Because of technological advances, including the internet and social media, a new agent can create the appearance of success, marketplace stature and marketing experience, far beyond the early stages of a real estate career. This gives new agents better odds at carving out a career for themselves. The timing of your decision to enter the field of real estate or advance your career could not be better. The industry has just come out of a significant market correction, and the number of real estate agents has been greatly reduced. However, the good news is that we're now re-entering a growth phase in real estate where home values are increasing and the number of homes sold is starting to climb again.

A real estate sales career paved the way to wealth, financial independence and exciting careers for both of us. It provided a solid income, many investment opportunities, an enviable lifestyle and a platform from which we've been able to help many others achieve their own goals and dreams in life.

About This Book

This book is about becoming a successful real estate agent, for sure. It's also about acquiring sales skills, marketing skills, time-management skills, people skills, technology skills and business skills. It's about gaining more respect, achieving more recognition, making more money and closing more sales. It's a guide that helps you achieve the goals and dreams you have for yourself and your family.

We're delighted to share with you the keys we've found for real estate success, and are keen to help you avoid the mistakes we've made along the way. (We're both firm believers in the idea that we often benefit more from failures than from successes. Funnily enough, 'failing forward' can be the quickest way to long-term success. But you can learn from our failures, without having to repeat them.)

The techniques, skills and strategies we present throughout this book are the same ones we've used and tested to perfection personally and with thousands of coaching clients and hundreds of thousands of training program participants. Although technology has had an expanding influence on the real estate market in the past decade, the foundational skills of sales, time management, marketing and people skills have not changed as much. This is not a book of theory but of 'real stuff' that works and is laid out in a hands-on, step-by-step format. You can also find time-tested scripts in most sales-oriented chapters. The scripts are designed to move prospects and clients to do more business with you. (If you're a junior member of the grammar police, you may find that some scripts don't sit perfectly with you or your own way of talking or writing, but don't stress. The objective of the sales scripts is not perfect sentence structure but rather maximum persuasion of the prospect or client. Just use these scripts as a guide, a template and a starting point, and change them to suit your own personality.)

If you apply the information contained in this book with the right attitude, and if you're consistent in your practices and in your success expectations, your success in real estate sales is guaranteed.

Throughout this book we incorporate a number of style conventions, most aimed at keeping the book easy to read and a few aimed at keeping it legally accurate:

- Throughout this book, we use the term *real estate agent* to refer to a real estate sales person. In some quarters, the term 'agent' refers only to a fully licensed agent or an agency principal, but here in this book, we will use the term to refer to anyone who has completed either the entry level industry requirements or alternatively has gone through to fully licensed status.
- The word *agency* describes the office in which you work. The word *franchise* describes the brand under which you operate and promote your services. In Australia and New Zealand, both franchise brands (such as Ray White, LJ Hooker and REMAX) and marketing brands

(such as The Professionals and Century 21) operate. These allow the licensee's name to appear in all marketing material and signage. There are other agencies, for example those affiliated as Jenman agencies, where individual agents' details do not appear at all. And, in addition, we've also seen a growth of independent agencies that choose not to be under a banner at all. As you can see, you have many choices and we will help you with strategies to know which one is right for you!

- The term *client* refers to a person with whom the real estate agent or agency has a written agreement and who is committed to pay for a service which the agent supplies. When clients list a home for sale, they enter a contractual relationship with the agent who will represent their interests. That agreement is called an *agency relationship* and the seller is bound into the contract with a *listing agreement*. Usually this agreement is with the agency and the individual agent is authorised by the Principal Licensee to enter into these agreements or contracts on behalf of the agency. Hence the clients always belong to the agency, unless an alternative arrangement is stated on the employment authority — this applies to commission-only agents as well as those on salary or similar.
- Agents have a *fiduciary (primary) duty* to put their clients' interests first at all times. In each Australian state and in New Zealand, agents have a unique set of laws and practices stipulating how consumers and real estate agents work in an agency relationship. These legislated codes of practice have been reworked and clarified over the past decade. Throughout this book, when we refer to agency agreements, we're describing the real estate agent's relationship with buyers or sellers, depending upon whether the agent is the listing agent or the selling agent.
- When an agent works with a member of the public with no written agreement in place and no money changing hands, this person is termed the *customer* — for example this could be the buyer. The sales agent works with the buyer but receives no money directly (unless a buyer's agent agreement is in place) This means that, in addition to the fiduciary duty to the client, agents have a duty of care to their customer not to engage in any activity that could put the customer at risk — economically, physically or emotionally.
- Bulleted and numbered lists present important information in a quick-skim format. Watch for lists marked by numbers or check marks. They contain essential facts to remember, steps to take or advice to follow.
- Whenever we introduce a new term, we *italicise* it and follow it up with a brief definition.

Foolish Assumptions

As we have compressed so much real estate experience and coaching advice into these pages, we had to make the following assumptions about you, the reader:

- You have already completed a course to become a licensed real estate agent — either at entry level or with your full real estate licence. If not, just google real estate qualification training for your locality and there will be both industry-run and private training companies for you to contact. Be sure to ask about their courses as (like most other things) prices and quality of service vary – look for feedback and testimonials from past students.
- You're interested in working in real estate sales rather than property management. This book is about maximising your income through accelerating your real estate sales. While property management has changed after the recent market downturn, with higher salaries now being combined with greater incentives and bonuses for people in property management, this area is beyond the scope of this book. For some useful tips on property management, you can check out *Property Management Kit For Dummies*, 3rd Edition, by Robert S Griswold (Wiley).
- You are looking to rev up your real estate business, whether you're just starting out or have been in the business for a while. Some of you may be deciding which real estate company to join. Others may have already launched careers and joined good companies and are now looking for advice on how to climb the success curve faster and higher. Still others are interested in refining specific skills, such as prospecting, selling, running their businesses more efficiently or building customer loyalty.

The tips, strategies and information we give you in this book will address all of these needs, no matter where on the spectrum you are.

Icons Used in This Book

This wouldn't be a *For Dummies* book without the handy symbols that sit in the outer margin to alert you to valuable information and advice. Watch for these icons:

Why reinvent the wheel? Whenever we present a true story or a lesson that we've learned from firsthand experience, this icon flags the paragraph so you can benefit from the recollection.

When you see this icon, highlight the accompanying information. Jot it down, etch it in your memory and consider it essential to your success.

The bullseye marks on-target advice and tried-and-true approaches that save time, money and trouble as you achieve real estate success.

When we highlight a danger to avoid or just a bad idea to steer clear of, this icon sits in the margin issuing a warning sign.

Beyond the Book

In addition to the material in the print or ebook you're reading right now, this product also comes with some access-anywhere goodies on the web. Check out the free Cheat Sheet at `www.dummies.com/cheatsheet/successrealestateagentau`. In addition, take note of the extra online articles, which you can find out how to access on each of the Parts Pages. These articles give you extra insight into the real estate world.

Where to Go from Here

The beauty of this book is that you can start wherever makes the most sense for you.

If you're a newcomer to the field of real estate sales, we suggest that you start with Part I, in which we consolidate all the start-up information that you're likely to be looking for.

If you've been in the trenches for a while and simply aren't having as much success as you'd like, start with Chapter 3 or 4 and go from there.

If you're pressed for time, facing a crucial issue or grappling with a particular problem or question, just turn to the table of contents or index to find exactly the advice you're seeking.

Wherever you start, get out a pad of yellow sticky notes, a highlighter pen or your note-taking app and get ready to make this book — and all the information it contains — your own key to success. We send you off with our very best wishes!

Part I

Getting Started with Real Estate Sales Success

getting started with real estate sales success

Visit `www.dummies.com` for great For Dummies content online.

In this part . . .

- We provide an overview of the skills you need to swing the odds for success your way. Find out the basic fundamentals that place agents on the right path to reach their target.
- We guide you through the process of evaluating, choosing and joining a real estate company.
- We show you how to act and work like a top-producing agent to make your goals a reality.
- We help you research and understand the marketplace in which you're working.

Chapter 1

Discovering the Skills of a Successful Sales Agent

In This Chapter

- Defining financial success
- Understanding the role and importance of a professional real estate sales agent
- Knowing the importance of lead-generation and sales skills
- Building your success as a listing agent
- Choosing the right path to real estate success

Each agent defines sales success slightly differently. Some agents set their goals in dollars, some are attracted to the opportunity to be their own bosses and build their own businesses, and some want the personal control and freedom that a real estate career allows. Achieving success, however, requires the same basic fundamentals regardless of what motivates your move into real estate. Agents who build successful businesses share four common attributes:

- **They're consistent.** They perform success-producing activities day in and day out. Instead of working in spurts — making 50 prospecting calls in two days and then walking away from the phone for two weeks — they proceed methodically and steadily, day after day, to achieve their goals. And, instead of slamming their Facebook friends with a barrage of posts over a two-week span, they consistently post, engage, respond and add value multiple times a week.
- **They believe in the law of accumulation.** The law of accumulation is the principle that says with constant effort everything in life, whether positive or negative, compounds itself over time. No agent becomes an overnight success, but with consistency, success-oriented activities accumulate momentum and power, and lead to success every time.

- **They're lifelong learners.** The most successful agents never quit improving. Their passion for improvement is acute, and they commit the time, resources and energy it takes to constantly enhance their skills and performance. You're reading this book because you have a desire to be better, but that quest can't stop with this book. It must continue with additional reading, watching, listening and attending events to improve your skills, strategies and systems.
- **They're self-disciplined.** They have the ability to motivate themselves to do the activities that must be done. Successful agents show up daily and put in a full day of work on highly productive actions such as prospecting and lead follow-up. They make themselves do things they don't want to do so they can have things in life that they truly want. Personal discipline is a fundamental building block for success. One of the greatest things about being a real estate agent is being an independent contractor. You're the master of your domain. You're the only one who can 'require' you to show up to work. That also has a downside if you can't force or discipline yourself to do the harder success-producing actions.

You're already on the road to real estate success, demonstrated by the fact that you picked up this book to discover what it takes to become a great sales agent. This first chapter sets you on your way to success by providing an overview of the key skills that successful real estate agents pursue and possess.

Our own inauspicious beginnings

Both Dirk and Terri began their real estate careers from inauspicious beginnings, but went on to become highly successful and respected agents. They came from very different backgrounds and life experiences, but what they had in common was a burning desire to succeed and the commitment to do whatever it took to reach their goals. This was the key to their success and it can be the same for you!

On Dirk's very first listing presentation, he went to the wrong house. Can you imagine arriving at the wrong address for your first presentation? The worst part is that the man who answered the door let him in. To this day, Dirk is not sure why he was let in and allowed to begin his listing presentation. Even worse, he was nearly halfway through the presentation before he figured out the mistake! The homeowner just sat quietly listening to Dirk talk about listing his home. He actually did have an interest in selling his home in the near future, so he just listened. Dirk finally realised that he was in the wrong house when he glanced over and saw the address on a piece of mail on the table. What he had done was transpose a number on the address, which put him in the wrong house. All the while, the real seller was waiting down the street. The good news was that, in spite of this mix-up, Dirk successfully listed the man's home a few months later.

Terri's beginnings were equally unimpressive! Her real estate career started out with fear and trepidation. She had changed careers midlife and so needed to get up to speed quickly. She listened to tapes constantly (in those days, CDs weren't available!), went to every seminar she could find, picked the brains of her principal and her colleagues, read numerous books and was almost an expert — or so she thought! Everything was great (in theory) until the day came when she actually had to show a real live person through a property. She worried about what she was supposed to say, and how she should ask them to make an offer. Terri stumbled through the inspection. Then the buyers wanted to do a contract! Oh dear! She drove them back to the office to find everyone had gone home for the day — she had never written out a contract before so found a photocopied blank form, filled it in and (thankfully) it was accepted!

So, you see, in the end, it really doesn't matter where you start in your career or what mistakes you make in the early stages. Everyone makes mistakes in new endeavours. What matters most is having a plan or process that keeps you moving down the track toward your goals. You will learn so much from every mistake you make. It's called 'falling forward!' Every mistake you make will take you further along the road to success. The only real failure is doing nothing — waiting until you are perfect before you get out there and have a go. Just remember to fall forward and you will be fine!

And this book will also give you awesome advice and strategies to keep you from spinning wheels, repeating mistakes and getting nowhere fast.

Having a Monetary Target

One of the first big steps toward sales success is knowing what you want out of your real estate career. However, 'financial independence' is not a specific enough answer.

We've been in real estate, either working in direct sales or teaching, speaking, training, writing or coaching people, for many years. Between us, we've met hundreds and thousands of agents, and nearly every one started selling real estate with the same goal of 'financial independence'. Countless times we've asked questions like: 'Tell me, how do you define financial independence?' What we usually hear in response is some variation of 'So I don't have to worry about money anymore.' Or we ask, 'Why have you chosen to be in real estate?' and the answer is usually 'To make money of course!' or 'Because I love to help people.'

These answers are too vague and, if you're using them, you could very well be setting yourself up for failure!

The key to attaining financial independence is to be very clear on what this goal means to you — that is, how much, how soon and, importantly, what do you plan to do with this new-found wealth? The answers to these questions will give you your big '*why*' — and knowing the big 'why' will fuel your passion, make you resilient and guarantee your commitment to whatever it takes to succeed!

The key to eliminating money worries is establishing a financial goal — an actual dollar amount — that you need to accumulate in order to achieve the quality of life you want to enjoy. Financial independence boils down to a number. (It can be a gross number, net income, created annually or monthly from your asset base.) Set that number in your mind and then launch your career with the intention to achieve your goal by a specific date.

By having your financial goal in mind, you find clarity and can see past the hard work that lies ahead of you. When you have to endure the rejection, competition, disloyal customers, and challenges that are inevitable along the way, your knowledge about the wealth you're working to achieve helps you weather the storms of the business.

Acting and Working Like a Top-Selling Agent

Real estate agents join doctors, dentists, attorneys, accountants and financial planners in the ranks of licensed professionals who provide guidance and counsel to clients. The big difference is that most real estate agents don't view themselves as top-level professionals. Many agents, along with a good portion of the public, perceive themselves as real estate tour guides, as mere cogs in the wheel of the property sale transaction. The best agents, however, know and act differently.

The internet and the open access to real estate information have accentuated the erroneous view that agents are simply people who can organise property inspections. Consumers in the real estate market are able to find so much information online that they often view themselves as the experts. Agents are no longer seen as the gurus, the sole keepers of the information. To succeed in these technological times, we must expand our offerings and demonstrate that our services go well beyond basic real estate information and access into homes. An important thing that can't be found on the internet is personal client service, along with strong marketing and negotiation skills.

Real estate agents are fiduciary representatives and financial advisors — not people paid to unlock front doors of houses for prospective buyers. A *fiduciary* is someone who is hired to represent the interests of another. A fiduciary owes another person a special relationship of honesty, commitment, exclusivity in representation, ethical treatment and protection. Build your real estate business with a strong belief in the service and benefits you provide your clients, and you'll provide a vital professional service while being recognised as the valuable professional you are. Your professional appearance, your area expertise and your great service will be the factors that show your clients you're worthy of respect.

Serving as a fiduciary representative

Real estate agents represent the interests of their clients. As an agent, you're bound by honour, ethics and duty to work on your client's behalf to achieve the defined and desired results. This involves the following functions:

- **Defining the client's objective:** You need to start with a clear understanding of the objectives your client is aiming to achieve through the sale or purchase of property. Too many agents get into trouble by starting out with uncertainty about the interests of the people they're representing. To avoid this pitfall, turn to Chapter 9 for advice and questions you can use when interviewing and qualifying prospects.

- **Delivering counsel or guidance:** In the same way that solicitors counsel clients on the most effective way to proceed legally, it's your job to offer similarly frank professional guidance and information so that your clients reach the real estate outcomes they seek.

  You need to be able to steer your clients toward good decisions regarding the value of their homes, the pricing strategies they adopt, the marketing approaches they follow and the way their contract is negotiated in order to maximise their financial advantage. The chapters in Part III of this book help you develop the knowledge you need in these areas.

- **Diagnosing problems and offering solutions:** A good agent, like a good doctor, spends a great deal of time examining situations, determining problems and prescribing solutions. In an agent's case, the focus is on the condition and health of the home a client is trying to buy or sell. The examination involves an analysis of the property's condition, location, neighbourhood, local schools, street appeal, landscaping, market competitiveness, market demand, availability for showing, and value versus price. The diagnosis involves an educated analysis of what a home is worth and what changes or corrections are necessary.

Some say that agents should present all the options available to their clients and then recommend the course of action they feel is best. This is a more collaborative approach. By doing this, agents allow their clients to take responsibility for making the final decision. An alternate approach is the diagnostic and prescriptive approach because it positions you better as the expert. However, using this approach leaves you vulnerable to receiving some or all of the blame when clients chose the wrong option. No matter whether your style is advisory or assertive, your success in guiding your clients to a successful outcome is based on your expert analysis and application of the variables to the marketplace.

Many agents get into trouble because they lack the conviction to tell clients the truths they don't want to hear. If a home is overpriced or not ready for showing, or if an offer is too low for seller consideration, it's the agent's job to speak up with sound advice. In these situations, you could get blamed for a poor outcome. You may also run the risk of doing all this work and not getting compensated for the time you invested.

To prepare yourself for the task, flip to Chapter 9, which helps you determine and advise sellers regarding a home's ideal price; Chapter 10, which helps you counsel clients regarding changes they need to make before showing their property; and Chapter 12, which helps you counsel clients through the final purchase or sale negotiation.

- **Troubleshooting:** Unavoidably, many times you have to be the bearer of bad news. Market conditions may shift, and the price on a seller's home may need to come down. A buyer may need to sweeten initial offers to gain seller attention. A loan request may be rejected, or you may need to confront sellers because the animal smells in their home may be turning buyers away. Or, a home that buyers really want may end up selling to someone else.

At times like these, your calm attitude, solution-oriented approach, and strong agent-client relationship will win the day. Chapter 14 is full of advice for achieving and maintaining the kind of relationship excellence that smooths your transactions and leads to long-lasting and loyal clients.

Guiding financial decisions

When you help clients make real estate decisions, your advice has a long-lasting effect on your clients' financial health and wealth. Their decisions based on your information and guidance will affect their short-term equity as well as their long-term financial independence. In most cases, home equity is the single largest asset that people own. Your ability to guide clients to properties that match their needs and desires, that fit within their budgets, and that give them long-term gain from minimal initial investment impacts their financial health and wealth for years to come.

In your early years, many of your clients may be first-time sellers and buyers who are taking their first steps into the world of major financial transactions. Guide them well and they'll remain clients and word-of-mouth ambassadors for years to come. See Chapter 14 for more information about keeping clients for life.

Don't give specific financial advice unless you're qualified to do so — that is, you hold a financial services licence and are a qualified financial planner.

Avoiding the role of Designated Door Opener

Before the advances of the internet, the consumer's only avenue to information about homes for sale was through a real estate agent. Every other week, agents received long lists presenting information on properties for sale, with each new entry accompanied by a small, grainy, black-and-white picture.

Today, consumers can go online instead of going to a real estate office to launch their real estate searches. With a few keystrokes and mouse clicks, they have access to a greatly expanded version of the kind of information that agents used to control. However, when consumers discover a home they want to see, they must contact either the owner or an agent to gain inside access. This is where things get tricky.

Ten years ago, only a tiny percentage of buyers found the home they wanted to purchase on their own through the internet. Nowadays, the vast majority of buyers find their home online themselves and then contact a real estate agent.

Often a consumer signs off the web and notes the open for inspection times or contacts an agent to get inside the home, as if the agent is simply an entry device. As an agent, you need to demonstrate special skills to engage the customer. Then you need to add value to your skills by having inside market knowledge, keeping up with trends in the marketplace, and being aware of technological advances. With this added know-how, you have an edge over other agents, which then allows you to convert the inquiry into a committed client for your services.

Agents as necessary evils: A mindset that comes and goes

The mindset that agents are overpaid and unnecessary to the real estate sale process takes hold of consumers every now and then. This mindset gains momentum especially when a robust market leads to low numbers of property listings and the quick sale of homes that often receive multiple offers during the short time they're on the market.

This mindset has also increased in intensity and breadth with expanded online access to real estate information.

As the real estate market continues to gain momentum, changes to a more normalised or even sellers' market will put additional pressure on agents to innovate and expand services. When times are booming, a segment of consumers and new homebuilders begins to question the value of the agent's services against the associated fees and commissions. During the best of market times, some home-builders even go so far as to sell their houses as private sellers, thus avoiding the agent's costs.

The silver lining is that when times are good, so many properties are moving that the few listings affected by the 'agent-is-unnecessary' mindset hardly limit opportunity. Plus, booms don't last forever. When the market swings back and forth, as it will many times during your career, you need to be prepared to adjust your offerings.

Winning Customers and Clients

Imagine that you're on a game show and you're given just seconds to provide the most important response of your career. Imagine that you're asked to write down the answer to this question: 'What is the function that makes or breaks a real estate agent's sales success?' Okay, time's up. How did you respond?

The moneymaking reply is: 'Creating customers'. How did you score?

Perhaps you thought the answer would be customer service. If so, you gave the same answer that more than 95 per cent of new agents give. Customer service is important, but the most important activity for you is to find your customers in the first place! Sadly, only a rare few agents see customer creation as the golden approach that it is.

Understanding the importance of lead generation to your business

You have to be excellent at customer development *and* customer service. However, in terms of priority, you have to first be exemplary at lead generation. Following are a few reasons:

- **You can't serve customers if you don't spend time and effort to attract them in the first place.** And because customer-service excellence results from customer-service experience, customer development is a necessary prerequisite to outstanding customer service.

- **Most consumers have been provided with such poor service that their expectations are remarkably low.** When service providers do what they say they'll do in the agreed-upon time frame, consumers are generally content with the service they receive. An internet-based customer, which is a growing segment, wants ease of service, faster service, and lower-cost service. The truth is that competing on the first two is better than the lower-cost service model. The real estate industry is more personalised in the service it renders than many other internet-based businesses. Responsiveness is one of the keys to success in the internet realm. Certainly you want to develop the kind of expertise that delivers exemplary, outstanding service, but if you commit from the get-go to do what you said you'd do when you said you'd do it, your delivery will be better than most.
- **Between creating customers and delivering service, customer creation is the more complex task.** Customer creation requires sales skills and ongoing, consistent, persistent prospecting for clients. It requires marketing, promotion and branding of yourself and your service offerings. To develop customers inexpensively and effectively, you have to gain the level of skill and comfort necessary to pick up the phone and call people you know (or even people you don't know) to ask them for the opportunity to do business with them or to refer you to others who may be in the market for your service. It also requires a level of encouragement and interaction via social media avenues. Plus, it requires watching for clues about life changes (think: New baby, kids going off to university, divorce) in those social-media interactions.
- **If you attract the right kinds of customers into your business, your clients will match well with your expertise and abilities, and service will become an easier and more natural offering.** If you attract the right type of customers, you'll also reap greater quantity and quality of referrals.

- **The only alternative to devoting your time and energy to customer development through some form of direct prospecting is to guide people to your website, social-media sites, office or phone line through promotion and marketing.** This can be costly and involve plenty of trial and error. The marketing approach can be effective, but it requires a lot of money and often generates leads with a long sales cycle. For new agents, this approach takes too long and many give up and move on to another career. This is especially true for internet-based buyer leads. Most new agents come into the real estate industry undercapitalised, so the marketing approach takes longer to implement. Making time for the tried-and-true fundamentals of direct prospecting is the best way to build your client base and do it inexpensively.

Developing sales ability to win customers

The single most important skill for a real estate sales agent is sales ability, and sales ability is how you win clients. Your sales ability is based on how effective you are in generating prospects, following up on those prospects to secure appointments, preparing for those appointments, conducting the appointments to secure an exclusive agency listing agreement and then providing service to that recently created client. People also base your ability on how quickly you can accomplish all of this.

Because you're holding this book, we're willing to bet that you've either just come out of training to receive your real estate license or you're in the early days of your career. In either case, decide right now to master the skills of selling in order to fuel your success.

In our view, sales skills in the real estate industry are not always at a high level. So much effort and emphasis has been placed on technology and social-media training in real estate that companies and agents have sometimes lost sight of the sales skills and sales strategies that are foundational to success in a sales-based industry.

We coach some of the best and highest-earning agents, and even they believe that continually upgrading their sales skills is vital. Many agents practice their prospecting strategies or listing presentations, but still never feel they've really nailed their sales skills. The difference between these high-earning agents and other agents is that the high-earning agents realise that sales skills are vital to success, and they continuously seek excellence in this area.

How times have changed

Look at the following breakdown of a great presentation today, compared to what one may have looked like in days long past.

The big difference: Today's best agents spend nearly three-quarters of the presentation giving prospects a reason to say yes — by focusing on the prospect's situation and needs and how the agent can provide the best solution. Yesterday's agents spent virtually no time defining their clients' situations or their own unique solutions. Instead, they spent nearly three-quarters of the presentation making the sale and going for a high-pressure close. We've come a long way!

Today's presentation time allocation	Time allocation in days long past
40% Building trust and confirming needs	10% Building rapport
30% Presenting your benefits and advantages	20% Qualifying
20% Discussing price	30% Presenting
10% Closing or getting confirmation	40% Closing

To follow the high-earning agent's example, make it your priority to develop and constantly improve your sales skills for the following reasons:

- **To secure appointments:** Chapter 4 provides practically everything you need to know about winning leads and appointments through prospecting and follow-up activities.
- **To persuade expired, withdrawn and 'for-sale-by-owner' (FSBO) listings to move their properties to your business:** Chapter 7 is full of secrets and tips to follow as you pursue this lucrative and largely untouched field.
- **To make persuasive presentations that result in positive buying decisions:** Chapter 9 helps you with every step from prequalifying prospects to planning your presentation. It's packed with tips for perfecting your skills, addressing and overcoming objections, and ending with a logical and successful close.

Knowing that the market doesn't dictate success

In robust market conditions, leads are abundant and relatively easy to attract, especially buyer leads. But when the market slows, as it inevitably will, real estate success becomes less automatic. Only great sales skills guarantee that you — rather than some other agent — will win clients no matter the market conditions. The best agents make more money in a challenging market than they do in a robust market. Agents who have great sales skills will also build loyalty and clients will stick with them in the boom times as well.

Regardless of economics, every market contains real estate buyers and sellers. No matter how slow the economy, people always need and want to change homes. Babies are born. Managers get transferred. Couples get married. People divorce. And with these transitions, real estate opportunities arise for those with the best sales skills.

The way to build immunity to shifting market conditions is to arm yourself with skills in prospecting, lead follow-up, presentations, objection handling, and closing. The information in Part II of this book guides you to success.

Becoming a Listing Agent

In real estate, the minute you stop prospecting (looking for listings) is the minute your business starts to go downhill. It is often easier in your early days to build your business by working primarily with buyers. However, this can't be your long-term business strategy (unless, of course, you're working as a buyer's agent). In time, you need to begin to secure your own listings — after that, you begin your climb to real estate's pinnacle position, which is that of a listing agent.

Listing a property is usually much more difficult than attracting the buyer and closing the sale. Without listings, you and your office have no stock to sell — which means no source of income! Listing agents are in high demand in an office, and unless you have purposely chosen to work primarily with buyers, then the position of top lister is what you should be aiming at.

In many agencies the commission split is weighted in favour of the agent who secures the listing, rather than the one who finds the buyer — yet another powerful reason to continually work to improve your listing skills!

Typically a larger percentage of referral business will be buyer-based. This means that you need to eventually develop a method outside of referrals to create and attract listings.

To create long-term success, a high quality of life and a strong real estate business, you need to set as your goal eventually joining the elite group — comprised of fewer than 5 per cent of all agents — who are listing agents. The advantages are many:

- **Multiple streams of income:** Listings generate interest and trigger additional transactions. Almost the minute you announce your listing by putting a sign in the ground, showing the property on your website, and placing the listing in generic real estate websites like `www.realestate.com.au`, `www.domain.com.au` or `www.realestate.co.nz`, you'll start receiving calls, emails and texts from active buyers; calls from neighbours; inquiries from drive-by traffic; and queries from people wanting to live in the area. These leads or inquiries represent current and future business opportunities that only arise when you have a listing with your name on it.
- **Promotional opportunity:** A listing gives you a reason to advertise and draw the attention of prospects whom you can convert to clients or future prospects. And when your listing sells, you can spread the word of your success with another round of communication to those in the neighbourhood, on social media, and throughout your sphere of influence.
- **A business multiplier.** Talk to any listing agent and you'll have this fact confirmed: One listing equals more than one sale, because showing a property creates opportunity to meet more prospective sellers.

Much of the information in this book focuses on developing listings, because to achieve top-level sales success, listings are the name of the game.

Selecting a Pathway to Success

Agents typically follow one of these four basic approaches in the quest to achieve real estate success:

- **Become a workaholic.** The vast majority of agents who generate a reasonable income achieve their success by turning their careers into a 7-day-a-week, 24-hour-a-day job. They answer emails, texts, private messages and business phone calls day and night; they make themselves constantly available to prospects and clients; and they work on demand with no restraints or boundaries because of technology.

- **Buy clients.** The second-most-frequent pathway to success is to buy business through marketing campaigns. Marketing can be a valuable tool, but you must monitor, track and count the results (or return on investment — ROI), because this is a risky strategy, especially for new agents. You have to be consistent in your marketing and branding. You can't start and stop campaigns. Some agents buy their way to top-level real estate success by investing in large branding or marketing campaigns — billboards with their names and faces on them, thousands of direct mailers, expensive ad schedules and all kinds of promotions. The challenge is the risk-versus-reward position, and earlier in your career the risk is even greater. Others buy their way to the top by discounting their commissions. By offering themselves at the lowest prices, these agents eliminate the need to emphasise their skills, abilities and expertise. (And by reducing their commission rate when asked by a seller, they demonstrate that their negotiating skills are not so good!)
- **Take the shady road.** Another avenue to real estate financial success is to abandon ethics and just go for the deal and the resulting money. Unlike the vast majority of agents who advise and advocate for their clients, agents who take this route choose not to be bound by ethics or any codes of conduct. They put their own needs first and put their clients' best interests in distant second place. Fortunately, these agents are few and far between — and their careers are often short-lived!
- **Build a professional services business.** The fourth and best pathway is to create a well-rounded, professional services business not unlike that of a doctor, dentist, attorney or accountant. The balance of prospecting and marketing is essential to reach this level. Very few agents follow this route, yet the ones who do are the ones who earn the largest sums of money — some exceeding $1 million annually while also having high-quality lives and time for friends and family. Plus, when they're ready to bow out of the industry, they have a business asset they can sell to another agent. (See the sidebar 'Mining gold from your professional services business' for more details on creating an asset you can sell.)

This is the route we urge you to follow. Each of the following chapters in this book tells you exactly how to build your own professional services business.

Mining gold from your professional services business

The best professionals provide ongoing services to loyal clients who wouldn't think of taking their business elsewhere. These professionals develop reputations and client loyalty that reside with that agent or with their agency. Doing more than just earning an income and building a clientele, these professionals build an asset that they can sell, which allows them to receive compensation from the value of the successful businesses they've built.

A real estate agent who builds a well-rounded, successful business can enjoy a similarly lucrative sale. In fact, your objective should be to build the kind of business that you can sell at the completion of your real estate career.

Chapter 2

Selecting the Right Company

In This Chapter

- Weighing the pros and cons of different types of real estate companies
- Knowing the roles of agency players and the rules of the house
- Choosing and joining your agency team

Before you sign on with a real estate company, you need to take time to look well beneath the surface and beyond first impressions to determine whether the company is, in fact, the right one for you.

Most agents, whether new or experienced, don't invest enough time in evaluating and analysing companies, principals, managers, and even the franchise reputation if they're looking at joining one of the big players. This is often because they have no idea of what they need to ask. In this chapter, we help you to do the homework, compare the opportunities, make the choice and establish a winning partnership.

Noting the Evolution of Real Estate Offices

When Terri is training new agents, she jokingly talks about her experiences in the 'olden days' — the mid-1990s — when no agents had computers (only the admin people did), none had mobile phones and no-one had even heard of 'open houses'. How times have changed!

Real estate offices have evolved from the sprawling buildings where every agent had their own workstation, cubicle or private office. Although some offices are still arranged this way, many real estate offices are morphing into a more stop-and-go model. Agents on the go share spaces for which they may pay a monthly fee, usually in return for a larger share of commission.

Many agents even work remotely from a home office and may only come into the office once a week for the sales meeting. Their activities are mobile because of technological advances in access to information and paperless documents and transactions. Even agents who need staff or help for administrative functions are investigating virtual assistants, who can work from any location — even overseas, from countries like the Philippines. This is proving very successful, especially if communication from both parties is clear and precise.

Some agencies who allow their licensed agents to work from home don't require these agents to even come to weekly team meetings or training sessions. If you're new to the real estate business, stay away from these offices — doing it alone is too hard!

If you're a new agent, you really need to be working within a team of motivated, enthusiastic professionals. This gives you the opportunity to not only be mentored and supported but also learn heaps, as you listen to other agents prospecting, negotiating and building client relationships. If you have little real estate experience, start in an office where you have to come into work every single day in a supportive environment. Although you can access some great online resources and webinars to build your skills quickly, working alongside experienced agents every day is the fastest way to learn your craft.

When you're experienced, you may like to try the 'work from home' option, although the downside of this freedom is that you need to be disciplined and self-motivated to access ongoing skills training regularly. Real estate today is a constantly moving field and it is vital to keep abreast of the changes.

Factoring All Your Options

An agent choosing an agency isn't a whole lot different than a consumer choosing an agent. All the choices can look good (often they all look very much the same!), and they all offer a wide variety of opportunities. What's more, they all tell you that they're the best. So how do you choose?

Choose by weighing the benefits to you, rather than focusing on aspects such as size and location. What advantages can you count on in terms of training, continuing education, lead-generation opportunities, opportunities to host open houses, social-media positioning, and access to good market share by joining one company rather than another? You should also check the search engine optimisation of the company website for your market (see Chapter 11 for more on how to do this).

Check the technology tools and systems that the agency provides for free as well as those you will need to pay for. Most successful agents these days could not imagine life without their customer relationship manager (CRM). A CRM is a flexible, easy-to-use, web-based system that streamlines everything you need to run a successful real estate agency day to day. The system lets you manage sales, listings, customer relationships, contacts and reporting, wherever you are and whenever you like. Many CRM options are available online, so you can take advantage of the one your agency uses or check out `mydesktop.com.au`, `www.lockedon.com`, or `www.propertysuite.co.nz`.

Check which CRM system your chosen office recommends. Is this an expense for you or is it provided free? Who trains you on the effective use of this technology? These are all important questions for you to ask.

Choosing residential or commercial

Differences abound in real estate companies: The biggest difference being whether the product the company focuses on is residential or commercial real estate. While real estate sales professionals can legally sell any type of real estate, whether residential properties or commercial properties or even businesses, usually a company will specialise in one of these areas.

Most licensing courses in Australia and New Zealand focus on residential sales skills, legislation and contracts, so if you're leaning towards a career in commercial real estate, be prepared to commit to very structured additional training and mentoring. This will be provided by the company you join.

Residential

A residential company primarily sells houses, townhouses, units and apartments. These properties may be 'off the plan', newly constructed or existing properties. Agents aren't precluded from other real estate activity in the commercial realm but usually find that leaving this market to specialists who have received training in this area is best.

Commercial

Commercial real estate companies tend to focus on larger commercial deals. They frequently leave the smaller-scale multi-dwellings (up to around four apartments) to the residential agents and companies because of lower sale prices and lower demand for complex financing options.

Commercial companies in large and mid-size markets do the majority of the commercial leases of retail, industrial and office space. They are the ones who handle the listing and sale of office buildings, retail centres, industrial buildings and large land sales.

Enthusiasm, coffee and muffins: Figuring out what makes a good office

One way to evaluate a real estate office is to pay attention to the following:

- **Energy and enthusiasm:** It takes passion to succeed at essential real estate activities like prospecting. If you surround yourself with agents who lack energy and enthusiasm for the business, it will affect your performance.

  When trying to determine whether an office has energy and enthusiasm, find out whether agents are excited to come to work. Notice the agents' demeanour and energy levels when you go in for your interview — is the office full of good vibes? Are the agents friendly but focused on their work? Notice whether the office has a whiteboard where listings and sales for the month are recorded and, if so, look to see if this board is full or empty. Are only a few names covering the entire board, or is the team represented evenly? If you can start with other new agents, it can help with camaraderie and commonality. When the going gets tough — and it will — it's good to have a buddy.

- **Experienced manager:** As a newer agent, you can benefit greatly from a manager who knows the ropes and has experience taking agents to higher levels of production. Ask the following question: 'Would I be having regular coaching or meeting with either the principal or the sales manager to help me to evaluate my performance and improve my results?' Succeeding on your own is hard, so the right answer can dramatically affect your career arc.

  You're looking for a manager who has a track record of building successful agents from new agents. Effective managers have low failure rates with new agents and see more than 40 per cent of their new agents become successful. Sadly, industry stats show that fewer than 20 per cent of agents last more than two years in the business. A manager who can give you time frames and statistics on his agents' success is someone well worth spending time with.

- **Listings inventory:** Do all inquiries for general property and/or listing opportunities go to the agents on *roster*, meaning whoever is on roster at the time of the inquiry gets the lead, or does the company spread them around to all agents? (*Roster time* is when agents are assigned times to take inbound calls or meet with walk-in prospects. The task is usually assigned on a rotating schedule in shifts that last several hours.) As a newer agent, you ideally want a company that spreads the wealth, as you may only be rostered for a minimum number of hours each week. As an established, successful agent, you want the opposite. An established inventory in an office gives you the opportunity to learn by assisting at open houses taking property inquiries. For guidance in increasing your listing inventory, turn to Chapter 4.

- **Reputation:** Although you can't count on your company's reputation to do your work for you, you can bet that a positive reputation will always open doors for you.
- **Training focus:** Look into how well the company handles the two major areas of training: Initial training (so you can earn an income) and ongoing training (so you can build and grow your business). Training options have exploded in the past few years, especially with online classes and programs, videos, webinars and other opportunities. The quickest way to increase your skills is to immerse yourself in as many of these as possible!

When they're selecting an agency, most new agents don't focus enough on the company's training programs because they get wrapped up in the 'what's my commission split' game. If, through good training, you're able to master the skills you need to excel, your income can be unlimited. However, if you don't, you have no chance.

Every company says it offers good training. It's your job to look under the hood to see for yourself. To do that, ask these three questions:

- **What's the loss ratio for new agents?** The *loss ratio* is the number of agents who fail after completing the agency's training program. This ratio tells you the effectiveness of the company's new-agent training program (if, of course, one is offered!). Looking at these numbers is the best way of discovering the success rate for new agents in that office — it may be difficult to discover but try asking the question in a friendly conversational way.
- **What is the per-person production ratio?** The average production by the salespeople in the company tells you who you're likely to be surrounded by on a day-to-day basis. It clearly illustrates the results of the training programs. You're looking for results. To have training for the sake of training is worthless. The question is what results are achieved in terms of income and quality service to clients. A company that claims to have excellent training but has low agent performance is fooling itself and its agents.

Check out premier online training

Online training is convenient because it can be accessed from your home. When Terri came into the industry, the training was almost completely from the United States, and mostly focused on general sales motivation rather than specific real estate sales skills. However, these days the training in Australia for agents is second to none, with the likes of Tom Panos, Mark Dwyer, Glenn Twiddle, Jet Xavier and so many more. The Brand You blog provides a handy list of Australia's best trainers (which includes Terri!) — just go to `brandyoublog.com.au/2012/08/19/20-most-influential-real-estate-trainers-coaches-and-leaders-in-australia-for-2012`. If you're based in New Zealand, check out `www.salescoach.co.nz` and `www.johnabbott.co.nz`.

Another popular way to learn is to watch the many YouTube training videos available. Just do a search for the topic you need on the YouTube website (`www.youtube.com`), or use your favourite search engine to search for 'online real estate training' — you will be amazed at how many opportunities there are.

- **How do the agents segment into income brackets?** The answer to this question tells you whether the company's ongoing training is building the capabilities of all agents or only a few. For example, you'd want to avoid the kind of agency where only a few agents are earning good amounts while everyone else is just scraping by.

Work out what your desired annual income is and opt for a company where a reasonable group of agents earns this — you then know that you earning the same (if not more) is entirely possible. If 80 per cent of agents are making less than $50,000 a year, the company is likely a poor fit for a success-oriented agent like yourself. This figure could be a result of poor agent performance, too many agents vying for the business or perhaps even the geographic area having little turnover of property.

Consider the rules you'll be playing by

In Australia and New Zealand, real estate agents follow two basic sets of rules:

- The first set are legislated by government bodies that are authorised to regulate the industry — for example, the Office of Fair Trading in Queensland, which oversees the *Property Agent and Motor Dealers Act 2000* with special emphasis on the PAMD Code of Conduct. (At the time of writing, this Act is soon to be replaced by the *Property Occupations Act*, which will just relate to real estate agents and letting agents.) Similar government bodies exist in each Australian state and territory as well as in New Zealand.

- The second set of rules has been established by the regulatory bodies that oversee the real estate industry in New Zealand and in every Australian state and territory. These bodies are generally focused on consumer protection, with published codes of conduct for all agents.

In Australia, the Real Estate Institute of Australia (REIA) is the peak body for the state and territory institutes, with each member institute required to accept a strict code of conduct. Check the REIA website (`www.reia.com.au`) for contact details for the relevant institute in your area. In New Zealand, check out the Real Estate Agents Authority (`www.reaa.govt.nz`).

The main difference between these two sets of rules is that the government ones are a product of legislation, and agents who don't abide by these codes are subject to fines and/or prosecution. On the other hand, the rules of conduct specified by the regulatory bodies are recommendations for best practice, but not legally enforceable.

The relevant government body can audit a real estate company's files at any time and, if paperwork doesn't conform to regulations, can levy fines or, worse, close the agency down until lapses are corrected.

As well as the codes of conduct set out by their relevant body, individual agencies will also have their own internal rules. When you're interviewing with a company, you can request a copy of their rules, their policies and procedures manual or their new-agent handbook or induction manual, to find out how they expect you to work, and then actually read it before you make a commitment to joining the company. If the company can't produce one, read the lack of response as a clue about its level of organisation.

The following sections fill you in on some other aspects of house rules you may encounter.

A dollar for you, a dollar for me: Commission split arrangements

In most areas, commissions are negotiable. You or your agency is the one who determines your fees — although in some areas, commissions are only negotiable up to a maximum cap. If the regulations don't outlaw it, some agents charge higher commissions because they're worth more. They can demonstrate to clients a higher level of value and service, which allows them to charge these higher commissions.

You then need to check how this commission is split between you and your agency.

New agents all seek a universal formula for commission splits (and one that's, of course, most beneficial for them), but none exists. Each agency is different.

The following list presents some of the most common commission options you may see in the industry:

- **The debit/credit system:** This is where new agents are given a certain amount of income each week. When they start to make sales and earn commissions, this income is recovered by the agency.
- **The graduated split:** The graduated split is the most common compensation package. You start at an approximately 50/50 split, which is increased to 60/40 and upward incrementally as you become more productive and your earnings reach company-established levels for graduation.
- **The 90 to 100 per cent commission:** Colloquially, this is known as the rent-a-desk arrangement. Agents on these high levels of commission pay a flat amount monthly to rent space and purchase services from the company. From there, they cover all their own costs and retain 90 to 100 per cent of all the commissions they generate.

  The 90 to 100 per cent commission arrangement can be risky for a new agent because you're committed to monthly fees whether or not you're making any sales. You really need to be well established and pretty successful (at least four sales each month) to do well under this system, and for that reason we don't recommend it for new agents. The risk is too great for beginners because of their lack of experience in creating leads and opportunities for income.

Brokerage or agency fees: Don't bite the hand that feeds you

After compensation arrangements are in place, most brokers and principals add fees to help cover their expenses. Among the most common fees to expect are transaction fees and franchise fees, as follows:

- **Transaction fees:** Just be aware that many agencies also charge agents a per-transaction fee of somewhere between $150 and $200 to cover the cost of processing the paperwork that accompanies a real estate sale.
- **Insurance fees:** Each agent is also covered by professional indemnity insurance. In a traditional commission split arrangement, this is absorbed by the agency principal for all staff, but in circumstances where the agent is an independent contractor within the agency — as in most REMAX agencies, for example — this is something that the agent must budget for.

- **Franchise fees:** If you join a real estate franchise, the individual agencies are expected to pay approximately 10 per cent of the gross agency revenue every time they complete a transaction. The percentage is established by the franchise contract. It doesn't graduate or fluctuate based on your productivity.

What really matters? Looking at size, online presence and market share

Sometimes, size can make up for other deficiencies in real estate companies, and here's why:

- **Companies with a large number of agents create a large listing inventory.** This may mean you're given the chance to work open houses for other agents in your office if they don't have the time to service all their own listings. While you may not be financially rewarded for this — the arrangement will be based on an individual agreement between you and the listing agent — it is a great opportunity to gain experience and possible client contacts for the future. (Again, this is up to your agreement with the listing agent — they may consider all leads belong to them.)
- **Large companies enjoy economies of scale, allowing them to provide a greater degree of service at a lower price per agent.** As a result, they can offer more training, more marketing and more exposure than smaller companies can afford to provide.
- **Because of their size, large companies can often negotiate better rates for online marketing ads, website-development costs and click-through ad banners.** However, large companies follow no hard-and-fast rule for how they direct these savings. Some companies decide to turn a larger profit margin for the company. Others — the ones you'll most want to join — pass on the benefits to their clients and agents.
- **Large companies often (but not always) hold a dominant portion of market share in their communities.** As a result, they have the most prominent reputations and earn the greatest slice of business. They tend to have more inquiries for appraisals, which can really help a newer agent.

Some boutique agencies work hard to control a small marketplace for themselves, which also can be very profitable and a very smart strategy. If you decide to join one of the larger agencies, you can still adopt the boutique mentality and strive to become known as the area expert. In other words, don't spread yourself too wide, because your client servicing ability will suffer.

In the end, you should base your choice on the office attributes (in particular office culture and training opportunities) rather than on the size of the real estate office. However, when two companies have equal attributes, let size tip your decision when you're starting out.

Prioritising your values and expectations

Before you can determine whether a company is a good match for you, you have to be clear about your own values and expectations so you can see if they're shared and supported by the company you choose to work with.

Know your values

Ask yourself: What are your core values? What beliefs and principles guide your life? What would you hold dear even if it proved to be a competitive disadvantage in the marketplace? Even if the marketplace or business climate changed, what aspects of how you work are non-negotiable?

When Terri started in real estate, she came from a professional background, and being seen as a person of integrity was vital to her. So she was immediately attracted to a real estate agency in Brisbane with the motto of 'Ethics in real estate'. Make sure the office you choose has a culture and values that resonate with your own.

When choosing an agency, know what you stand for, what you honour and what you believe in. After you study yourself, you can then study the values of the company you're considering to ensure that your belief systems align.

Establish your expectations

What do you expect from yourself over the next 6 to 12 months? What do you expect from your company over the same time period? What will your new company expect from you? What does it consider to be the minimum standard for new-agent production? What does it consider to be average, or good, production? What do you need to earn in income to make this worthwhile for you? What is the most that anyone has ever produced in the company? What is the most anyone has done in your market? Taking some time out to consider these questions for yourself will help you succeed.

Also, beyond expectations for the next year, we suggest looking a few years down the road. What are the market predictions for your area over the next few years?

Before you choose a company, align your expectations with the company's by taking these steps:

- **Set your goals and expectations for the upcoming year.** Establish your targets for gross income, number of transactions, number of listings taken and sold, and number of buyer sales. These are your *key performance indicators* (KPIs), and they can help you keep track of where you're sitting each month.
- **Know the expectations and typical production levels that exist within the company you're considering.** If your targets are high, you need to join a company where established inventories and support systems help you jump-start your business for quick success. If your aims are lower, you need to be sure that they match company expectations for new agents.

After you establish your goals, keep them in front of you at all times. Carry them with you. Put them on your screen saver, program them into your smartphone, and write them on index cards and stick them on your sun visor, bathroom mirror or anywhere else they'll catch your eye repeatedly throughout the day.

Narrowing Your Agency Short List

When you've done an overall 'due diligence' on your agency options (refer to preceding section), you want to shrink your list down to your top two or three firms quickly so you can really study each one. The upcoming sections help you with your decision.

Do your homework

Follow these steps as you research each of your top-choice companies:

1. **Rank your top-choice agencies based on your views as a consumer.**

   Before you colour your opinion with facts or market statistics, ask yourself: What is each company's reputation? Based only on information available to the general public, what impression does the company make? We suggest you do this because when you join a firm, you automatically acquire this reputation.

2. **Evaluate each company's market share.**

   Determine the portion of all real estate business that each firm captures in its geographic area. Then figure out what percentage of the market it commands in the specialised area in which you'll be working. (See the sidebar 'Determining market share' for some how-to information.)

Determining market share

If you're into figures and stats, you'll likely get a kick out of determining an agency's market share. Even if, like most agents, you tend to go with your gut feel, taking a step back and looking at market share is worthwhile.

Before selecting a real estate company, find out how well it competes in its market area by determining the share of the market it commands. (If the company you're considering has more than one office, work out the numbers for the office you're likely to join.)

To assess market share, find out how many listings the company you're considering took last year. How many listings did it sell? How many houses did it fail to sell?

Then ask each company you interview with to provide you with its statistics. Any company with a competitive advantage knows and wants to share its statistics, and many are also willing to provide comparisons between themselves and their competition. Compare each agency's statistics, looking not just at listings the agency took on, but also how many it sold.

When just starting out, Terri chose inner-city Brisbane as her target area — not only did this area feature many heritage-listed and character homes (which she personally loved), but it was also an area that was attracting an increasing number of young professionals, anxious to move close to the city lights and renovate their dream home. The market was continually moving upwards — an exciting trend to experience! So Terri focused on a narrow geographical area, and then researched and drove that area daily. Soon she was the area specialist, and many more listings came her way!

3. **Assess how production is shared within each company.**

   Ask whether a number of agents contribute to the company's success or whether a few agents or even just one person carries production.

   Terri has seen offices that advertise amazing results but, when you look deeper, these results don't look so amazing — they're achieved by the top one or two agents, with the majority struggling to survive. Beware of offices like this, because the top agents have market share based on their personal profile and this does not necessarily spill over to the other team members.

4. **Go online to evaluate presence.**

   Use search engines to see the ranking of the company's website. The higher the ranking, the more the leads. Also search on key real estate sites like `www.realestate.com.au`, `domain.com.au` or realestate.co.nz to figure out the company's position on sites with listing inventory. You can evaluate the listing quality, as well as price ranges, locations, marketing materials, virtual tours and so on.

5. **Drive around your market area to determine each company's visibility.**

   In today's technological world, you can do much of your research online, but if you're still stumped, hit the street and count the number of signs you see for each firm you're considering. Also, evaluate the quality and array of homes presented by each company. You may discover that a firm has a lot of signs, but they're all concentrated in a small geographic area or a specific price range. Beware of these firms because they could limit your opportunity. For example, if a company's business is concentrated at the lower end of the marketplace, securing higher-priced listings may be more difficult.

6. **Evaluate each company's marketing.**

   Monitor media exposure for at least a month to gain a good perspective of the scope and nature of a company's marketing campaign and its exposure. Check out your local area listings on sites like www.realestate.com.au or www.realestate.co.nz. Is the company using traditional methods of marketing as well? Print media, such as newspapers and home magazines, aren't as effective as they used to be, but some sellers still want their homes to appear in them. While monitoring the media, do the following:

   - Study the ads carefully. Is the company using classified or display ads? What is the size and exposure? Do the ads feature individual agents? Could you see yourself in these ads?
   - Go to the local stores and pick up copies of real estate magazines. Are the companies you're considering featured? What do their ads look like?

   If you see lots of marketing featuring the listings of a number of agents from your selected company, you know that the agency has a very visible presence, which could be of value to you as a member of the agency team.

7. **Visit the company's website.**

   More than 90 per cent of all consumers now search the web for properties. Is the company's website easy to use? Are the listings easy to find and navigate? Are agents featured on individual pages within the company site?

Act like an online shopper and find out whether the site performs well in online searches. Go to major search engines and directories, such as Google and Yahoo!, and conduct a search for real estate in your market area. How well a company's site ranks in the search results may affect the number and quality of leads you generate. Just keep in mind that a site ranking may not be half as important as the leads you attract from your own efforts and presence in the community.

Ask key questions

Your moment in front of a prospective broker or principal is a pivotal one: They're sizing you up to determine whether you fit well in the company. Instead of treating the session like a job interview, use it to ask questions and obtain information that enables you to understand the unique attributes of the agency. Just make sure you listen — don't take over the conversation and come across as cocky!

Ask the following questions:

- **What is your training program for new agents?** The old-school approach of 'Here's your desk. Here's your phone. Off you go.' won't prepare you for success. If possible, you should be looking for a legitimate, established, multi-week training program that extends beyond contract writing and gets into the fields of prospecting, lead follow-up, sales presentations, objection handling and closing techniques.
- **How many new agents would your group recruit and train annually?** Find out the success rate of the agents who complete the program. Ask what percentage of trained agents continues with the company for at least one year. What percentage lasts two years?

  Companies that regularly recruit and train new agents usually have better training programs than those that don't.

  As you evaluate the responses, take into account that you have to attribute some of the agents' lack of success to market conditions rather than to training program quality or agent skill.
- **Would it be possible to talk with a few of your agents?** Try to get the perspectives of two to four agents, including a fairly new agent, an agent who is struggling to perform, a solid performer, and a top-performing agent. This diverse group provides a wonderful view of the company's training, education, support and pathway to success or failure.

- **Would you be helping me to generate business?** Ask this question and then wait. Expect to hear responses that fall all over the map. Some make specific mention of open houses and roster times to take incoming calls or meet with walk-ins. Some discuss the frequency and scope of marketing efforts. Some offer to pay for business cards. Some send marketing materials announcing your association with the company to those in your sphere of influence.

  Use the answers to this question to assess

  - Whether the company is committed to helping you succeed.
  - Whether the company has a system or process that works to generate business for new agents.

- **Who do I turn to when I have a question or problem?** As you climb the steep learning curve ahead of you, you need to know who will help you find solutions to your problems. You need assurance that the person will be accessible. Make sure to ask whether this person is available during regular office hours.

- **Is any computer and software provided for me?** Some companies make numerous high-quality computers available to agents. Some companies support agents with company database management programs, intranet sites, internet sites, and even electronic marketing pieces or e-cards. With other companies, you're completely on your own to purchase the technology tools you need. You'll need your own computer, tablet and smartphone, as well as anything the agency supplies.

- **Do you have regular office meetings?** Even though, many companies have moved away from weekly sales meetings, if you're a new agent you really need these weekly meetings to keep you motivated and on track. You could ask whether the meetings are training or informational sessions. Are they done online, or do you need to be present in the office? If you are a new agent, you really need to be part of in-office sessions.

- **Do you have an agent coaching program? If not, could you recommend one for me?** Find out whether the company you're considering embraces coaching as a way to increase agent performance.

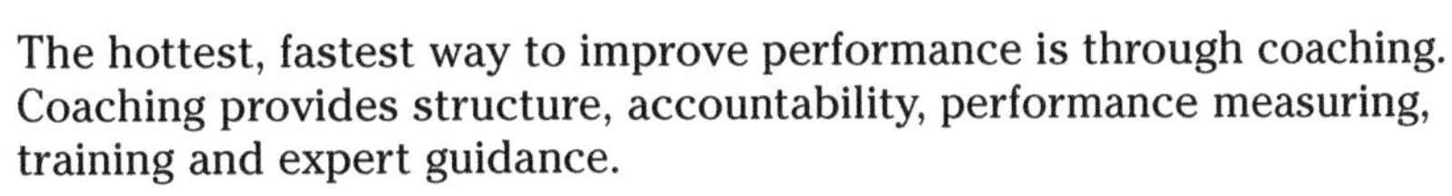

The hottest, fastest way to improve performance is through coaching. Coaching provides structure, accountability, performance measuring, training and expert guidance.

- **What does it cost me to be working with you?** Most agents enter real estate with limited cash to invest in a new business. Yet they may need to fund business cards, phone calls, petrol, licensing fees and more — these expenses can easily total more than $1,000. Some of these costs must be paid up front, and others may be withheld from your first commission cheque.
- **What's my commission split?** When considering the split offered, just keep in mind that whether you receive a 50/50 split or a 60/40 split for the first year means very little over the course of your career. What's more important to your success is the investment the company is willing to make in terms of your training, education, services, leads and opportunities. The company deserves a return for the investment it's making and the risk it's taking.

Save this question until late in your interview. Certainly the answer affects your immediate-term income, but I think far too many agents put undue emphasis on the commission split as they make the decision to 'hang their license' with a certain company.

Left-side/right-side your research

After you complete your interviews, put your assessments down on paper. On a single sheet, list all your final company candidates, along with their one-to-ten rankings in each of the following key areas:

- Competence of the principal or manager
- Initial training
- Lead generation
- Market share
- Marketing
- Marketplace reputation
- Office environment
- Ongoing education
- Other agents in the company or office
- Web presence

As you compare companies, weigh a few areas more heavily than the others. Especially in the early phase of your career, put special emphasis on a company's training and education offerings. As a close second, pay attention to how much the company is prepared to help you with lead generation and online marketing.

Pick a winner

As you add your scores for each company, give extra points to companies that rate particularly high in training and lead generation.

Then compare your findings with your initial, first-take impression of each company's consumer reputation. Do those with the best reputations also rank the highest in your assessment?

If two companies rank extremely closely in your assessment, you may want to re-interview the brokers or other high-ranking managers. Explain that you're deciding between two companies. We even suggest that you inform each company of your other top contender. This enables them to describe their benefits in direct comparison to the other company, which in turn gives you an indication of their ability to train you in selling based on their presentation against a direct competitor. Then, if you sense that you've made a favourable impression, you could ask why you should select their company over the other (humour and a smile works well here!). And carefully weigh the answer.

When you make the final selection, send handwritten thank-you notes to the companies you didn't select. Thank them for the considerable time and help they provided you. This act alone will position you in the top 5 per cent of agents they've ever met. It also keeps the door open in case you seek to work with another firm in the future.

Forging a Good Start

When joining a new team, your objective is to blend in with the team. As an inexperienced agent, you should expect scrutiny from your associates. Many will greet you with a wait-and-see attitude for the simple reason that fewer than one in five agents succeeds in the long term while the rest wash out of real estate sales. Your fellow agents are waiting to see which category you'll fit into.

Building a relationship with your manager

We rarely see a principal or manager with high expectations of a new agent. Instead, they focus on potential. They believe that a new agent can become a top producer, but they cautiously reserve judgement until they see the quality of the agent's action. The key to success is to quickly move from 'potential' to 'performance'.

Even though they're cautious of judging your performance, your managers are on your side, rooting and pulling for you to realise your goals, dreams and potential. Your success is their success.

The best way to build a relationship with your manager is to achieve results by taking the following steps along the way:

1. **Involve your manager as you set your goals.**

   As you establish specific, concrete, attainable and exciting goals, ask your manager for input regarding what you should do daily, weekly and monthly to achieve your desired outcomes (or your KPIs).

2. **Seek your manager's input as you lay out an activity plan.**

   Gain advice regarding which avenues you should follow to achieve success and what you should do daily to bring you closer to your goals.

3. **Ask your manager to help monitor your activities.**

   By asking your manager to monitor and coach your performance, you separate yourself from 90 per cent of the other real estate agents. Although nearly all agents want to improve, few are willing to make the changes necessary for success.

4. **Request a weekly meeting.**

   Aim to sit down with your manager at the same time and on the same day each week. Some weeks the meeting may last only 15 minutes, during which time your manager can review your performance based on the contacts made, leads generated, appointments booked, appointments conducted, and properties listed or sold. Other weeks you may work on specific training topics.

5. **Ask for help with marketing and lead generation.**

   Creating prospect opportunities can really separate the high producers from the marginal ones. Although service may be the same or similar, the person with the most leads usually wins.

Understanding your manager's role in your success

Of course you hope for a positive manager who supports you with a high level of encouragement, but even a negative manager can play a positive role in your success. It's counterintuitive, but when a sad-sack manager tells you that you can't accomplish your aims, the comment often ignites conviction and taps into a huge reservoir of 'I'll show you' attitude.

A number of years ago, Dirk coached an agent named Sheila Gunderson. She had a burning desire to close $24 million in sales over the next year. This amount was up from a current sales volume of about $10 million and was well above the top performance level of any agent in her area to date.

Together, Dirk and Sheila constructed a business plan outlining how she would achieve her $24 million goal. With total excitement she took it to her principal. He laughed, telling her that no-one in the market area had ever come close to $24 million, and asked her, 'Who do you think you are?'

When Dirk heard her manager's comments, he immediately knew that they would only fuel Sheila's fire. And they did. She blew right past the $24 million that she had projected and closed the year at more than $27 million, adding more than $17 million in sales to her previous year's performance.

Whatever input your manager gives you — even if it's negative — use it to fuel your fire.

Earning respect from your manager

Follow this simple formula to earn respect from anyone, including your manager:

- **Do what you said you would do.** Get to your office early each day, whether it's your home office or real estate office, and be proactive about prospecting and generating leads. The vast majority of agents wait for business to come to them and then make excuses for why it never shows up. Take action instead.
- **Improve your knowledge and education.** Many agents attend training courses just to earn continuing education points (or continuing professional development (CPD) credit), rather than to master specific new skills or abilities.

  The training you do should be focused on improving your skills rather than just satisfying the industry requirements.

  To earn your manager's respect, attend courses and education sessions that teach you how to make more money. Then implement what you discover after the session.

Forming partnerships

To get the real estate job done, you'll form many partnerships — some of these will last as long as a single deal and others will last for years and years.

Earning respect from your peers

The sales arena — and certainly the real estate sales arena — is a magnet for those with big egos. To earn the respect of other real estate agents, you have to perform and succeed. Your peers will base their respect for you on how they feel you perform in the following three areas:

- **Production growth:** When you produce, you get noticed. In fact, many of your associates will notice your success even before you see a commission payment because they'll notice your name on the company listings board and on the For Sale and the Sold signs in your local area.

  At first, they may attribute your success to luck, saying 'He got good lead calls' or 'She hit a hot streak,' but as your listings keep appearing, their respect will build.

  Few agents perform consistently over the long haul. Most have a good month, quarter or year, but only a rare few constantly finish at the top of the income list. However, when you do, your peers will most definitely notice and share their respect.

- **Business ethics:** Because the commissions can be large, some people feel that acting unethically is acceptable. For many agents, money, or the opportunity to make money, too often exposes character flaws.

  Be an exception. Maintaining your values even in the most competitive situations enhances your own self-respect, while also earning the respect of your peers.

- **Life balance:** Agents notice and respect other agents who have their priorities in order, who manage not to be controlled by their businesses, and who carve out good chunks of time to spend with their friends and families. Few agents manage to earn a large income while also protecting their personal time. You'll be recognised and respected as one of the best agents in the country if you can strike this important balance. (Check out Chapter 15 for more on making the most of your time.)

Working with agents in your office

Many agents these days are independent contractors earning a higher commission split but no base salary, and depending entirely on their own skills, actions and activities to create income. This pay structure breeds competition within the industry and within each company. The trick is to balance that competition with cooperation.

Striking the balance between competition and cooperation isn't always easy. Invariably, you end up competing with agents inside your own firm for clients and dollars. One example is finding that the agent in the next cubicle is working on the same lead you are. This situation is usually the result of a prospect who chose to work with several agents at one time but who didn't reveal the lack of allegiance to any of them. Later, when one agent writes the contract — after both agents showed the home — well, you can imagine the office arguments that occur. This situation certainly presents a moment where a good principal makes a difference. A good principal (and a good policy and procedures manual) can shed light on the issue and mediate the issues between the agents, making sure that the client is getting good service while handling the interpersonal issues between the agents.

To succeed in this competitive office environment, follow this advice:

- **Use the other agents as mentors.** Nearly all agents owe a debt to some other agent who helped them along the road to success, and they feel a sense of obligation to repay the favour by being similarly helpful to a new agent like you. Find a mentor. When you do, be respectful of the mentor's time, take action on the mentor's advice or counsel, report back on the success you achieve, and say thanks over and over again.
- **Help other agents serve their clients better.** Agents often announce their 'haves and wants' — the homes they're working to sell and the homes they're seeking for clients — and few agents even tune in. Be an exception.
- **Hold open houses for other agents.** Open houses can be burdens on the schedules of busy agents. Open houses are popular, and many sellers expect agents to conduct one. Offer to serve as a stand-in host, supporting your associates while also giving yourself an opportunity to create prospects and business. Just make sure you agree on the specifics beforehand with the listing agent — don't presume anything.
- **Ask other agents to work with you on listings.** If you lack skill or experience in a certain price range or geographic area, you risk losing a listing to a more established agent. Be pre-emptive instead. Ask a more established agent in your firm to co-list the property with you. Through this short-term partnership, you capture the opportunity to expand your business while you learn and earn. Don't focus on 'what percentage' you're giving away. Focus on how much you can learn.

Cooperating with agents in your marketplace

At times you may choose to work jointly with agents from other firms to achieve sales. Check with your principal to find out the rules around this practice in your own office. Each office will have a different policy — for example, some offices never work with other agents on auction properties, and some don't allow any joint agreements in the first week of listing a new property. As you work with these agents, form cooperative relationships by following this simple advice:

- **Deal with the other agents honestly and fairly.** Most offices have a general policy to ask for details of other agents' clients first, because you may already be dealing with this person. Give other agents the information they need about your client or property without giving too many details. Always remain aware of the fiduciary responsibility and privacy protection you owe your client.

- **Involve principals when necessary.** If problems arise between you and the other agent, enlist the help of your principal. If paperwork comes back too slowly or you feel you're not getting the full facts, get your principal, or the other agent's principal, involved. Move quickly if you sense that a lack of cooperation is affecting your client's security in keeping the transaction together.

Developing strategic partnerships

Mortgage brokers and loan officers lead the list of strategic partners who can help you get real estate deals done. These people play an essential role in securing your clients' loans. They can help you expand your business through several avenues:

- **They can help you serve lower-credit clients.** Mortgage brokers who are skilled and have a broad line of loan products are open to loan requests from a broadly diverse economic segment, which increases your pool of prospects.
- **Mortgage brokers can help convert leads.** Most agents make the mistake of getting the mortgage broker involved in a transaction too late. They wait until after they've secured the client relationship to introduce their loan partner. Make the introduction earlier in the lead-conversion process. Tandem lead conversion is a powerful strategic-partnering technique.

  The odds of lead conversion rise significantly when two strategic partners are working the same contact. When one of you achieves a face-to-face meeting, you both win, because either of you can cross-sell the services of the other.

- **The mortgage broker can play the role of a prospect's professional advisor.** Although most prospects view agents as salespeople, their psychology toward mortgage brokers or bankers is quite different. They tend to see and trust them as consultants rather than as the salespeople they truly are. By forming strategic partnerships with your mortgage broker, you can put that psychology to work and secure more clients more quickly. We've seen agents greatly increase their closed transactions through this simple tandem lead-conversion approach.

Chapter 3

Becoming a Marketplace Expert

In This Chapter

- Collecting and analysing information on your market (or *farm*) area
- Putting the advantages of market knowledge to work in your business
- Using market knowledge to build your clientele and your personal reputation

Here's a fact: Most real estate agents know too little about the markets in which they operate. This is one reason that consumers think they know more than — or at least as much as — their agents do, and why they don't hold their agents in higher regard. This is especially true with the unlimited access to real estate information in our new technological world. Consumers can now access information and conduct real estate searches without an agent ever knowing that they're doing their own legwork.

Consumers can use a variety of information sources to find all kinds of data on practically any property. For example, a buyer can tap into sites such as `www.rpdata.com`, `www.pricefinder.com.au` or `www.terranet.co.nz` and access the history of a property, find out the previous purchase price, make note of the current land valuation, the rates, and view aerial maps and satellite images of the property. Buyers can even look at public access websites where they can find information about distressed properties and forced sales, foreclosures and repossessions. With all this information freely available to consumers, unless agents can improve their service and their skills, they could soon be made redundant!

Now, here's a tip: You can give yourself an edge over other agents and establish yourself as a regional real estate expert simply by doing your homework, researching your market area, and gaining a good understanding of the realities and trends that affect the real estate decisions of your buyers and sellers.

This chapter begins with a look at the realities that affect real estate in every market, regardless of location. Then it leads you through the steps involved in compiling a profile of your specific market area, including where to find facts and figures, how to analyse your findings, and how to put your knowledge to work to build both your reputation and your clientele.

Knowing the Three Truths That Rule Every Real Estate Market

Whether you're in a major inner-city marketplace or a small town, and regardless of the country, the economy, or even the day and age in which you're doing business, when you're in the field of real estate, three core rules apply to your business:

1. **Real estate is governed by the law of supply and demand.**

   This rule is absolute and without exception. The ups and downs of a market, the expectations of buyers and sellers, and the velocity of market sales are all dictated by the supply of — and the demand for — real estate for sale.

   As a recent example, we saw rapid appreciation and a frenzied response by buyers in the Australian and New Zealand real estate markets from 2002 to 2007. This response was caused by the fact that demand for real estate was at an all-time high while the supply was limited. This caused rapid appreciation, with home sellers receiving multiple offers within days or even hours. At one time during that period, homes were selling at auction well above the listed price — the result of a market condition where demand outstripped supply.

   Terri was selling property in the tightly controlled character suburbs of inner Brisbane during the early to mid-2000s, and exciting was the only word for it. She could hammer in a for-sale sign in front of a cute little Queenslander and have three offers by phone before she even got back to the office! How easy was that? However, the downside was that many new agents flooded the market, looking for the quick buck. Their skills were often virtually non-existent and they 'stretched the truth' in their efforts to make a killing fast. As a result, the reputation of the industry and all agents went downhill. Those who chose to work ethically had to prove themselves over and over again. But, when the market turned (as it always does) those greedy agents didn't survive. After that bubble burst in 2008, the real estate market made a big shift because supply outstripped demand. The big lesson here is that, as a real estate expert, you have to clearly understand supply and demand levels and monitor them at all times. You have to expect, and prepare for, these dips — otherwise, your bank balance and your sanity may not survive!

2. **Real estate is governed by the law of cause and effect.**

   Put differently, positive situations cause positive outcomes, and vice versa. For example, vibrant economic growth leads to a vibrant real estate market and strong appreciation of homes, while job loss and a languishing economy produce exactly the opposite effect.

   Prior to the recent economic slump, the availability of loans with fewer documentation requirements (commonly called *low-doc* or *no-doc* loans) and for buyers with lower credit scores led to an increase in buyers who could qualify for mortgages. Banks created these loans, and then financial markets bought the repackaged loans. But many consumers took on more mortgage debt than they could really afford. These buyers then purchased houseful of expensive furniture on a 'no deposit, no payment for three years' plan. This created a perfect storm, with banks having to foreclose on a large volume of homes. Many homeowners found themselves in serious financial difficulty, having to offload their homes to repay their debt. Many homes in the luxury market, particularly along the eastern coast of Australia, were forced to sell at hundreds of thousands of dollars less than their original purchase price.

   This *cause* created an *effect* of price depreciation, such that an influx of investor buyers is now driving the lower segment of the housing market. Investors now account for a significant proportion of all homes sold. The vagaries of the stock market have led to many investors (particularly those with self-managed super funds) turning back to 'bricks and mortar' as one of their key investment strategies.

3. **History will repeat itself.**

   Any marketplace has cycles. Periods of rapid real estate appreciation are followed by stagnant periods where values stabilise or even decrease. By acquiring marketplace knowledge, you can foresee trends both for your own benefit and for the benefit of your clients.

By knowing your market and watching regional statistics, you're prepared and proactive. The following section helps you acquire the necessary information.

Acquiring Knowledge about Your Marketplace

Think of your marketplace as your playing field, not unlike how an athlete views a footy field, a netball court, or a cricket pitch. The better you know every inch of that playing field, the more you can exploit it to your advantage.

Terri's sons all played soccer at a high level in Coffs Harbour, a thriving town in northern New South Wales. They were taught to focus not only on their own performance, but to be aware of the whole playing field, to note where each player was positioned and to accurately predict the next move to set up the goal. You must do the same. Market conditions change all the time, sometimes predictably but sometimes seemingly out of the blue. So be prepared — keep your eye on the whole playing field.

Real estate is like any other competitive endeavour. If you find out all there is to know about your playing field, you'll acquire a competitive advantage that will distance you from the competition and build the basis of your success.

Collecting marketplace information

The most challenging aspect of gaining market knowledge is determining what facts to collect and where to find the information you need. Fortunately, a number of readily accessible resources are available to agents. All you have to do is contact the right people and ask the right questions. The following sections help you on your data quest.

Your local industry board

The Real Estate Institute of Australia (REIA) is Australia's professional association and has branches in every state. In New Zealand, the top regulatory body is the Real Estate Institute of New Zealand (REINZ). Membership of these organisations is voluntary but they are an invaluable source of up-to-date industry knowledge, and make available to members a wealth of statistical information. The facts you can obtain from these local bodies include:

- **The number of agents working in your marketplace:** This information helps you understand your competitive arena. It also enables you to track whether your competition has expanded or contracted. In the past few years, the number of agents in every marketplace has fallen dramatically . . . good news for you.
- **The production of the average agent in terms of listings and settled sales:** By obtaining this information and comparing it with your own key performance indicators, you can contrast your performance against the other agents in your local area. This information is useful in your effort to calculate your share of the market. (See Chapter 13 for more on this topic.) It also helps you understand how you stack up against the other agents that your prospective customers might be considering (your competitors). The average per-agent production is a

key comparative stat to use for marketing and positioning yourself in your local area.

- **The experience levels of agents in your marketplace:** You should also be able to find information regarding the percentage of agents recently licensed and those with three, five, and ten years in the business. This information provides you with another factor against which to measure your competitive position. Experience levels are currently rising because so many less-experienced agents exited the business in the downturn.

Knowing stats about your marketplace, and how you compare to other agents, is useful, but don't get so bogged down in searching for and noting these statistics that you neglect your real work — meeting and qualifying prospects, listing and marketing properties and negotiating sales. Analysing figures and stats can become your comfort zone — when building client relationships and networks needs to be your main priority. Otherwise, your sales (and your stats) will suffer.

The REI (Real Estate Institute) magazines provide a national view of real estate sales: What's happened in terms of sales and days on the market, what people are purchasing, what financing they're using, what trends are emerging, and what predictions experts are making for the future. This is a powerful tool in the hands of a successful agent. If you aren't currently receiving and reading the magazines available, put them into your information arsenal immediately.

Other sources of marketplace information

Consult your broker/principal about company-compiled statistics on trends and plans in your region. For example, is any infrastructure planned that you should know about or are companies closing down or relocating? Both of these changes will have direct impact on your client base, and also on your firm's market share and market penetration.

Especially if you work for a regional or national real estate company or franchise, your organisation has likely commissioned studies that are useful to your fact-gathering efforts. Take advantage of this information as you go about your most important activities and KPIs — the actions that will make you money.

Analysing the facts and figures

After you have access to solid facts and figures, it's time to interpret your findings to arrive at conclusions that steer your business in the right direction.

The following sections help you seek and analyse answers to three important questions:

- Which nearby real estate markets are influencing your market area?
- What migratory patterns is your market area experiencing — are buyers moving in, or sellers moving out? If so, ask yourself why.
- What market trends are you seeing that can help you prepare yourself and your clients for success?

Determining the influence of other regional markets

Real estate in your market area is affected by influences outside of your own region. For example, people priced out of a nearby market area may start looking to buy in your area.

To determine how neighbouring regional markets are affecting your market area, study migratory patterns and then research the reasons behind the population movements you discover.

In Australia, for example, significant numbers of people have always moved from the southern parts of the country to more northern parts, where the climate is more favourable. These moves often happen during winter months so being aware of this trend — and perhaps marketing any properties up north to the prospects down south during this time — is worthwhile. Just market far-north Queensland properties to Melbournites who are shivering away in a cold, miserable winter!

Australia has also seen huge demographic changes to the population in mining areas. At the start of this trend, every available home was purchased for the recently arrived workers and their families. Rents skyrocketed — which was great for investors but not so good for the locals who were not receiving the inflated mining wages. Then spouses and families got tired of living in remote country areas so they moved back to the bigger centres and the workers began FIFO (fly in, fly out) patterns. The country towns suffered with this itinerant population and many of them have never recovered. It is not hard to imagine the impact these changes had on local real estate markets.

Studying population migration patterns

To quantify population migration trends that affect the buyer and seller pools in your market area, determine the answers to these questions:

- Is your marketplace growing in population or losing population?
- Are people migrating into your area or leaving your area?
- Where are new residents coming from geographically?

- Where are current residents going when they move away?
- At what rate are people arriving to or leaving your area?
- What economic factors (for example, unemployment rate, new business start-ups or business sales growth) are driving population changes in your marketplace?

If your answers lead you to believe that a population boom is pending, prepare yourself and your clients to take advantage of a sellers' market and the positive effects of a high-demand, low-supply market situation.

Conversely, if your answers lead you to believe that a population exodus is beginning to take place, you can steer buyer and seller decisions with that knowledge in mind.

Identifying and capitalising on market trends

To understand your marketplace and its economic condition, compare current market activity with correlating statistics from the previous year, using the following guidelines:

- **Compare the number of sales and total sales volume, on both a year-to-year and year-to-date basis.** This helps you understand and forecast trends in your marketplace.
  - Is the number of sales going up or down?
  - Is total sales volume going up or down?
  - Is the marketplace ahead of or behind the pace of sales from the previous year?
- **Compare the number of listings taken.** The available inventory in a marketplace is the supply half of the supply-and-demand equation. Ask:
  - Is the number of listings up or down? Fewer listings indicate a sellers' market; more listings indicate a buyers' market. Is competition for buyers more or less than in previous years?
  - Is the selection better for buyers than last year at this time?
  - Is the inventory of homes for sale growing or shrinking as compared to this time a year ago?
- **Compare last year's average sale price to this year's average sale price.** Determine your market's average sale price by dividing total sales revenue by the number of homes actually sold. Then consider the following:
  - Is the average sale price going up or down? If a marketplace is healthy and vibrant, the average sale price will be increasing.

  - Is your marketplace appreciating or depreciating in value? For instance, if the average sale price has gone from $249,000 to $257,000, your marketplace is appreciating in value. Be aware that the average sale price must be viewed on at least a quarterly basis. A one-month change in this particular statistic doesn't indicate a sustainable trend. This is especially true in small market areas.

    Additionally, you need to check the mix of sales. If a large volume of high-end properties sells in a given month, those sales can heavily influence the average sale prices for the period. Don't make assumptions based solely on a rise in the average sale price; be sure to check the mix of inventory to confirm.

  - How well is the inventory of homes aligned with demand? If you have an appreciating marketplace, the inventory probably is lower than the demand for homes. In a flat or depreciating marketplace, the inventory or supply probably exceeds demand.

- **Compare the percentage of appreciation of average sale price this year versus last year and year to date.** Ask:

  - Is the appreciation percentage increasing or decreasing compared to this time last year?

  - Is the marketplace gaining strength in appreciation or losing its power?

To understand your marketplace and its economic condition, create a market-trend analysis by comparing current market activity with correlating statistics from the previous year.

Compiling a marketplace analysis

Before delving into your own marketplace analysis, check to see whether your local REI compiles monthly reports on your marketplace. If so, save yourself a lot of time by using the statistics they can provide on the current homes for sale in your area — often broken into regional geographic areas.

If the essential data isn't available, sharpen your pencil, clear some calendar time, and get ready to construct an analysis on your own by amassing the following facts and figures on a monthly basis:

1. **Segment your marketplace by area.**

   You need to acquire both a macro view of the whole marketplace and a micro view of selected neighbourhood or school boundary areas. The broader view is helpful, but the close-in view on specific market areas is essential when you're showing particular properties to clients.

You can use the same segmentation as featured in your newspaper's real estate classified ads, because that aligns with common market knowledge.

2. **Determine available inventory levels.**

   Know the level of competition for your buyers' dollars by tracking the number of active listings on the market and look at the average days on market (see Step 4 for more on this). If the number of days on market is shortening, as was happening in 2014 in Queensland, you must prepare your sellers for early offers and market intensively in the first couple of weeks to nab that good buyer.

3. **Calculate the number of transactions in the past 30 days.**

   To get an accurate picture of marketplace activity, look at the number of pending transactions for properties that are in the process of settlement and transferring ownership. In most markets, a property remains as a pending transaction for 30 to 60 days, after which time the money and ownership is transferred, and the deal is referred to as settled or sold.

   It's important to analyse the market based on pending rather than settled or sold properties because the completed transactions reflect the activity of the marketplace 30 to 60 days ago rather than right now.

4. **Calculate the average time on market for listings in your area, or approximately how long it will take for the currently available inventory to be purchased.**

   You can find this information by tracking the current listing history of properties on sites like `www.rpdata.com.au`, `www.pricefinder.com.au` and `www.terranet.co.nz`.

   This last calculation is an important one. By looking at the current stock level and dividing it by the number of properties to settle in the coming month, you can calculate how many months' worth of inventory is for sale in your market area. This provides a snapshot of current supply and demand.

   Now ask yourself these questions:

   - Which market do you think is appreciating faster?
   - Which market allows the seller greater control?
   - In which market will homes spend fewer days for sale?
   - In which market do buyers have the least control and the greatest need to meet seller demands in order to make the purchase?

- Which marketplace inspires the greatest seller greed?
- In which marketplace do sellers put more pressure on agents to cut their commission rate?

The marketplace with an average of one to two months' worth of inventory is the right answer to all these questions.

If you know the numbers, you know the future of your marketplace. The trends are predetermined by your monthly analysis. Don't leave your office without one!

Projecting trends on the horizon

Most real estate trends are a reaction to the law of supply and demand. As you project trends, study your market analysis for hints of changes in your market's inventory. At the same time, study your region's economic growth and stability for hints at what is taking place to influence consumer demand.

In general, a low inventory of homes leads to increased appreciation and more competition for 'high demand' properties, which include homes that are in superior condition and in superior locations. In a low-inventory marketplace, sellers can often overreach in terms of pricing. We call this *blue-sky thinking*. Be wary of this. When inventory levels are high, the competition for buyers slows appreciation. This situation also extends days on the market and can even reduce sale prices because of a lack of purchaser urgency to 'buy now'.

Comparative market analyses (CMAs)

The most common question asked of agents by prospective sellers is 'How much is my property worth?' It is not enough to guess this answer or say what you think your prospect wants to hear. What you need to do is offer an opinion of price, based on current market evidence. A CMA requires you to compare the seller's property with at least six other comparable properties — three past sales within the previous six month period and at least three similar properties currently on the market. This evidence helps you to build a picture of what the property is worth, rather than a quick and often inaccurate 'guesstimate'.

Chapter 9 goes into more detail about answering this price question and gives you some great tips.

Putting Your Findings to Work

Most agents, even the good ones, are far from being experts in their field. They've created clients and sales through strong relationships rather than through superior knowledge. This in itself is not a bad thing, but many agents are working hard to build these relationships. To differentiate yourself, acquire a deep understanding of current and emerging market trends and then share your findings with prospects, current and past clients, and others in your sphere of influence. Doing so helps you position yourself as a leading expert in your market area. Being a 'nice' person is no longer enough.

In the context of being seen as an experienced industry professional, one of the biggest lessons in Terri's career came early on. She had done an appraisal and a listing presentation one Saturday for a client and his wife. Their rapport was excellent, they laughed at her jokes and listened intently to her campaign strategies. The listing was 'in the bag' — or so she thought. She left without being assertive enough to ask for the business then and there, and instead called the sellers on Monday to confirm the time to complete the paperwork. Imagine her feelings when they told her that she hadn't got the job — they had given it to a prominent male agent and the reason was that, although she was a 'lovely' person, they didn't think that she was tough enough to get them the price they wanted! From that moment on, being 'nice' was always secondary to her goal of being seen as the area expert and tough enough to negotiate until she achieved the very best result.

Whether you're making contact by phone or in person, get the conversation going by presenting questions that prompt interest, inspire urgency, and convey your market knowledge and authority. For example:

- 'Did you know that we have less than six weeks' worth of inventory in the price range you're looking for?'
- 'Did you know that the average home price has appreciated more than 6 per cent the past six months, and that this same home you called about today would have cost $30,000 less six months ago?'
- 'Has anyone mentioned to you that on average, a high-demand house is on the market less than 30 days in today's environment?'

The preceding examples are for illustration purposes only — you must do your own research to fill in the numbers for yourself. Check your facts before quoting any statistics — don't just make them up or exaggerate them because, if they're wrong, your credibility will go gurgling down the drain.

When you seize a potential client's interest, immediately ask for an appointment to meet soon because of the marketplace inventory being low or high, or appreciation being low or high, or the days on the market being low or high, or other market conditions that work in your favour.

Here is a script example:

> *Bob, did you know that the average home price in your area has risen more than 10 per cent in the past six months? Here's what that means to you. This same home we're talking about right now would have been $30,000 less if you had called me six months ago. Based on the trends in the marketplace, would it be useful to you to get an updated idea of the worth of your property in the current market? I'm just off to an appointment, but I do have openings on Wednesday or Thursday this week.*

The use of key statistics, such as list-price to sale-price ratios and days-on-the-market averages, demonstrates your mastery of marketplace knowledge. It also creates a competitive gap between you and your competition by establishing you as the one who can use market forces to your clients' advantage, raising the probability of a higher sale price, a shorter time on the market and increased net proceeds for your sellers. Armed with the information, your buyers can benefit in negotiations with sellers, or just feel more comfortable when the market dictates that they have to offer the sellers' asking price because the market numbers aren't in their favour.

To put your findings to work, take the following steps:

- Use your marketplace knowledge to prompt prospects to act now rather than procrastinate until a time when market conditions may not be so ideal.
- Share your market analyses as a way to stay in contact with past clients and others who can positively influence your business.
- Each quarter, share your most recent statistical findings with your business contact list via an email newsletter and social-media posts.

Part II

Generating Leads for Buyers and Sellers

	OPEN HOUSE PLANNING WORKSHEET	
	Planning Step	Notes
	ADVANCE PLANNING Select the right property/Factors to consider High-demand area Attractiveness of home Street appeal Proximity to major street Set open house objectives Number of visitors Number of leads Number of buyer interviews Set the open house hours Plan neighborhood events, including: Sneak peak event Establish date/time Determine number of invitations Decide whether to mail or hand deliver Other neighborhood events Plan directional sign strategy; choose sign locations Plan advertising and write ads Assess street appeal; advise seller re: suggested improvements	
	DAYS BEFORE THE OPEN HOUSE Place open house ads Prepare and produce flyers or home feature sheets Research up to six similar properties to share with prospects Advise seller of hour to depart prior to open house	
	OPEN HOUSE DAY Prepare house by opening blinds, turning on lights, and arranging music, candles, and so on Place guest book or sign-in sheet and pen in entry area Put out flyers or home feature sheets Put out and carry a supply of business cards	
	FOLLOWING THE OPEN HOUSE Send hand-written note to each attendee Send requested or promised material to prospects Make phone calls to set appointments	

Find out more about generating leads for buyers and sellers with a free article at www.dummies.com/extras/successrealestateagentau.

In this part . . .

- We unlock the secrets of client relationships. Learn how, when and why to market yourself and prospect for business.
- We show you how to put technology to use in your real estate marketing. Find out how to use social media and other technology to make your marketing campaigns stand out from the rest.
- We give you the goods on how to mine gold from referrals and win business from expired, withdrawn and FSBO listings.
- Discover how to plan the perfect open house and how to use open houses as the ultimate prospecting approach.

Chapter 4

Prospecting Your Way to Listings and Sales

In This Chapter

- Targeting the right prospects and keeping in mind the basic rules
- Knowing and meeting your objectives
- Thinking of prospecting as a never-ending, business-building cycle

Prospecting is one of the easiest but most misunderstood concepts in the field of sales. This is especially true with the explosion of online lead generation. Attempting to balance prospecting and marketing has never been more difficult.

Sales trainers constantly try to sell their 'prospecting-free systems' on speaking circuits, email blasts and social media, basically saying, 'You'll never have to prospect again if you use my system.' And because salespeople secretly don't want to prospect, they readily buy into the too-good-to-be-true, no-prospecting philosophy. If it sounds too good to be true, it usually is! Everything demands your own efforts. Both marketing and prospecting have a place in your business. The correct positioning is to be prospecting focused and marketing enhanced.

As a salesperson, if you buy into the myth of a prospecting-free or marketing-only system, you're failing to master sound prospecting approaches, and you're abandoning the need to continually develop new leads. You're risking your very livelihood in the real estate business.

In this chapter, we take you through the basics of prospecting, how to put it to work, and how to track your success.

Knowing Why to Prospect

The purpose of prospecting is to develop prospective clients for your business. The real estate prospecting process involves two steps:

1. **Identify and create leads.**

   You create leads by establishing contact with people who have interest in what you're offering and the ability to become clients of your business. Prospecting can be making connections with your friends and past clients and specifically asking for referrals. The key is the last statement: 'specifically asking for referrals'.

2. **Secure face-to-face appointments.**

   Make sure you book in a pre-determined time in the future.

Real estate agents seek two categories of clients: Sellers, who become listing clients, and buyers, who become real estate purchasers. The following sections provide tips on how to prospect for clients in each group.

Getting a feel for the importance of prospecting

Terri's experience with the early discipline of prospecting was incredibly valuable as her career took off. She did her research carefully — this was a midlife career change — and joined an agency with great systems, processes and structures in place. Her first principal was a very experienced business owner and agent, and a great mentor. Her first three months were spent prospecting and gaining appraisal appointments for the more experienced agents. This experience was invaluable and within a short space of time she was one of the top listing agents in that office.

As a new real estate agent, Dirk joined an office full of experienced agents who were doing well. He knew that to succeed he needed to prospect. He didn't know much more than that, but did understand the value of prospecting based on the results he'd experienced in previous sales jobs.

Dirk would come into the office at 7 am, and by 8 be talking to expired listings, private sale by owner prospects, people within his sphere of influence — whoever he could reach on the phone. The snickering from the other agents didn't escape his notice, nor did it redirect his efforts. The laughing died down within six months when Dirk's listings and sales put him on top-performing lists — and it stopped altogether when he made over six figures in his first year in the business. He became the number-one agent in that office after his third year in the business, and his commitment to prospecting hasn't stopped yet.

Prospecting for sellers

Listing leads come from past clients, those in your sphere of influence, expired listings, FSBO (for-sale-by-owner) conversions, open houses, notices of mortgagee in possession default, absentee-owner homes, networking and lead cultivation and door knocking — but they rarely come without some effort, and here's why. The tendency when people are sending you referrals is to send you prospective buyers. The public's perception is that real estate agents sell houses — that we put people in our cars and drive them around and find them a home to buy. If you evaluate thousands of agents' businesses, as we have, you'll see that most referrals are buyers.

To find sellers, you have to do some pretty active prospecting work:

- Seller referrals don't come naturally. Specifically ask those within your sphere of influence, your circle of past clients and your referral groups to share the names of people who might be needing or wanting to sell their properties.
- To achieve a greater listing inventory and develop a specialty as a listing agent, cultivate listing prospects by working expired and FSBO listings.
- To prioritise your efforts, see the sidebar 'The prospecting hierarchy of value', later in this chapter, for help assessing which sources of listing leads are the most productive for your business.

Prospecting for buyers

Prospecting for buyers is easier than prospecting for sellers, in part because referrals arrive more naturally and in part because open houses attract prospective buyers and provide you with such a great prospecting platform. Additionally, buyers are more naturally created from your marketing efforts. Most agents will have far more buyer opportunities than seller opportunities or leads.

If you're short on buyer prospects, increase the frequency of your open houses. The real estate industry has shifted to a more do-it-yourself buyer. Nowadays, most buyers look at properties online — in full-colour detail — before they come to view the home in person. The vast majority utilise open houses because they think that they don't have to reveal themselves as buyers or register their contact information. However, every good agent will be asking for contact details and even photo IDs at open homes. You can ask permission to contact those inspecting the property to get feedback for sellers and follow through on all buyer interest.

The types of houses you choose to show determine the kinds of prospects you generate. Obviously, higher-priced and more-exclusive properties draw more-discerning buyer prospects, and lower-priced properties attract less-affluent prospects.

To build your business quickly, work to generate leads from more first-home buyers by planning more open houses in the low range of your marketplace. The benefits of developing first-time buyer prospects include:

- First-home buyers can be sold into homes quickly because they aren't burdened with the need to sell homes in order to make purchases possible. There may even be government schemes available that give money to these purchasers to help buy their first home. These grants change from time to time and you should keep up to date with the offerings in your particular area.
- They often lack experience with other real estate agents. They don't have current agent affiliations, nor do they approach a new real estate agent relationship with baggage that may have been acquired from a less-than-stellar past experience.
- They acquire strong loyalty when good service is rendered, allowing you to establish a long-term relationship that may span 10 to 15 years and multiple home sales and purchases during that period.
- They provide you with an opportunity to establish relationships with their friends who are also considering first-home purchases.

Understanding the Four Pillars of Prospecting

For long-term prospecting success, apply these four disciplines that are common to agents who consistently achieve their revenue and quality-of-life goals.

Set a daily time and place for prospecting and be prepared

You can't work your prospecting around your day. You have to work your day around your prospecting. You have to establish the habit and engage in the discipline of prospecting on a daily basis and from a controlled environment where your prospecting tools are available and readily accessible. Even two hours of solid prospecting a day can pay off big time for you. We often ask agents who are just starting or who have renewed their focus for prospecting, 'When does prospecting happen during your day?' We can see they made their contacts, but what we really want to know is did the contacts happen during a scheduled prospecting time, or did they just do it ad hoc 'when the mood felt right'? That's better than not completing the prospecting, but it's not sustainable in the long run. Somewhere along your ride to success, the will to do it will have to be replaced with the habit of doing it. Without blocking out prospecting time each day, procrastinating is too easy, as you wait for 'the right time' instead of just taking action.

Terri's prospecting process started the night before each session, when she would plan which prospecting options to use. Going through her list of prospects, she worked out which people to call, which ones to send emails to, and which areas to letter-box drop or visit in person. She printed out lists of phone numbers and email addresses and had these set out ready on her desk. Another vital part of her process was having her diary handy to make appointments immediately if she got a 'live one' — that is, a prospect interested in taking the conversation further. She also created templates for her thank-you letters, ready to personalise and print out or email straightaway to confirm the appointment. The last part of her strategy was to set herself targets for how many prospects she'd contact during each session, and to track these numbers to see how many resulted in a listing and subsequent sale.

When contacting prospects, having some set phrases or scripts on hand can be helpful. For example, instead of asking prospects 'Are you thinking of selling?' ask 'Have you thought of moving from where you are now?' This often can lead to a productive conversation.

In a prospecting area around a property that has recently sold, you could try a script something like the following:

> *Hi, this is _______. I wonder if you would have a couple of minutes to help me out/talk with me? . . . I'm with _______ here at _______. Have you ever come across us? . . . I just wanted to let you know that we have*

> *recently sold a home in your immediate area. We had great interest in this property but, unfortunately, we couldn't satisfy all our buyers. One in particular just loves the area where you are and has asked me to see if I can come across anyone else nearby who may be thinking of making a move. Have you heard of anyone round this area who may be good for me to talk with?*

In a prospecting area around a property recently listed, you could try something like this:

> *Hi, this is ________. I'm with ________ here at ________. If you have a few minutes, I just wanted to let you know that we have a brand new listing in your area at ________. I'm not sure whether the local market may be of interest to you — or this particular house — but perhaps you'd like to keep an eye on what homes are selling for in your area? I would love to invite you along to our first open house for this property. You may know of someone who this home may suit — this often happens and I'd be really pleased if you had the time to come along.*

These kinds of prospecting calls have multiple purposes:

- Building your profile and name recognition
- Adding to your pipeline of present and future sellers
- Providing a valid reason for future calls — always end this first call (and all future calls) by asking if the contact would mind you keeping in touch every so often with market information for their area

A headset can be a vital prospecting tool, allowing you to stand up and gesture while on the phone as if you're talking to the prospect in person. It can also dissuade your colleagues from interrupting you with questions or chit-chat. However, if you're making an investment in a headset, don't get the cheapest one you can find. Spend a few hundred dollars to get one of high quality. Otherwise, you'll end up with such poor sound quality that your prospect won't be able to hear you clearly — hardly a formula for prospecting success.

Fight off distractions

The truth is, most agents welcome distractions that take them away from prospecting obligations. An inbound phone call, a text message, a social-media message or post, a problem transaction, a home-inspection question, an incoming email, an agent who wants to talk, a broken nail — anything will do. It's called creative avoidance or procrastination, and agents generally excel at the art.

Whether you're just starting out or you're a top agent, distractions never just go away. Real estate professionals face more distractions than ever because of the technology driving the real estate industry. In fact, the best agents have even more potential for distraction because of the volume of business, the number of staff, the size of client transactions and the scope of responsibilities they juggle. The difference between prospecting avoidance and prospecting success comes down to the question, what do you do when the distractions hit? Do you postpone prospecting while you put out a fire? Do you decide to make just a few calls to settle the pending issue? Do you justify not starting your prospecting at the appointed time? If you said 'yes' to any of those questions, you're practising creative avoidance.

To fight off distractions, you have to bar their access:

- Turn off your email, so the new mail alert doesn't tempt you.
- Ask the receptionist to take messages for inbound calls during your prospecting session.
- Turn off your mobile and make sure you change the message to let callers know when you will be available next.
- Close down social-networking sites.
- Put a sign on the door that basically says, 'Talk later; I'm prospecting'.
- Tell anyone who asks for a meeting during your prospecting period that you already have an appointment, because you do — working to find a potential prospect.

Follow the plan

Success boils down to taking the right steps in the proper order.

To get your prospecting steps and order correct, you must follow a prospecting plan. You must know who you're going to call and for what reason. The best approach is to set up each day's prospecting plan a day in advance.

If you wait to put your prospecting plan together at the beginning of your prospecting session, you'll waste precious time just getting organised and chances are too high that you'll talk yourself out of more calls than you make. Your self-talk will get in the way of action, causing you to think things like 'This person will think I'm calling back too soon . . .' or 'This person won't buy or sell right now . . .'

If you establish a plan in advance, you'll be ready for action instead of second-guessing. Follow these steps:

1. **Do your research; establish your plan and set up for the next day's prospecting one day in advance.**

   Before you leave your office for the day, determine the prospecting calls you're going to make the next day. Assemble everything you'll need for the calls and put the information on your desk so it's ready for your attention as soon as you walk in the door.

2. **In the morning, quickly review your calls and daily goals.**

   A word of caution: Don't take too long! You could be setting yourself up for creative avoidance (procrastination!).

3. **Get familiar with your scripts, dialogues and objection-handling techniques.**

   You may even want to have the scripts in front of you. You don't want to rattle them off like a parrot but they can help remind you to keep on track — you're not calling for an idle chat.

4. **Review a few affirmations to put you in the right frame of mind.**

   Consider the following:

   'I'm a great prospector — I connect with lots of people who want to sell their homes.'

   'When I prospect, people love to talk with me and set appointments with me.'

   'I will generate leads and appointments before I'm through today.'

You're now ready to pick up the phone with focus, intensity and an expectation of success.

Be faithful to yourself and finish what you start

Stay faithful to your daily objectives by completing all your prospecting contacts down to the very last one.

When you're running a race, you have to run the whole way. No-one remembers who was ahead at the 80-metre mark of the men's 100-metre race at the Olympics. The winner has to complete the full circuit before he can claim his medal.

Don't drop out early; finish what you start.

Putting Prospecting to Work

You can work harder. Or you can work smarter.

Most successful agents don't go into a secluded room, pick up the phone and toil away making hundreds of random calls over a non-stop eight-hour period. Few people would even consider that approach. This used to be the training method favoured by many in days gone by — but no longer, and we would never recommend this!

Instead, those who win at prospecting begin by targeting who they will call and why. They don't waste their time or effort calling iffy contacts that may or may not even be in the real estate market.

At its best, prospecting is truly effective when it generates a lead from a truly qualified prospect — someone who is interested in what you offer, needs the service you provide, and has the ability and authority to become a client of your business, or to refer you to someone who could. Don't disregard the fact that every single person you connect with can be the beginning of a relationship that could lead to future business or a referral. But you need to work to make this happen.

And that's where targeting and goal setting come to your rescue.

Targeting prospects

A great area to begin targeting your prospecting is in areas where young families congregate — for example, sports clubs, schools, gyms and clubs. Focus some 'under the radar' prospecting in these areas — join these clubs, or sponsor school activities or local sports clubs. Your potential clients get to know, like and trust you before you even begin to talk real estate. Take every opportunity to wear your name badge and you will be surprised at how conversations around real estate will start automatically. Be patient and your patience and perseverance will pay off big time.

Another area to focus on is where older people are likely to be found — again, local sports and recreation clubs present a great opportunity to offer free advice and become known as a trusted advisor. When the time is right and your contacts require a real estate agent, because of your efforts you'll likely be the only agent called in.

Setting and achieving prospecting goals

In setting prospecting goals, focus on three core areas: The number of contacts you should make each day and week, the number of leads you should develop, and the number of personal appointments you should set.

Start with easily attainable numbers for your prospecting goals, so you can build up your energy, intensity, focus and discipline slowly and steadily. You wouldn't run a marathon without working up your daily and weekly distances over time, and the same premise applies when establishing and meeting your prospecting goals.

Number of contacts made

A contact is a personal conversation with a decision maker who can make a purchase or sale or refer you to someone who can. A contact is not a conversation with the babysitter, a ten-year-old neighbour, a friendly teenager or an answering machine.

When we take on new coaching clients, we almost always start them with a goal of five contacts a day, and we suggest the same for you. Make a goal of five contacts a day without fail, resulting in the completion of 25 contacts a week. This is easily achievable.

It will take three to four weeks for contact with five prospects a day to become a habit. After you achieve the goal for three consecutive weeks without missing a single workday, you can raise your goal to seven or ten.

Number of leads established

Leads are contacts who have demonstrated through their dialogues that they possess the basic motivation and desire to make a change in their living arrangements — for example, they're thinking of selling. In prospecting, you have to make some assumptions until you either pre-qualify a client yourself or they secure an appointment with a lender that determines they have the financial capacity to make a purchase.

To advance your business, aim to develop at least one lead per day and five leads per week.

Number of appointments secured

An appointment is a face-to-face meeting with prospects, during which you discuss their needs and wants, share how you work, and aim to gain their commitment to work with you in an exclusive relationship to sell their home or find them a home to purchase. An appointment is the launch of the agent–client relationship. It's *not* a meeting during which you show a property.

Like your lead-generation goal, your appointment goal should be set at a reasonable level — a goal of one appointment a week is a solid start. If you acquire two appointments, terrific, but make sure that you're able to secure at least one.

If you're thinking, 'Hmm, five leads and only one appointment a week from all those calls . . .' realise that these are starting goals. It's far better to begin with aims you can actually achieve rather than ones that overwhelm you from the onset. As you gain consistency and skill in prospecting, both your numbers and your ratios will improve.

Even if you only maintain the starting goals, you'll have a good year as a newer agent. At the end of the year, you will have made 1,250 contacts and created 250 leads. You also will have set and conducted 50 appointments — and gotten two weeks off with your family to boot. How good is that?

Even if only half of the appointments turn into listings or sales, you'll have 25 deals in your first year. In most companies, that will make you rookie of the year. You'll also likely earn in excess of $100,000 in gross commission income. We don't know too many people in real estate (or in any other profession) who make that type of money in their first year.

The prospecting hierarchy of value

In prospecting, some approaches involve a shorter contact-to-contract cycle than others, therefore delivering a greater return on your time investment and a higher value for your business. In order, here are the factors that most influence the value of your prospecting approaches:

1. **Past clients:** The highest-value form of prospecting is calling past clients and those in your direct sphere of influence. These people have either used your services in the past or know you and your character. Asking them to do business with you again is described as *canvassing.* Asking them to refer their friends is described as prospecting for *referrals.*

   These calls are the easiest to make because they reach those with whom you have established relationships. Typically, real estate agents experience less resistance when placing calls to this group than to any other. They also make the calls with high expectations that their efforts will generate leads. How long it takes to acquire leads with this approach varies greatly. You can secure a lead on your very first call or on your 100th contact, so the ratio of leads generated to time invested is difficult to anticipate.

2. **Expired listings:** We can make a case for this being the number-one highest-value prospecting approach, as well, because of the ease of locating expired listings, and the relatively quick contact-to-contract cycle. You can easily monitor listings and track those that are expired. Check out www.rpdata.com.au, www.pricefinder.com.au or www.terranet.co.nz. Many expired listings go back on the market with another agent — either as a private treaty sale with a listed price or as another auction campaign — within a week, so the sales cycle is short, which is a key reason that expired listings offer such a high rate of return for the effort. The sellers are usually frustrated, tired and discouraged so are open to getting a firm offer as soon as possible so that they can move on with their lives. In essence, the big question you need to be broaching is, 'If we could get $XYZ for your property, even if it isn't your wish price, would that be enough for you to move on with your life?'

   Few agents engage in calling expired listings, largely because the sellers, who haven't experienced success with their last agents, can be hostile toward new agents. Agents in general tend to avoid situations where they may be verbally abused, which is natural — but you must get past this hesitation. Walk in the sellers' shoes, understand and let them vent their frustration, remembering it's not aimed at you personally. Many agents also feel it's 'beneath them' to contact these prospects — which further contributes to the opportunity for the ones who do.

3. **FSBOs:** Converting sale-by-owner contracts requires more work than securing expired listings. You have to seek out these sellers through newspaper ads or private seller sites such as www.buymyplace.com.au, www.owner.com.au, www.homesell.co.nz or www.sellahouse.co.nz. After you target a sale-by-owner property, figuring out whom to call takes another round of effort, which is why these sellers are farther down the value hierarchy.

   The sales cycle for-sale-by-owner properties is four to five weeks on average. These sellers generally try to sell by themselves for that time frame before engaging the services of a real estate agent. During that period, you must be willing to follow up weekly to secure an appointment four to five weeks away.

4. **Open houses and door knocking:** These face-to-face techniques require greater time investment than phone contacts, simply because you can't see as many people face to face as you can speak with over the phone. The advantage: It's harder for people to reject you face to face.

5. **Cold calling:** This technique, tried and true since the advent of the phone, has lost effectiveness over the years because of the preponderance of busy two-income families and the onset of Do Not Call registries. But some agents still make money, and a lot of it, by cold calling. It's not something we recommend highly because you have so many other techniques that provide higher returns with less effort. It is, however, better than waiting for the phone to ring.

Leveraging your success through technology

The key to increasing your effectiveness and efficiency is leverage: Putting yourself at an advantage above others. Leverage in prospecting is the ability to shorten the time spent doing research and increase the actual talk time or number of contacts you make in a day.

When Terri started in the industry in the early 1990s, technology was in its infancy. She used 6 × 4 contact cards and wrote letters and cards to her prospects and clients. It was effective but very time-consuming. Nowadays, technology has elevated real estate success to a whole new level. One email about a new listing can reach thousands of contacts with one press of the button. You can market properties online with multiple images, floor plans, aerial views, virtual tours and even maps of surrounding areas. The sky is the limit.

Customer relationship managers (CRMs) are now specially designed to make an agents' life simple. A CRM is far more than just a software application. It is a business solution that gives you the ability to connect with and understand your customers. The system combines people, processes and technology and covers every interaction with your customers across your entire business.

Utilising your CRM well ensures that all the information you require is available to all areas of your business — you can easily access prospecting plans, letters, scripts, appointments and follow-up activity plans. This provides a platform for building and maintaining loyal customers, while helping you to enlist new ones. Your CRM can even help you to set trackable goals and KPIs (key performance indicators), and keep abreast of your commissions.

Your agency may have a CRM they prefer their agents to use. If not, many are on the market now. Check out `mydesktop.com.au`, `www.lockedon.com` or `www.propertysuite.co.nz`. Or you can search online for options and to read through reviews. Another way to check out different CRMs is to join a Facebook real estate group (just type **real estate group** into the Facebook search field) and then ask other agents what they'd recommend.

Shattering the myths

You've likely heard at least some of the reasons agents give to avoid adopting sound prospecting techniques. 'My market is different' or 'You don't understand how we do things here in Sydney' (or Auckland or wherever you happen to be) are among the many. The truth is, the techniques in this chapter work in every market area, everywhere in the world, at any point in time. So bury the myths, starting with the ones that follow.

Try this magic pill . . .

Real estate success is built on a series of fundamentals. One of those fundamentals is prospecting.

Plenty of people are working to sell agents on some magic pill they can take to avoid the fundamental need to prospect. They are greeted by a willing market because many agents secretly hope for a prospecting-free existence, just as we secretly hope those guys on the late-night infomercials are right that we can buy a home for no money down at below market prices, or take a tablet and eat whatever we want and not work out and still lose weight.

Dream on. You'll never find a magic mailing program, social-media ad campaign, calendar, magnet, marketing piece or website that will make up for the fundamental need to pick up the phone and actually talk to a prospect.

Here's an approach that's too good to be true . . .

Agents are quick to share with you how they got where they are today, passionately describing their techniques, people who helped them or products that made the difference.

While a few of these agents can tell you the cause-and-effect link between their actions or techniques and their sales and revenue, more than 95 per cent truly have no idea or can't quantify their success for you.

Your job is to pull the curtain back. In the movie *The Wizard of Oz*, Dorothy, the tin man, the scarecrow and the cowardly lion are all mesmerised by and scared of the great and powerful Oz. It takes a dog, Toto, to reveal that Oz is just a little man pulling levers and using a sound system to produce the semblance of greatness and power.

In the future, when someone approaches you with great and powerful business-generating techniques, pull back the curtain with these questions:

- How many transactions does this technique generate for you annually?
- How much time do you need to invest personally to set this up and maintain it?
- What does it cost you to use this marketing service to generate leads?

- What is the conversion ratio on this technique?
- What percentage of your business comes from this activity?
- How many buyers did you get from this approach?
- How many sellers did you get?
- What is your net profit from this activity after all your costs are subtracted?
- Have you included the value of your time in that equation?

Most people (whether they are other agents, your broker, other trainers or sales gurus) can't answer most of these questions. However, they're all positive that what they're advocating is the magic bullet for you and your business.

Be wary of things that sound good but may not stand up to scrutiny. Say you receive a marketing piece from an agent touting his approaches to business. The agent outlines that he sold 60 homes in his third year in the business — a respectable number. Based on his personal success, he's promoting his lead-generation model as better than prospecting because he did 60 deals and generated more than 1,200 leads a month. The average agent would be frothing at the mouth to achieve those numbers.

But have a look at these types of figures more closely (grab your calculator if you need to). In this example, the agent generates more than 14,400 leads a year, which means his 60 transactions represent a lead-conversion rate of .004167 — less than half of 1 per cent. Put differently, he has converted only one person for every 240 leads generated through his so-called prospecting technique.

You can only come to two logical conclusions here: Either the leads he's generating are marginal at best, or he's really poor at securing face-to-face meetings and subsequent deals. We'll leave you to pick which scenario you think is more likely.

If it seems too good to be true, it probably is.

Top producers don't prospect . . .

This myth is based on some truth. Many top-performing agents *don't* prospect in the same way, after they've 'made it' as agents. But you'll be hard pressed to find top producers who got where they are without prospecting at earlier stages in their careers. And you'll be even harder pressed to find top producers who can weather the swings and changes of the marketplace without going back into prospecting mode at least on an occasional basis.

To become a top producer, you must prospect. And to remain at the top of your game, you must continue to prospect. Don't quit prospecting ever!

As you become more and more successful at real estate sales, you may even do more prospecting, in part because prospecting becomes more natural and easier than ever. As you acquire name recognition and market presence, the people you contact are increasingly honoured and pleasantly surprised to receive your calls. Prospecting becomes fun rather than a chore. They know you're busy and successful, and they respond not only with their own business but also with many referrals.

My clients and friends don't want to be bothered . . .

Agents who use this excuse are focusing almost exclusively on the canvassing or referral portion of the call, rather than on the connection the call allows with a long-established associate or friend.

Wouldn't you be delighted to get a call from your accountant, doctor, dentist or insurance agent, asking how you and your family are, thanking you for your business, and seeing if they can do anything for you?

We bet you can count on one hand (or less!) the number of times in the last 20 years you've received a call like that. If you did, you'd probably be stunned and appreciative. Your sphere, past clients and other associates will feel the exact same way.

Every time we work with a new client, we can be almost guaranteed to hear the same excuse: They don't want to bother anyone. Then they make calls for a week and when we talk with them again, they always say the same thing: 'I was amazed how easy it was. My clients were really happy to talk with me. I couldn't get them off the phone. It was great to catch up.'

Finding Safety and Success in Numbers

Sales is a numbers game. Prospecting is a numbers game, as well. The problem is, too few agents actually know their numbers and how to track them.

The following sections help you understand and set objectives for your ratios of contacts to leads, leads to closings, appointments to contracts, and contracts to closings. Knowing this information moves you almost immediately into the league of our industry's most productive agents.

The law of accumulation

The law of accumulation basically says that achievement is the result of ongoing and constant effort. Everything in life, whether positive or negative, compounds itself over time.

An illustration of this is money. If you want to be a millionaire, all you have to do is save a little on a consistent basis and the law of accumulation will take over.

If you put away $2.74 a day from the time you are 20 until you are 65 and receive an average rate of return of 9 per cent over those years, you'll be a millionaire. You will have saved about $45,000 over those 45 years; the law of accumulation does the rest. If you ask most people whether they'll trade $45,000 for $1 million, they'll say yes, but few people actually make the effort.

You can expect an equally uneven return when you invest in prospecting. The tricky part is that the reward for your miniscule investment of prospecting effort doesn't happen overnight. You have to prospect for 90 days before the law of accumulation does its thing. As Dirk's good friend Zig Ziglar used to say, 'Life is like a cafeteria. First you pay, and then you get to eat.'

The power of consistency

Marginally successful agents take a binge approach to prospecting. Highly successful agents are far, far more consistent in their efforts.

Dirk often gives this example of the success that comes with consistency. Rich Purvis, a man Dirk met a few years ago, had entered the field of real estate after 25 years in a fire-fighting career. His goal was to earn $100,000 a year, but when Dirk met him in March his income was a disappointing $2,500. Dirk told Rich, 'If you call ten contacts within your sphere of influence each day, you'll get your $100,000 before year's end.' Rich did just that — Dirk can count on one hand the number of times that Rich failed to make the ten contacts. He blew by his goal of $100,000 in less than nine months and ended up earning more than $120,000 that year. The next year he crossed the $200,000 mark. It was all the result of his extraordinary consistency. Moral of the story — set your targets and keep to them!

The never-ending prospecting cycle

Agents can easily find time to prospect when they have no listings, no pending transactions, and no buyers to work with. The secret is to continue to prospect even when you're busy with all the other activities.

Look at a typical agent's annual income stream and you'll see that it goes up and down like a yoyo. Most agents have four to six good income months per year. The rest of the time — nothing much. If you overlay their revenue streams with their prospecting numbers, you'll see that revenue decreases when prospecting tapers off, leading directly to the business void that follows.

Your job as a salesperson is to fill a pipeline of leads so you always have new prospects to work with. And the only way to keep a healthy pipeline or conveyer belt of leads is to prospect consistently.

The importance of tracking results

Any business in sales can be broken down to a series of repeatable numbers that, over time, produce a pre-determined result. When you establish goals and track your performance over a few months, you can determine the activities you need to earn the income you desire.

Terri's goal was to sell six to eight properties a month in her second year of operation. She worked the figures, looking at the conversion ratios of appraisals that resulted in listings and the ratio of listings that resulted in sales. She worked out that 20 appraisals led to 12 listings, which led to 6 to 8 sales per month.

Working backwards, she then looked at, on average, how many prospecting contacts resulted in a good lead. It turned out that she needed to speak in person with at least 20 people each day, or 120 each week. From this, it was simple to set her prospecting plan.

Use Figure 4-1 to establish and track your prospecting numbers.

The law of averages evens out your numbers over time. Don't evaluate yourself on a single day's achievements. Even a week is too short a period for evaluation. Some days you may not set a single appointment. Other days, you'll set up more than your target. As long as you're consistent, your numbers will always stack up.

DAILY PROSPECTING GOALS AND RESULTS

ACTIVITY:	GOALS:	RESULTS:
Prospecting contacts made		
Leads obtained		
Listing appointments scheduled		
Qualified listing presentations made		
Buyer interview appointments scheduled		
Buyer interview appointments made		
Qualified offers written		
Total "real working hours" invested		
Prospecting hours		
Listing hours		
Showing hours		
Offers hours		

Rate your day (1 – 10) __________ Comments:

Figure 4-1: Use a tracking sheet such as this one to monitor and evaluate your prospecting efforts.

The challenge of managing contacts

To store your prospecting information and assure prompt and ongoing follow-up, employ real-estate specific contact-management software such as My Desktop, Top Producer, LockedOn or one of the many other CRMs on the market today. These systems will be invaluable to you and are designed to help you with your sales functions and also with business management, including creating market reports, generating correspondence and tracking your settlements.

Regardless of the system you select, you must be able to access your contact database with reliability and ease.

While you're budgeting . . .

As a newer real estate sales agent, you need to budget for ongoing self-improvement.

Start with a budget for a wardrobe that presents you as a successful agent. Some people will make assumptions about you based on the way you dress, so don't wait — dress for success now. This doesn't need to break your budget. A well-cut suit and business shirt, or polo shirt and smart casual pants for men and smart (not too colourful or way out) outfit for women will speak volumes to your prospects. Most agencies have a dress code and some a uniform — you can check this at the initial interview.

Just as important, budget to attend every business seminar you can make time to attend. Your personal education and skills-based training is fundamental to your climb up the ladder of success. Not only will you learn heaps, further education and training is a great opportunity to meet and mingle with your colleagues — which can be an amazing source of mutual help and cooperation. In between, buy books, CDs and DVDs, download podcasts, and get your hands, eyes or ears on every piece of media that can help you develop sales skills, mental focus, leadership, discipline and motivation.

The most significant asset in your business right now is you. Ten years from now, the most significant asset in your business will still be you. Don't fail to invest in yourself.

Your CRM isn't the place to apply a shoestring budget. Minimally you want to invest in a computer (preferably a laptop) and all the software necessary to build and run your business, including contact management, MLS (multiple listing service) access and agency management.

Staying in Touch

Use your contact-management system (or your CRM) to trigger the next call to a prospect and make staying in touch automatic and easy:

- Each time you end a prospecting call, determine when the next call will take place. Find out your prospect's time frame and when it's convenient to speak again. Then schedule the contact right then and there.
- When talking to a past client or sphere member, schedule the next call without even asking. Then, the next time you call, they'll be pleasantly surprised to hear from you.

- In addition to making calls, send emails to thank contacts for their time and to reiterate your service offer.
- Get permission to add contacts to your blog or email newsletter mailing.
- Follow up first-time contacts with a copy of your agency brochure or marketing piece. Or send a 'Just listed' or 'Just sold' card to demonstrate your success as an agent.
- Craft a personalised business letter, perfectly proofread and presented on your letterhead and sent out in a matching envelope.

But wait! Great as all the preceding suggestions are for your business, none of them beats the all-time winning touch of a handwritten thank-you note that says to the receiver, 'You were so important that I took the time to pen this in my own hand instead of touching a few buttons on my computer or spitting out a pre-planned, standard-issue, regurgitated letter that I've sent to 1,000 other people just like you.'

Most of us get hundreds of emails a day, most of which we don't even want. We all receive junk mail, each one wanting to sell us something.

The handwritten thank-you note breaks through the clutter. It looks like an invitation to something special. It enhances the personal relationship and keeps it active until you talk again in a few days. It's still the best way to keep in touch in our technology-driven world.

Chapter 5

Using Social Media to Create an Online Presence

In This Chapter

- Using your personal Facebook page to generate leads
- Setting up a Facebook page for your business
- Creating a blog to highlight your real estate expertise
- Looking at Twitter and LinkedIn for your business

Not so very long ago, social media was considered the exclusive domain of the young, and was used primarily for social networking. However times have changed and agents have changed with them. You can now use such tools to find and communicate with prospects; market yourself, your services and your listed properties; and converse with your past clients and sphere of influence.

You can successfully use social media in lead generation, and sales and brand building through use of mass audience social platforms. You can share videos, new listings or local news with your communities and prospective buyers or sellers. Social media is an exciting new world — one that you need to be part of.

Social media has greatly influenced some real estate agents' time management. While the greater use of social media has many positives, if used unwisely the overinvestment of time in social media can reduce revenue rather than increase sales. It can be a great (and unprofitable) time waster! If you ask most agents, they're likely to say that social media accounts for a much larger portion of their business than it actually does. For many agents, the time invested in social media generates an inequitable return. It is fun, it does build relationships, but you need to think about who you're actually building relationships with. The hour or more each day posting comments could get you better known within the real estate community, but how much of this actually results in a listing or a sale? Perhaps you're just relating to your colleagues, who certainly aren't going to be passing on their leads to you.

So, although social media is no doubt becoming an increasingly important lead-generation tool, especially if you can ask your satisfied clients to post their testimonials on your online page, allocating the right time, strategies and communication systems helps you maintain the correct balance between traditional business strategies and new tech-savvy strategies. Remember, both are important.

Although real estate agents have many social-media options, including established sites like Twitter and LinkedIn, for generating leads and finding buyers Facebook and blogs are the most commonly used tools in real estate. Fast-growing social-media newcomers like Instagram and Pinterest have a young audience, but a big portion of that audience is still living at home with parents. Many of those users aren't ready to purchase or sell homes. Other sites will come and go, and it's nearly impossible to use every social-media tool without spending all day in front of your computer. That's not a recipe for success in a business where face-to-face interaction still matters.

So we devote the majority of this chapter to the social media that is going to be most powerful for you — Facebook and blogs — and how you can use these forms of social media to increase leads and, ultimately, sales. We also look briefly at using Twitter, LinkedIn and YouTube to your advantage.

Personal or Business? Using Facebook Effectively

Facebook is the most used social-media tool in the world. Using Facebook in real estate is a great way to build relationships and stay at the forefront of the technological world. But because real estate agents often use both their personal and business relationships to conduct business, the line between the two can become muddled. We personally believe you need to keep your business page on Facebook totally separate from your personal one. Establishing a personal profile enables you to post your personal history — your likes and dislikes, photos, stories and so on. This is the most common experience on Facebook, which now has more than a billion personal profiles. This type of profile is a one-person profile that highlights your interests and connections with others.

Your personal profile may still be viewed by current and potential clients, and your personal contacts are often a good source of business. Don't think for one moment that your clients aren't searching for you online and researching whatever Facebook posts they can access before they decide to give you their business. So make sure you don't post any photos that could embarrass you! One slip could cost thousands in lost dollars.

From a business perspective, Facebook enables you to brand your product or service. (Just a hint . . . the product or service is still *you* until you grow a larger market presence and leverage yourself through other people or a team.) Facebook gives you numerous free methods to interact with prospects, clients and people you know. This allows you and your 'company' to connect and encourage people to 'like' the page so they receive valuable information and updates.

Using your personal page to create business

On your personal Facebook page, you need to achieve a balance between communicating your business interests and sharing personal updates. Your personal profile should be mainly personal with a sprinkling of business information.

Your photo is one of the most important first decisions. Facebook is a casual and informal media. Your profile and cover photos should reflect that. You don't need the glamour shot, professional headshot or air-brushed shot; in fact, it's probably better not to use those. This is your personal page, but you'll get crossover from personal contacts with whom you do business, so it's important to choose a photo that represents who you are in a casual setting, but that isn't too hobby driven or inappropriate.

Your profile photo will appear in most posts, communications and connections. Choose one that shows you as both the warm, personal person next door and the professional. The mistake we see too frequently is a picture that makes someone appear unapproachable or arrogant.

Walk the fine line with business on your personal page

Too many agents cross the line. They post every new listing on their personal timeline. Most of your friends don't want an overload of property listings invading their newsfeed. The rule of thumb is four to five personal posts for every business post you make. Err on the side of caution. If you think you may have overdone the business posts this week, you probably have.

One option that is softer than an 'in your face' listing announcement is a congratulations post to a new buyer who settled on a property. Check whether your buyers or sellers are happy for you to post a photo and perhaps a testimonial from their purchase or sale on your Facebook page — if they agree, this is a powerful way to cross over to business from personal. Be sure to tag the happy buyers so all their friends are informed. This enables you to engage with a large, growing group of friends and followers. You can even send friend requests to the people who comment or post. This is a simple way to use your personal page to generate business and say thank you to clients.

Watch for life changes

One of the best ways to use Facebook is not posting but listening. Just review your friends' posts to see what's happening and changing in their lives. The coolest part of Facebook is how quickly you can pick up on clues and cues of change. Set aside some time to quickly review personal posts — but don't get too involved in this or it will take over and your results could be affected dramatically!

The right message or comment can lead to a wealth of new business. Telling someone how pleased you are about the announcement of a new child can lead them to mention that their home is now getting cramped. You generally won't have to say too much, because your warm greeting will jog their memory about your real estate business. If you need to lightly or casually remind them of your profession, do it after a few comments back and forth. A great idea is to use Facebook's private message function to contact the person if you don't want to publicly seem like you're pouncing on a lead opportunity — you don't want to come across as always having an ulterior motive for your comments.

Set up a watch list

One of the least used but most important features of Facebook is the list function. You can create lists of people that categorise them so it's easier to listen and watch. Use the 'smart list' suggestions in Facebook to separate some of your lists. These smart lists break your contact list down by city or high school, for example. These are helpful, but setting up your own lists is even better.

Set up specific watch lists around the type of business you want to do. You can set up a buyer watch list or seller watch list. Put in people who are high-level prospects with whom you interact and who have shown an interest in a different home ownership situation. Others on the watch list may be going through a life event, as we described earlier in this section.

Watch lists make it easier for you to monitor these peoples' posts. They still remain in your newsfeed, but they also appear in the list area on the left side of your Facebook page. All you have to do is click on the specific watch list and the recent posts of all the people on that list will be organised on your screen. It creates a smaller, more organised set of posts to review each day. This approach is much faster than scrolling through your whole newsfeed to see what a group of people you deem to be viable prospects has posted today.

Creating different lists is easy. Go to your newsfeed and select Friends from the left side, and then select Create List. A pop-up menu asks you to name the list, and then you can select the friends whom you want to be part of the list.

You can send posts directly to these lists as well, rather than to all your friends. For example, you can create a post targeted to the people on your list of potential buyers. Maybe you read a great newspaper article about rising interest rates and why people should buy now. You can post the article but target it to your buyer group. You're sending information of value to the group that is most likely to use it.

Post for pleasure (and business)

Keeping people up to date with both your personal life and business can be a chore. Here are a couple of tips on how to keep up with posting and creating variety for you and your friends:

- **Share what's up:** Don't be afraid to share about your family and what's happening. This makes you approachable and shows that you're just like your friends, clients and prospects — just be careful not to invade your family's privacy, because they may not want their lives splashed all over Facebook. As your production grows and you become an elite producer, it's even more important to remain approachable. Share your likes and dislikes with your friends (staying away from controversial topics like politics that offend and so impact your business). If you ask questions that create interaction, you can improve your position in the newsfeed of others who answer and comment.
- **Don't share inappropriate or sensitive views:** Be careful with religious views, as well as perspectives on hot-button social issues. Any photo of you that doesn't align with your professional image is also a no-no. Avoid the revealing bathing suits, the giant margarita or the less-than-flattering hangover picture.
- **Share your photos:** Most people prefer to see visuals rather than text. Your photos can be either personal or community photos. Create the

reputation of being your community expert. Photos of local places and events create an image of you as 'the man (or woman) about town'.

- **Share interesting articles or links:** The key is sharing links to things your network will find interesting. They can be notices about local events and issues, or they can be real estate articles from respected sources such as Australian Property Investor (www.apimagazine.com.au) or New Zealand's *Property Investor* magazine (www.propertyinvestor.co.nz). This demonstrates that you're well read, educated and on top of the market trends.
- **Acknowledge others:** If you've received great service, or if someone in your network has achieved success by winning an award, opening a business or similar, acknowledge that. You're spreading the wealth of who you know to aid others in achieving their dreams.

If you're comfortable with others knowing your whereabouts, use the check-in feature when you visit stores, restaurants and travel destinations. This allows your location to pop up on your Facebook feed. Check-ins can create conversations or spur memories from others that will open dialogue between you and friends. The more interesting you seem in your check-ins and experiences, the wider the net you cast for posts from others.

Creating your business page

Facebook created business profiles to reduce the business promotion that was happening on personal pages. The purpose of a business page is to engage with the people who 'like' your page, interact with the community where you live and do business and, finally, to share valuable information that relates to real estate investment and sales. The difference between the business page and your personal page is that the business page can be viewed by anyone. Most people set the privacy settings on their personal pages so that those pages can be viewed only by confirmed Facebook friends. But people don't have to 'like' your business page to see your posts there.

A Facebook business page should be part of your overall online marketing strategy. Agents try many different strategies for Facebook business pages. Some agents have one business page where they drive much of their online interaction. Others segment their business pages to align with different aspects of their business. However, if you're just starting out, this is probably more complex than you need to get.

The keys to a powerful Facebook business page are:

- Frequently update the content of your pages. The more you update and refresh the information, the more your 'likes' will grow and the more people will come back to see what's new. People who have 'liked' your page receive a notification when you post something. By posting regularly, you keep your face and message in front of your prospects, clients, sphere of influence and past clients.
- Create posts that lead to interaction. Using questions to engage your followers in conversation is also a way to create interactivity. When you create engaging content that gets people talking, reposting and sharing, you know that you've been successful in expanding your reach.
- Generate leads by creating posts that lead back to your own or your company website. Because so many consumers start dreaming about home ownership online, you must always develop strategies that leave a trail of crumbs for them to follow.

Figuring out what to post on your business page

You should post quality content to entice new 'likes' and retain the current group of followers. Before you get all fired up to promote your page to the world, make sure you're posting good content and a reasonable amount of it. No-one wants to like a page that has limited information and value. You don't need a truckload of posts, but you need some value that can be seen and digested. The more powerful the content, the more it will be shared. Sharing is one of the most useful aspects of Facebook. It explodes your reach exponentially.

You have a number of options when looking to post valuable content. You may want to post market data, for example, to update your followers on the state of the marketplace. Share numbers for the inventory of homes for sale and sold properties. Also talk about what segments of the market are hot in terms of price range, geographic areas, key neighbourhoods and types of properties. Posts about staging, home improvement, decorating and design also attract eyeballs.

Practising consistency

A key to posting is consistency and frequency. You need to post at least five times a week, but these posts don't need to be long — sometimes just one sentence or a great quote is enough. When you post, use photos, videos or links on a handful of those posts and you will see growth. You can't set the standard for yourself that every post is earth-shatteringly brilliant. The truth is that not every post will create the attention you want. Your job is to build a voice and build a habit. When it comes down to it, success comes to people who are consistent more than it comes to the brilliant.

Finding the right mix

The right mix in your posts fosters community and connection. The focus of 40 per cent of your posts should be to engage others in conversation and communication. Use 20 per cent of your posts to link to other content that positions you as well informed and that has value to your followers. Another 20 per cent can be general business or economic news that influences the greater real estate market. The final 20 per cent can be real estate specific about trends nationally, regionally or locally. Local trends should outweigh the regional and national.

You can post listings, but don't overdo it. What you want to do in posting listings is to tell a story. Don't just list general information, such as the number of bedrooms and bathrooms and the price . . . boring! Share something that makes the listing unique, desirable or different. Maybe it has an interesting, historic story: Did someone famous or infamous once live there? Does it have unique amenities, such as a rare type of hardwood floor or one-of-a-kind design features? Use those aspects to draw people in and they will most likely connect with you and respond. And don't forget videos are always good.

Getting people to share your posts, business or personal

No technique can make up for poor content. The first rule of getting more shares is to post something worth sharing. You can increase the sharing if you make the post visually stimulating as well as mentally stimulating. Be sure to use photos and videos as much as possible. The share numbers go through the roof when you do.

If you're going to use a photo, select an interesting shot that will catch the audience. Just make sure that the image size is correct — nothing is worse than looking at a picture or a quote that's cut off at the bottom.

Creating a great headline is another way to increase shares. Many people only read the opening headline, but if it's provocative and engaging you can get them to share.

Anecdotal stories that align with what's happening in the real estate marketplace can be good shares. Also think about posting general market updates, funny stories, announcements of big sales and pictures of hot new listings.

When all else fails, ask. The adage 'ask and you shall receive' is still in play. If you softly ask your followers to 'help you out', 'share if you would like to' or 'feel free to share with your friends', this can increase your shares as well.

Understanding the Basics of Blogging for Real Estate

Blogging today is what newsletters were ten years ago. The biggest difference is the interactivity you can create with a blog. Although many agents agonise over what to write for their blogs, the basic rule is like any other social-media platform: Consistency is key. If you're going to blog, you must do a couple of blog posts each week rather than once a week or month.

Blogs are like short stories. They can be a great source of information about your market and an opportunity to display your knowledge of this market, but they also allow you to show a little creativity. For example, you could offer clients some information on interest rates, particularly when they could be favourable for purchasing property. Or you could talk about new and planned infrastructure in your area, or add links for current listings, which can be a great way of sending people across to these listings on your website. Blogs are also great for SEO (search engine optimisation), because they keep fresh content directly on your website.

Nothing is worse than going to a blog that hasn't seen any new posts in months. It shows a lack of attention to detail on the part of the agent. We know coming up with something meaningful to say and write about a few times a week can sometimes be hard. But you don't have to have written a number of books to be effective at blogging.

In fact, you don't have to write much at all. You can actually do a video blog for most of your blog communication. A simple HD webcam on your computer, smartphone or tablet can even do the trick in creating simple but effective video blog communications. For some of your blogs, you can also do an online search to find relevant articles you can use short extracts from — just make sure you acknowledge the original author and ensure most of your blogs are still your own.

Creating the look and feel of a professional blog

Blogging is much easier today than ever before because of the wealth of programs, apps and software that can incorporate a blog into your website. A simple WordPress site with a template layout is easy, quick and worth checking out — this site is our preference because of the ease of use. Most blog designers use it, as well, and it really is the best option for agents. Blogs are effective in helping you climb in search-engine rankings because search engines like the new content that a blog provides.

Add credibility and variety to your blog. What about featuring a guest blogger each week? When you think about it, you will have access to an unlimited number of guest bloggers — for example, your mortgage broker can blog about what information they look for when someone applies for a loan, or your favourite building or pest inspector can blog about the benefits of having these kind of inspections done before buyers come through. What about some advice from home stagers, interior decorators or conveyancing solicitors? The list is endless. If the consumer thinks you're an agent who knows how to add value to a deal, you're already ahead of the pack.

Setting up your writing and posting schedule

Setting up your blogging schedule or theme days is one of the most important first steps to having a successful blog. You can set aside time each week to create half a dozen blogs and then set these posts to go out automatically and on schedule across a defined time. Posting new content a couple of times a week can really enhance your readership. Also, posting at the same time each week will create anticipation for your posts. Decide on a schedule to post but also to write. If you don't carve out a set time to create new content, you'll always be doing it last minute. The quality will suffer, and the pressure you feel will explode.

You can set up different segments or even different days that you post about certain topics. You can do a 'photo Friday' theme. You can blog about your community, using photos to illustrate your topic. You can highlight restaurants, businesses and new attractions in your community on a certain day. You can regularly deal with zoning or planning issues that affect your community. You can feature a real estate column each week where you share rate alerts, give tips on home values, talk about the current state of the marketplace, give the pros and cons of home ownership versus renting, or discuss your keys to your marketing plan.

Always be ready to gather observations in your daily life. Don't go anywhere without your digital camera. Your smartphone can take pictures, but most digital cameras are far better. Post what you observe and craft a blog from it — a new park or playground, a great garden, a horrendous traffic jam and so on. Be a gatherer of experiences and photos for later use, as well; file them away on your computer, tablet or smartphone. The other option is to use an app like Evernote to store photos with your brief observations so you can reconstruct your feelings, thoughts and ideas at a later date when you want to incorporate the photos into your blog.

Positioning yourself as the marketplace expert

The vast majority of consumers think that they know more than real estate agents. It's why we typically score so low in any poll of trusted professionals. We must change that. The best method is to demonstrate market knowledge. A blog is an effective way to continually demonstrate your knowledge. Share list price to sale price ratios, days-on-the-market numbers and real estate trends.

Real estate values and market activity are controlled by supply and demand. When either of those changes, you'll see a corresponding reaction in the real estate market. If supply goes up and stays up, prices will usually moderate, flatten or start to move downward. If the demand increases because the number of buyers increases, you may see the opposite results. By regularly commenting on these trends, you establish yourself as an expert.

Your market data and trend projections should explain, educate and forecast what the law of supply and demand is reflecting in your real estate market. Using your blog a handful of times a month for this targeted purpose can inform your readers and position you as the expert.

Don't forget to include a *call to action* with these types of blog posts. A good call to action is 'If you're looking to move into the upper end, it's a buyers' market at the moment, so call me right away' or 'A large volume of mortgagee-in-possession listings have just hit the market, so if you're looking for a great deal, call me or text me now'. You want to move people beyond readership to the actionable steps of calling and reaching out because they see a clear opportunity or a heightened fear of loss.

Positioning Yourself on Twitter

Twitter is another amazing way to keep connected to your clients. Twitter gives you 140 characters (or less) to provide updates to your followers. Use it to engage your contacts and keep strengthening your relationships.

You can use your tweets to provide quick information and tips to your followers, such as the following:

- Tips to help sellers prepare their property for sale or get a higher price for their property
- Information on how the local market is going
- Ideas about how to select an agent and what to watch out for
- Local news and events of interest in your area

Short bursts like this are easy for your followers to read but set you apart as an area expert and someone to go to for guidance when buying or selling.

Twitter isn't really an avenue for promoting your listings or boasting about your latest results. Your focus when using it should purely be on building relationships with people who want to know, like and trust you for the future.

If you don't have a Twitter handle, check out this great blog from social media guru Krista Bunskoek: `blog.wishpond.com/post/47480842552/how-to-make-a-twitter-handle-for-your-business-13-easy`.

Using LinkedIn as a Business Tool

LinkedIn is a great professional platform for agents to connect with a very valuable target audience — businesspeople buy and sell their own houses and properties too. That means LinkedIn is another great tool for residential real estate professionals to build relationships that lead to sales.

Most agents are pretty familiar with using Facebook and Twitter for personal and hopefully business use, but many are at a loss with LinkedIn. If this is you, the first thing to do is to create a business page and a business profile. Include a good summary, introducing yourself and outlining the benefits of choosing you as a real estate agent (both to buy from, and to sell through).

Join local LinkedIn groups and participate in them. Like with Twitter (refer to preceding section), the purpose is to build connections, not to sell anything. Keep connected with your followers, and ask for referrals through the site (just as you would in person).

On LinkedIn, recommendations are equivalent to testimonials, and like all testimonials, these recommendations can lead to referrals and so can be a critical piece of the agent's profile.

Every extra piece of exposure helps! Undoubtedly, you can be more powerful as part of a team than alone, so if you work with a franchise or agency, make sure the details of these are included in your profile.

Using YouTube to Accelerate Your Growth

Many successful agents now make it a rule to have professional videos done for every new listing. You can post these videos on your website, email them to prospects and allow them to (hopefully) go viral by posting them on YouTube. You can also post a short video on YouTube to introduce yourself (you can embed this onto your website too). Or you can post videos that show off the best features in your neighbourhood, reinforcing your local presence and setting yourself up as the 'area expert'.

YouTube is a powerful marketing tool, and an effective method of showcasing properties and generating leads for your real estate business.

Chapter 6

Generating Referrals

In This Chapter

- Understanding the pluses and minuses of a referral-based business
- Developing a client base and implementing a referral strategy that works
- Establishing and maintaining relationships with your referral base

Salespeople love referrals. They're the sincerest form of compliment and a remarkably cost-effective route to new business.

The idea of attracting referrals is so popular that sales trainers who promote themselves as referral gurus make fortunes promoting magical systems that supposedly deliver more referrals than an agent can handle, all in return for tuition at a three-day seminar. What they talk about for three days is really a mystery to us. Referrals are really pretty simple stuff. In this short chapter, you can find 90 per cent of what you need to know. The rest you can only acquire through perfect practice of your scripts, over and over, for the referral-generating and referral-cultivating tactics in the upcoming sections.

Knowing the Referral Truths and Consequences

Before you turn even a moment of effort away from prospecting activities and before you put all your hopes into winning business through a full-tilt referral-generation program, be aware that in addition to all the benefits that come with referrals, a 100 per cent referral-based business has some downsides. Proceed with awareness of these ironclad truths:

- **Truth #1:** Especially for newer agents, over-reliance on referrals results in slow growth simply because a newer agent doesn't have a large enough database of existing clients and contacts to draw upon.

- **Truth #2:** Relying entirely on referrals for client development is a narrow, exclusive and unbalanced approach. For one thing, if incoming referrals decline, you won't have other prospecting systems in place to bail your business out of trouble. What's more, when referrals do come in, most will be for buyer prospects rather than seller prospects. What the referral gurus never say is that their approach develops buyers' agents — although sellers' agents are the ones who experience the greatest success and build the strongest long-term real estate sales businesses.
- **Truth #3:** The percentage of referral-based business is on a downward trend over the last few years. Consumers are shifting to the internet and other social forums to find a real estate agent. Although referrals should always be the most important part of your lead-generation and business strategy, maintaining a deep well of prospecting strategies (refer to Chapter 4) and marketing tools (see Chapter 11) is vital to success.

Building a Referral-Based Clientele

A referral-based business is one that generates most leads as a result of contacts provided by friends, family, clients, colleagues and other associates. Sounds great, doesn't it? It *is* great, if — and here's a big if — you have a large sphere of influence and enough patience to wait out a lag time of at least 90 days, and often longer, between when you begin to cultivate referrals and when referrals begin to generate revenue for your business.

Building a referral-based clientele is a long-term strategy rather than a quick-fix tactic. If you're looking for immediate results (and what new agent isn't?), you're better off developing clients through a traditional lead-development program that involves prospecting (go straight to Chapter 4 for step-by-step advice), conversion of expired, withdrawn and for-sale-by-owner (FSBO) listings (see Chapter 7) and open houses (see Chapter 8).

Relying exclusively on referrals, especially when you're a new and undercapitalised agent, is a quick form of business suicide that will drive you out of the real estate industry within a year, guaranteed. Instead, consider referrals a second-stage strategy — one that follows your initial round of business development, and contributes to the long-term growth and health of your business.

Defining referrals

At its core, a referral is a recommendation.

In its best form, a referral is a high-quality lead and a high-probability prospect who is introduced to you by someone both you and the prospect regard highly.

Finding sources of referrals

Most referrals come from family members, friends, current clients, past clients, people you've met through networking situations, and people you know through social or business dealings. They come from people you either have a personal contact and connection with or know through online and social-media platforms.

When working with referral sources, make it your objective to secure names, addresses, and home, mobile and work phone numbers, as well as email addresses for those in the market to sell or buy. From there, you can reach out to pursue the leads. Ask the referral sources to make a personal contact on your behalf — meeting with or phoning the prospect in advance of your call to share your name and a little bit about the success you helped them achieve. Some people are uncomfortable turning over contact information for a potential prospect to a real estate salesperson, or any salesperson for that matter. They're afraid the salesperson will turn into a pest. You could start by adapting the following script, which really works well to put the referring individual more at ease:

> *Bob, I appreciate the referral opportunity and you offering to give your friend Suzi my business card, but I will tell you it's rare when a referral actually calls the agent. My real concern is that in our marketplace more than half of the agents have been in the business less than a handful of years. The average agent does fewer than 8 sales a year. The probability is that your friend is going to get an agent who doesn't understand the marketplace and may not be as skilled. I'm sure that's not what you want to have happen. Would there be a way we could work out that would allow you to be comfortable with giving her number to me so that I can make a soft introductory call?*

The upcoming sections provide information for working with different groups of potential referral contacts.

Current clients

Current clients are people you're actively representing, right now, in real estate transactions. Current clients are a rich pool of referral opportunity mainly because, more than any other group, they have real estate on their minds. They're in the midst of deals that they're constantly talking about with their friends, associates, family members and neighbours. They're posting pictures of their dream home or their new home on Instagram and Facebook. They're pinning real estate pictures on Pinterest boards. Their online and offline conversations revolve around their real estate wants and needs, their moving plans, real estate trends and market activity. They're churning the waters for your next prospect with every post, tweet and pin.

If you don't ask your current clients to recommend you to their friends or to refer their friends to you, you're really missing out on a huge opportunity to reach potential prospects. You can bet that your name comes up in your clients' conversations, even if it's just to say that they have an appointment or that they're awaiting information from you. Putting in a few good words about you and the great service you're providing is a natural and easy thing for them to do. Keep in mind that many potential clients are wary of real estate agents, with the labels they use to describe them not always being complimentary. However, you have a huge opportunity to turn this to your advantage by being the kind of agent that people know, like and trust.

You talk to your clients regularly to communicate about selling their home, finding a home, monitoring their transaction progress or working toward closing. During the course of those conversations, ask for referrals — it can be that easy.

Don't forget to have your clients include you in their social-media world. Getting your clients to post about their experiences and tag you on their Facebook pages brings you into their circle of friends. It opens the door to them liking your business page and forming a service relationship. Be sure to engage in posting and include your clients in your posts.

Past clients

These are the people you've helped through real estate transactions in the past. They have first-hand knowledge of the quality of service you provide. You need to tell them that you want to provide the same level of excellent service to their friends and family members by requesting their referrals.

Clients you've recently served provide the most fertile opportunity, both because their experiences are fresh in their minds and because they're still buzzing about their recent move to everyone they know. The new social-media environment makes this group a gold mine — it's on fire with posts, tweets and pins of their new home.

Social media increases the speed of the news, widens the scope of people who know about it, makes the news easier to share, and makes the news more visual through pictures and videos.

Networking contacts

In sales, networking is a buzzword for building business contacts into referral alliances.

The objective of networking is to meet success-oriented people with whom you can exchange referrals, advice, counsel, contacts and even wisdom. Ideally, networking results in professional relationships with others who are committed not only to their success but also to your success.

The truth is, most salespeople talk about networking more than they actually do it. They don't really understand what true networking is about. They attend a Meetup group, a networking group, or a group like Rotary or Lions, have an enjoyable lunch, visit with a few friends, and chalk the time up to 'networking' even though no new alliances were formed, no existing alliances were deepened, and no referral resources were generated. In other words, no worthwhile relationships were formed and no real networking took place.

To make networking work for you, follow these tips:

- **Network with the right mindset.** When you network, make up your mind to develop prospect recommendations, not just the names of leads.

  Ask questions and be genuinely interested in the answers — this will build bridges, which could lead to business at some stage. If all you do is exchange business cards, you're probably wasting your time. Many referral alliances are established with the single objective of generating leads. Attendees learn the names of new businesses, new managers, newly arrived residents, or others who are possibilities for your future contact. Now a lead from a referral alliance is better than no lead at all, but it's a long cry from the name of a prospect provided by a networking associate who shares extensive background and then offers to put in a few good words on your behalf.

- **Acquire warm referrals.** A warm referral begins when a networking associate makes contact on your behalf with a person who is in the market for your services. Warm referrals involve calls or correspondence that convey your qualifications, the quality of your service, and reasons why prospects should at least interview you for the opportunity to represent their interests in real estate transactions.

When establishing networking relationships or referral alliances, work to gain a mutual agreement that those in the network will engage in the practice of exchanging warm leads.

Business and social contacts

Many people you meet socially or through business dealings will never become clients. They may have previously established agent relationships, or they may not be in the market for a real estate transaction. Nonetheless, they're important to your business because they're in a position to give and receive referrals.

Notice the words 'give and receive' in the previous sentence. The law of reciprocity is alive and well in 21st century business circles. It's the old saying of 'I'll scratch your back if you scratch mine.'

In his book *The Seven Habits of Highly Effective People*, Stephen Covey talks about emotional bank accounts into which successful people must make deposits before making withdrawals. Apply that wisdom as you build your referral network. Start by sharing business referrals, counsel, help and wisdom with others, and before long the recipients of your kindness will repay you with like efforts. Help your friends, family members and associates build their businesses; in time, they'll help you build yours.

When dealing with your referral sources, make it your goal to provide service and value in excess of expectations and to keep your accounts with others in the black, rather than the red.

Constructing a referral database

One of the best ways to start generating referrals is to construct a referral database composed of all the people who are likely to help you by referring your services.

If you're like most agents, your first list of business and social contacts will look embarrassingly short. That's because few people dig deep enough to think of all the people with whom they have business and social ties. To jog your memory, use the worksheet in Figure 6-1. Then list the names of people in each category who know and respect you and may be willing to refer prospects your way.

Referral Database Worksheet *Create a list of contacts in each category who may be willing to refer prospects your way.*			
Accountant	Construction	Laundries	Property Management
Advertising	Consulting	Lawn Care	Rental Agencies
Aerobics	Contractors	Libraries	Resorts
Airline	Cosmetics	Limousines	Restaurants
Alarm Systems	Credit Union	Loans	Roofing
Animal Health/Vet	Day Care	Management	Schools
Apartments	Delivery	Manufacturing	Secretaries
Appraisers	Dentists	Mechanics	Shoe Repair
Architects	Dermatologists	Medical	Siding
Art	Doctors	Mobile Phone Suppliers	Signs
Athletics	Electrician	Mortgages	Skating
Attorney	Engineering	Motels	Skiing
Automobile	Firemen	Museums	Skydiving
Babysitters	Fishing	Music	Soccer
Banking	Florist	Newspapers	Softball
Barber	Furniture	Nurses	Software
Bartender	Gardens	Nutrition	Spas
Beauty Salon	Golfing	Office Machines	Sporting Goods
Beeper Service	Groceries	Office Furniture	Surgeons
Boats	Gymnastics	Optometrist	Teachers
Bookkeeping	Hair Care	Orthodontist	Telecommunications
Bowling	Handicapped	Paediatrician	Tennis
Builders	Handyman	Pedicures	Theatres
Cable TV	Hardware	Pest Control	Title Company
Camping	Health Club	Pets	Training
Carpet Cleaning	Health Insurance	Pharmacies	Universities
Chiropractors	Horses	Phones	Video
Church	Hospitals	Plumbing	Waste
Cleaners	Hotels	Podiatrist	Weddings
Clubs	Insurance	Pools	Wine
Colleges	Investments	Pre-Schools	
Computer	Jewellery	Printing	

Figure 6-1: List the names of contacts in as many of these social- and business-contact categories as possible to form your referral database.

Following the three golden rules for cultivating referrals

To win referrals, you have to follow three important rules. In this arena, close isn't good enough. Follow just two of the three rules and the growth of your referral-based business will be stunted. Follow all three, and you'll open the floodgates to success.

Be referable

Generating large numbers of quality referrals is impossible unless you're referable. Being a pleasant person isn't enough. To attract referrals, follow these tips:

- **Do what you say you'll do, and do it with excellence.** People known for mediocre results never win the kind of accolades that lead to recommendations.
- **Know your clients' expectations.** The only way you can know what your clients expect from you is to ask. The typical agent thinks a client simply wants to get a home sold or find a home to buy, when in fact that end result tells you nothing about the client's service expectations. Ask your clients these questions:
  - What do you expect from the agent you choose to work with?
  - What are the top three services I could provide that would add value when working with you?
  - If you've worked with other agents in the past, what did you like best and least about the experience?
- **Deliver exemplary service that exceeds expectations.** Meet and exceed the service expectations of your clients and they'll become ongoing sources for referrals. Chapter 14 is full of tips for using service and follow-through to win clients, and their praise, for life. Also, follow these steps:
  - Survey your clients on a regular basis to find out whether their needs are being met and how you can serve them better. Sending a survey is so easy in today's world. The advent of online survey systems, such as SurveyMonkey (`www.surveymonkey.com`) makes it fast and inexpensive. For as little as a few hundred dollars a year, you can create surveys for current buyers and sellers, clients who just moved, past clients, people who used your website, and a host of other options.
  - Become a recognised real estate expert and share your expertise by calling clients regularly with reports on market trends, equity growth and investment opportunities.
  - Continue to serve your clients after the sale settles.
  - Get to know your clients beyond their real estate needs.

- **Say thank you.** This step is so simple, yet in our 'what's-in-it-for-me' world, most service providers overlook the power it possesses. When was the last time you were thanked by your lawyer, accountant or banker for your business? When was the last time the person who makes your coffee, handles your dry cleaning or packs your groceries thanked you for continually directing your dollars into their pay?

  Now think of those in your circle who do take the time to thank you with a smile — perhaps your hairdresser or barber, your beautician or your gym trainer — how does this make you feel? Translate this to your interactions with your own clients and your referrals will accelerate — everyone likes to be made to feel special and appreciated.

  Extend your thanks verbally. Put your thanks into handwritten notes. Find simple and creative ways to express your appreciation to the people who put food on your table, fuel in your car, dollars in your retirement account and more. Your thanks will be rewarded with referrals.

- **Admit and correct mistakes.** Should your service fall short, admit it, apologise and make amends . . . fast!

  Sometimes, the most loyal past clients — and the strongest referral alliances — result from perfectly corrected mistakes. When things go awry, too many people put more effort into covering their tracks than righting the wrong and helping the client. Follow these steps instead:

  - Find out what the problem is and solve it quickly.
  - When the problem has been identified, admit it was your fault. Diffuse frustration or anger by saying, 'You're right; I blew it and I'm sorry.'
  - Tell them how you'll make amends. When they know that you're committed to their satisfaction, the healing of the relationship can begin.
  - Follow up to see if the problem is resolved to the client's satisfaction and to see if you can do anything else.

Mine your contacts

The first step toward mining — or extracting value from — your referral contacts is to segment your database into manageable subgroups.

To use your resources effectively, you have to put most of your effort toward contacts with the highest referral potential. Contrary to popular opinion, you can't afford to treat all referral sources with equal attention. Unless you establish priorities, you won't have the time or energy to devote to the contacts who will benefit your business most.

Segment your database of referral contacts with the following in mind:

- **Create a top-level or platinum group of contacts.** This category includes clients who were a delight to work with, people who are in key strategic positions, and friends and associates who are strongly likely to refer business your way. Go through your complete database looking for those with the following traits:

  - People who understand your need for business referrals
  - People who really like you and want to help you
  - People who did business with you in the past and were highly satisfied by your service
  - People who previously sent referrals to you, even if the referrals never resulted in a commission cheque

  This is your best group of referring partners or referral alliances, and you must treat them accordingly. They deserve personal attention and personal interaction from you on a regular schedule.

  You can even create a top-20 or top-50 list within this group of top-level contacts. This super-elite list merits your highest level of attention. Send them special and personal correspondence a couple of times a year, and see them on a face-to-face basis a few times a year as well. Invite them to special client-appreciation events, or invite them in very small groups to attend functions or special activities with you to deepen the relationship and hopefully generate future referrals.

- **Create a second-tier or gold level of contacts that you want to cultivate into platinum affiliates.**

  This group includes influential people who are likely to refer you if you meet a few conditions. You may have to ask them consistently over a period of time before their referrals come through. Or you may have to achieve greater familiarity or top-of-mind consciousness before they're comfortable with the idea of sending business your way.

  To develop this group, take time to establish your credentials and competitive position (the information in Chapter 13 will help). By proving how you save money for your clients, sell their properties more quickly and for top price, and handle smoother and better transactions, in time you'll develop advocates who will serve you with referrals for years to come.

- **Create a silver level of contacts for future cultivation.**

  This group includes contacts who *may* refer someday, but the jury is still out regarding when and if. Still, because you know them and they know you, they deserve your attention and follow up.

  The people in this group are in a position to refer business, but they may not be overly excited about you or, in some cases, any service provider. Include in this group people you've only recently met, people with limited social circles, and people who are tremendously analytical or demanding and whose need for proof and perfection may put the brake on their willingness to share referrals with others.

Anyone who doesn't fit into the platinum, gold or silver category has limited referral value to your business. Some trainers advocate purging iffy contacts out of your database, but we don't share that view. After all, how hard is it to include the extra names when you distribute your email newsletter monthly, at absolutely no extra cost? When the data is collected and contact permission is obtained, the hard work is over. All you have to do is hit 'send' on a regular basis, backed by an occasional snail-mail communication.

When continuing to send emails to contacts, just make sure that you abide by any opt-out rules for your area — otherwise your emails will be counted as spam and you could be prosecuted. For Australian agents, the best way to learn more about this vital requirement is to go to `australia.gov.au/service/do-not-call-register-service-directory`. New Zealand agents can check out the Do Not Call List information on `www.marketing.org.nz`.

Consider creating a bronze category for your contact database just to keep remote possibilities in your contact circle. Especially when your overall database is small, you want to wring potential out of every hope. Inexpensive, regular contacts are a step in the right direction toward engaging the interest of these contacts and developing them into future referral sources.

Leverage your relationships

In your everyday dealings, you come into frequent contact with people who, with a little effort, you can lead up your relationship ladder and cultivate into referral sources.

For many newer agents, these daily encounters are centred on the lives of children — through meetings with teachers, participation in school events, visits with other parents, sideline conversations at gymnastics, soccer and cricket practices, and the list goes on and on. Beyond that are all the people you meet in church groups, golf or athletic clubs, book clubs, neighbourhood associations and other social outlets. Cast your net carefully and you'll bring many of these people into your referral circle.

Be aware, contacts from your everyday relationships don't develop into referrals automatically. Far from it. It's your obligation to let people know what you do, why you're the best and how you deliver successful outcomes. Chapter 13 helps you define and present your competitive strategy.

As you proceed to leverage personal relationships, start by setting a high expectation for the quality of communication and service you'll deliver. At the same time, set moderate to low expectations for quick referral results. Cultivating acquaintances into referral affiliates takes time, patience and persistence.

Developing Your Referral Strategy

To develop referrals, start with a referral mindset. This exists when

- Every prospecting, marketing and customer-service action is accompanied by the realisation that the contact could lead not only to new business but also to positive word-of-mouth advertising and the recommendation of your service to others.
- You create, believe in and implement strategies that purposefully generate referrals as a regular part of your business-development activities.

- You know that prospecting is a key route to referral success. In the same way (and often at the same time) that you prospect for client leads, you need to prospect for referrals. Chapter 4 is jam-packed with advice on how to keep this strategy working for you.

Generating referrals is among the easiest, most cost-effective ways to gain new business leads, but success doesn't happen overnight. Even your platinum-level referral sources need to be constantly contacted and reminded to send business in your direction. The upcoming sections help you set your objectives and develop a system that first delivers the kind of service that wins recommendations and then transfers that value, through ongoing communication, into new business opportunities.

Defining the type of referrals you seek

Before you launch a referral-generating effort, know what you're looking for. In a sentence, you need to be able to focus your referral sources on an idea of what your ideal real estate prospect looks like. Include the following information:

- **Moments when people become great prospects.** Help your referral sources notice the signs that indicate friends are in the 'thinking about moving' stage. This is the point at which you most want to enter the game, before the transaction is already underway. Universal signs to watch for include pregnancy or adoption, promotion or job transfer, trouble with ageing parents, a recent empty nest, and trouble in a marriage or relationship.

  Left to their own good intentions, people will call to tip you off about people they've just learned are in the buying or selling process. By the time a mutual friend hears that people are actively looking to buy or are in the midst of selling, it's too late. By then, the prospects probably already have an agent relationship.
- **Your interest in helping people sell their homes.** The standard consumer view of real estate agents is that they put people into their cars, drive them around and sell them houses. If you don't expand this initial impression, most of your referrals will be for people seeking to buy rather than sell homes. Buyers are great clients and important sources of revenue, but the best agents build their businesses through listings. By cultivating referrals for those thinking about selling their homes, you'll put your business on a faster growth track.
- **Your real estate niche.** If you're particularly effective serving a specific niche of real estate clients, such as investors, seniors, younger-generation buyers or first-home buyers, let people know. Likewise, if you want to gain more of a certain kind of buyer, you need to inform your referral sources about your expertise in the desired segment and what prospects in that area look like.

  When communicating your market niche interests, start by sharing your overall competitive market advantage and inviting all referrals. Then explain how you've developed a particular niche market expertise that you want them to know about so that they'll think of you when they learn that their contacts have interest in your specialty area.

  When outlining your real estate *niche* (that is, what you want to be known for or where you think your best business is going to come from), your point isn't to get referral sources to screen leads for you. You still want them to recommend the name of anyone with interest to buy or sell property. The more the better. But your sources may be able to 'sell' you more effectively if they know your particular areas of expertise and success.

Setting your goal

In a really effective referral-development program, you may aim to achieve two referrals a year, on average, from each of your platinum-level sources, one a year from those in your gold group, and one every other year from those in the silver category. Referrals from sources at the bronze level are too hard to project, but for all other categories, you need to give yourself an annual goal to aim at. In the beginning, you may just pluck your goal from thin air, but after you establish your first-year expectations (or hopes), you'll have a good benchmark against which to measure progress and set your aim in future years.

As you set goals and track progress, consider these tips:

- The number of referrals you aim to generate from platinum-level sources should be double what you expect from gold-level sources, and your expectations from gold-level sources should be double what you expect from silver-level sources.
- Whenever you receive a referral, note whether the source is listed in your platinum, gold, silver or bronze categories. This helps you track whether those in each category are performing at the projected levels. If not, you'll know to enhance communications and referral-generation efforts accordingly.
- As you qualify and work with referrals, note which of your database groups — platinum, gold, silver and bronze — are delivering referrals that lead to business. If you notice that some categories are generating referrals that are dramatically more or less qualified than other categories, study your own communications to see how your messages to those in various groups may be contributing to good or weak leads.

Approaching your referral sources

Marketing for referrals with mailers, calendars, magnets, recipe cards and other outreach and appreciation efforts is nowhere near as effective as prospecting for referrals by making personal calls and requests.

The hard truth is that most consumers stand a far better chance of finding a poor agent than a great one. When you can personally convince them that you're among the best in the field, referrals follow.

When cultivating referral sources, realise that most people who send referrals your way do so for a variety of reasons, but above all they recommend you for the following two reasons:

- **People want to promote friendship and trust.** People like to help people they like and believe in. Take time to get to know those in the platinum and gold levels of your database and to let them get to know you. Share the vision you hold for your business. Let them catch your enthusiasm and buy into your dream. The result is a vested interest in your success and the desire to help you achieve your goal.
- **People want to be champions.** Each time you deliver superb service and an excellent outcome, you create clients who are willing to champion your business. What's more, based on your exemplary performance, you create clients who know firsthand that by recommending you to others, they'll become champions in the minds of their friends and family members.

It's never too early to begin building referral relationships. You can start during the first meeting or phone call with any prospect, using a script such as this:

> *Joe, I build my business primarily based on referrals from clients. The benefit to you is that my focus will always be to give you the best service possible. The reason is that I want to be able to talk with you in the future about who you know that would benefit from my service. The only way I deserve to have that conversation is based on the job I do for you. I hope that if you're happy with my service, you'll be able to help me and your friends out.*

The consistency of your communication with potential referral sources is key. Be in front of referral sources and at the top of their mind at all times. Be consistent in calls, mailings and social-media interactions. You can't go dark or quiet for extended periods of time.

One of the new advances in communication that is highly effective and personalised is video email. This is more common in the United States but is starting to be adopted in Australia and New Zealand. Many agents feel that video email will be a game changer in relationship building. You can also use YouTube or other videos for your own listing promotions and profile marketing — this is a very powerful tool to keep your name and your reputation current. Another advantage of this is the ability for people to share and post your video. Your reputation can be spread far and wide — a huge benefit!

When approaching referral sources, keep some important rules in mind:

- **Rule #1: Respect the referral process.** When you're asking for referrals, keep in mind that this is a privilege, not a right — you must provide service that impresses before someone will refer you to their friends or colleagues.

  Don't ask for referrals by simply adding a throwaway line onto the end of another conversation — saying, basically, 'Oh, by the way,' before you ask for a business referral. That tactic minimises the importance of the referral, instead of raising it to the high level of respect it deserves.

  You may find asking for referrals difficult — perhaps you fear embarrassment or looking stupid. The best strategy is to be upfront. Terri used to preface her request in a casual manner, saying something like, 'If you were happy with how I worked for you, would you mind giving me a referral when you hear one of your friends or colleagues talking about selling?' People were usually happy to agree and Terri would follow the conversation up with a little note (enclosing some spare cards), thanking them again in advance for helping her with any referrals from anyone in their circle.

- **Rule #2: Ask for help.** If you're soliciting referrals, you are, in fact, asking for help. So say so. The trouble is that egos get in the way and won't let the words out of most agents' mouths. 'I need your help' or 'I would really appreciate your help' are powerful keys for opening the referral floodgate.

- **Rule #3: Ask permission.** In particular, ask permission to explore your client's contact database — not by rifling through computer files but by becoming aware of and gaining access to associates you may be able to help. When asking for permission, use a script like this one:

  I'm glad that we've been able to get this great result for you. I was wondering about others you might know who could also benefit from my service. Can you think of anyone in particular who I might be able to help?

  The final question in the script is an important one. Too many agents ask for referrals and then leave all the burden of thinking up names on the shoulders of their clients. The truth is, your referral sources don't want to work that hard. They'll work that hard *with* you, but not alone.

- **Rule #4: Get specific.** Don't just make a general request for referrals and leave it at that. Saying 'Do you have anyone you might like to refer to my business?' is sort of like an assistant at a clothing store who asks, 'May I help you?' The automatic response, 90 per cent of the time or more, is 'No, just looking.'

  Sharpen the focus of your request by leading clients into areas or niches in their lives where they have day-to-day relationships. Ask them about potential referrals among the families in their church, people they know through their children's soccer team, and prospects they've met through school affiliations. If they're members of associations or groups, pull out the member roster and spend a few minutes talking about the names on the list.

Asking the right questions at the right time

After they've asked for and received a referral, most salespeople stop and wait for the magic to happen. In fact, this is when Phase 2 of the referral-generation process kicks in. Follow these steps:

1. **Thank your referral source, immediately!**

   Say thank you the moment the referral comes through, and say thank you again when you follow up with a handwritten note. Terri used to send a bottle of wine as a thank you and then, if she got a sale through the referral, send something else — for example, a voucher for a meal at a great restaurant or even an overnight stay somewhere nice. You can easily find deals for these kinds of vouchers on sites such as `cudo.com`, `scoopon.com` or `wotif.com` — these gestures make for great loyalty.

2. **Determine the nature of the referral.**

   To increase the probability of a successful first call, you need to determine the level of the lead you're dealing with. Slot the referral into one of four referral tiers:

   C Level: This is really a cold referral. Your referral source has provided you with the name and phone number of a potential prospect but doesn't want you to use his or her name to create an opening.

   B Level: This referral is lukewarm. You have the prospect's name and phone number and permission to use the name of your referral source to open the door, and from there you're on your own.

A Level: This is a warm referral. You have the prospect's name and number. You have permission to use the name of your referral source as a door opener. Plus, your source has given you time to ask questions about the lead that will improve your odds of connecting with the prospect on the first call.

AA Level: This is the whale in the referral fishing game. With an AA-level referral, you have all the resources that you have at the A level, plus the insider's edge because your referral source agrees to contact the prospect in advance of your call to introduce you. This advance contact paves the way for a welcomed first call. It can also lead to a lunch or face-to-face meeting where you, your referral source and your new lead get together to transfer the relationship into your hands.

To significantly increase your conversion odds, spend a few minutes with your referral sources finding out the answers to the following questions:

- How would you describe your relationship? Is it a business or personal one?
- Do you know if they have ever used an agent's services before? If so, do you think they were happy with the experience?
- Is there anything that you can see that we have in common?

Get more than the prospect's name and number. Ask some questions and go the extra mile to move the referral lead up to a higher probability of conversion.

3. **Thank your referral source again.**

   Offer your assurance that you'll provide the same level of quality service that your referral source has received from you in the past.

Handling the referrals you receive

Not all referrals turn into transactions. In fact, not all referrals possess the necessary desire, need, authority and ability to qualify as likely prospects for your business. That doesn't mean that every referral isn't important to your business; it just means that not every referral demands the same follow-up approach.

When handling referrals, take these steps:

1. **Qualify the lead and determine the odds that your investment of time and resources will result in a commission cheque.**

   Turn to Chapter 9 for help with qualifying prospects.

2. **Develop only qualified referrals into client prospects.**

   When working with referrals, agents often feel compelled to work with every lead, regardless of the person's qualifications or willingness to commit to an exclusive agency relationship. We believe this is an error. Ask yourself: If this person came from an ad call, sign call, open house, or any other lead-generation system, would I pursue the business given the person's qualifications and commitment? Don't change your standards, expectations or code of conduct simply because the lead was referred to you.

3. **Thank and reward your referral sources for every single lead.**

   Too many agents reward referral sources only when the leads they provide produce a return in the form of a commission. That is a huge mistake. If you train friends and associates to think that you only value referrals that result in a listing or a sale, you run the risk that they'll start trying to pre-screen leads, passing along only the ones they think will result in sales. Reward and acknowledge each and every referral you receive.

4. **Keep your referral sources informed of the lead's progress.**

   Especially if you're faced with the need to drop a prospect, let your referral source know what's happening. Explain that although this time the match didn't work out, you sincerely appreciate the recommendation and are honoured by the referral. Try to avoid the gory details as you walk the tightrope, sparing yourself from wasted time while preserving the strength of your established referral relationship.

Developing Referral Relationships

After you've received a referral, gathered information and ranked the lead (refer to preceding section), it's time to pick up the phone. The advice and scripts in the upcoming sections help you with each step of the lead-conversion process.

Making first-time contact

The first call is the hardest one. Until you make first contact, you don't really know the quality of the lead. It can turn out to be a huge business opportunity — or nothing at all. You have to hope for the best; the referral lead could result in years of business and an important new referral alliance. Or it could go into the rubbish 60 seconds after you make the call. As you initiate contact with a new referral, heed the following advice.

Know the two objectives of your first call or visit

The primary objective of your first contact, like the objective of any other first sales call to a new prospect, is to book an appointment. The first appointment may take the form of an exploratory session aimed at determining the wants, needs and desires of the lead, or it may be an appointment to conduct a buyer consultation or listing presentation.

The secondary objective of your first contact is to open the door, establish trust and respect, demonstrate your knowledge and establish your position as a reliable resource.

In your first contact, you're not trying to make a sale; you're just trying to achieve a face-to-face meeting.

Use the name of your referral source to open doors

The best way to get beyond your prospect's defences is to share the name of your referral source. By presenting the name of your mutual associate, you establish immediate rapport and credibility. In your opening statement, include a reference to your referral source by using a script such as this:

> *Hello, Mr Smith, this is [Mary Smith] with ABC Real Estate. The reason for my call is that your name came up in a conversation yesterday with your friend Jane Brown.*

Then continue by using a linking statement such as:

> *'She said you're neighbours' or 'She said you used to work together' or 'She said your children go to gymnastics together.'*
>
> *Jane Brown is a very valuable client of mine. Jane knows I primarily work with referrals; she suggested I give you a call. She thought it would be worth a few minutes of our mutual time to see if we should meet.*

You can also use a variation like:

> *Jane was pleased with the service I provided to her and her family. She thought you'd like to evaluate how I might be able to assist you in the future.*

Converting referrals into clients or referral sources

After you establish a solid opening connection, it's time to ask probing questions that help you determine the wants, needs, desires and expectations of the lead. Depending on your findings, the lead may result in a qualified prospect whom you convert into a client. Or, you may determine that although the lead isn't ready to buy, sell or commit to an exclusive agent relationship, the person is a valuable resource to be added to your referral database.

Use the techniques we share in Chapter 4 to assess the lead's business potential and gather the information you need.

Personal visits and calls

Leads generated through referrals come with a higher client-conversion probability than leads received from ad calls, sign calls or any other cold sources. Because of that fact, consider investing some additional time as you launch the relationship. Instead of or in addition to a personal call, consider stopping by to personally meet your new leads in their home. After they attach a face and voice to your name, they'll find it more difficult to reject you or select someone else to represent their interests.

If a personal visit isn't possible, aim to enhance the sense of personal connection through an increased number and frequency of calls. It takes, on average, four to six calls for you to leave a lasting impression. Just make sure you read the signals from your contact — don't continue to intrude with your calls if the signals are telling you your calls aren't really welcome.

Written notes, email messages and mailers

Between calls and personal visits, build a bridge with personal notes and email messages. Written communications will never replace the personal touch of phone calls or face-to-face visits, but, in between live contact, they do a great job of keeping the connection alive.

Send market updates, testimonials, letters from other satisfied clients, information on your current listed properties, and news about key awards or recognition you've received.

Beyond that, treat referral leads as if they're already clients by adding them to your newsletter list and to insider mailings that share news from your office (just remember the Do Not Call and opt-out requirements — refer to the section 'Mine your contacts', earlier in this chapter, for more information).

Chapter 7

Traditional Lead Targets That Work: Expired, Withdrawn and FSBO Listings

In This Chapter

- Understanding the appeal of targeting expired, withdrawn and FSBO listings
- Converting expired listings into new listings for your business
- Bringing withdrawn listings back to life
- Securing for-sale-by-owner, or FSBO, listings

Certainly technology plays a big role in a real estate agent's success, there can be no doubt about that. Throughout Part II, you can find numerous ways to leverage and use technology and social media such as Facebook, Twitter and LinkedIn. However, going 'old school' and using traditional methods of generating business is still effective. When you blend these traditional lead-generation strategies with new technological tactics such as using social media and information from real estate listing websites, your company website and perhaps your personal website, you have a powerful force.

The main reason you want to evaluate and implement traditional strategies is that these three tried-and-true methods lead to new listings: Expired listings, withdrawn listings and for-sale-by-owner listings (FSBOs). The value of a listing can't be overstated in building your business. Whoever has the most listings usually wins the game.

Keeping this in mind, you must have at least three sources from which you create leads, revenue and listing opportunities. Expired and withdrawn listings and FSBOs can be time consuming if done correctly, but they're certainly worth it. You have to find a mix that works well with the amount of time, effort and energy you plan to spend working these and other areas of business generation. The truth is that you can't attack ten different lead-generation models at once. You have to select the best handful to use to generate your listing business.

If you like the idea of being a successful agent who works these areas, read on. This chapter reveals why and when to pursue expired, withdrawn and FSBO listings, and how to convert others' real estate sales failures into your own success stories.

Three Reasons to Work Expired, Withdrawn and FSBO Listings

If you've been in the real estate business for any time at all, you've probably already sensed that many agents have a preconceived negative impression of expired and withdrawn listings and FSBOs. These agents act as if these listings represent second-hand goods that aren't worthy of their interests and abilities. These same agents may also look down on fellow agents who work any or all of these three listing opportunities. As a result, they turn their backs on tremendous revenue potential and literally thousands of annual listings. And that's good news for agents like you who can reap great success by converting expired, withdrawn and FSBO listings to new listings for your business.

We honestly believe that agents who work, or have worked, these potential listings with successful outcomes are the best salespeople in the real estate industry. They prove they're skilful in sales, time management, prospecting, lead follow-up, presentations, objection handling and closing. They know how to put their sales skills to work to book appointments, make presentations and persuade potential customers to become clients. As a result, they make more money and have more listings than agents who don't work these three areas.

Any new agent with aspirations to climb all the way to the top tier of sales success in residential real estate should consider working expired, withdrawn and FSBO listings for three good reasons:

- **They're easy to find.** Take, for example, FSBO listings. You don't even have to ask the owners if they're considering selling. All you have to do is notice the 'For Sale by Owner' ads and signs, scan the private sale ads in your local paper or check out the listings on the many websites now targeting private sellers such as www.buymyplace.com.au, www.forsalebyowner.com.au, www.owner.com.au, www.homesell.co.nz and www.sellahouse.co.nz. Another option is to do an online search to find sites with listings in your own marketplace.

Finding listings that have been withdrawn or have expired is also pretty simple. You can just track listings in your local area via a website like www.rpdata.com.au, www.pricefinder.com.au or www.qv.co.nz in New Zealand, keeping an eye out for properties that are withdrawn or don't sell (either through auction or the private sale process). You can also access the listing archives in your own agency for properties that have recently been withdrawn or not renewed.

Use a technology service, such as your own customer relationship management (CRM) system, to help you compile data in an organised and efficient manner. With a few clicks of your mouse, you can add expired and withdrawn listings and FSBOs into your database with a separate folder for each.

- **They exist in any kind of market conditions.** You read that correctly! If you're skilled at converting expired, withdrawn and FSBO listings, market conditions will have little bearing on your income and overall success. Here's why: In a market that's experiencing sluggish sales, buyers are in control and listings move slowly, if at all. As a result, a large number of listings expire each day, week, month and year, providing you with a near-endless supply of conversion opportunities. On the flip side, when the marketplace is robust and listings are moving briskly, sellers enjoy quick sales, high list-to-sold ratios and multiple offers. In this environment, an abundance of FSBOs sprout up. Consumers, because of what they see and read in the media, think selling a home is easy. So, they devalue the services of real estate agents and try to sell on their own.

Agents who work expired, withdrawn and FSBO listings can make their businesses bulletproof by simply shifting their listing emphasis to fit market trends — focusing on expired and withdrawn listings in sluggish markets and on FSBOs in brisk markets.

- **Working expired, withdrawn and FSBO listings provides the best training an agent can get.** No question about it, if you're going to convert four, five or even six expired, withdrawn or FSBO listings a month, you're going to become a great salesperson. We're not going to whitewash the truth: You'll work hard getting there. But the rewards — in terms of self-discipline, time management, sales skills, personal confidence and, last but certainly not least, a whole lot of money — make the effort well worth the investment.

The ABCs of Expired Listings

When a homeowner and agent agree to work together to sell a property, they sign a listing agreement that is valid for a specific length of time — the required length of time varies depending on where you operate, so check with your local real estate regulatory body or your agency principal for exact dates. Unless the home sells and settles within the specified time period, or unless the owner and agent agree in writing to extend the time period, the listing expires.

When a home is taken to auction (usually with a 30-day market campaign) the listing agent will normally take a 60-day listing authority. This gives the agent time to still sell the property if it doesn't sell at auction — either by auctioning a second time or with a private treaty sale and a listed price. If you're targeting these listings, ethically you should ask the seller if they still have an exclusive authority with the original agent before taking the conversation any further.

Securing an expired listing is a pretty simple process that many agents make more complicated than necessary.

Basically, to win an expired listing, all you have to do is make a phone call or series of phone calls (first checking that the listing is not still in an exclusive authority with the original agent), make personal visits, send marketing pieces or connect via private messages on social media—although direct mail can also be effective. The direct mail that some agents send can be cute, clever and even corny packages, postcards and letters. Some agents create envelopes that look like they contain express deliveries. Just be careful not to be too cute or this tactic could work against you big time.

Don't let your social media or direct mail do all your talking for you. This can be seen by the seller as evidence that you don't really want to risk a face-to-face rejection — not a good start if you're trying to impress with your negotiating skills. Personal visits and phone calls are still the most effective way of proving yourself and your skills.

Agents who rely exclusively on direct mail to win expired listings come in a distant second behind those who call directly or use a call and mail combination. A homeowner with a ready-to-expire listing can be flooded with direct mailers from real estate agents, all competing to be the one who grabs the owner's attention and interest. However, it's personal contact that really grabs attention. Our advice is to take the risk and call in person.

Treating expired listings as high-probability leads

With the seller's information in hand, you're ready to proceed with what we call a *high-probability lead*. Leads come from many sources: Internet inquiries, pay-per-click campaigns, social media, ad calls, sign calls, referrals, open houses, direct mail and even cold calls. Some deliver possible leads; others deliver probable leads. The difference lies in the likelihood that the leads will convert to business. For example:

- Possible leads convert less than half the time.
- Probable leads convert far more often.

Working probable leads is much more efficient, and finding a more probable lead than the owner of a home with an expired listing is difficult. The owner has demonstrated the desire or need to sell and shows the existence of a problem you can help solve. The problem, of course, is that after waiting out the entire listing period, the owner's home didn't sell. However, the problem in most owners' eyes is that the previous agent didn't perform well or the market didn't meet their price expectations. More than half of the time, these homes go right back on the market with a different agent — why not you?

If the property didn't sell because the previous agent took on the listing without properly qualifying the seller's motivation and especially their willingness to meet the market within a reasonable time, just be careful that you don't fall into this same trap! Time is money for you – don't waste precious time trying to work with an unmotivated seller.

Engaging an expired listing

Working expired listings is an all-or-nothing game. However, this shouldn't be the only way you generate leads. Instead, make expired listings just one of your pillars of business.

You can't proceed in a half-hearted, here-today-gone-tomorrow fashion. Either you work expired listings — every day and on a consistent basis — or you don't. You can't try to work expired listings for a few days when you find yourself low on listings, and then quit for a few weeks only to return to the effort again later. You won't find a business card stating that an agent is 'kind of' in the business of working expired listings. If you want to capitalise by converting expired listings, be ready to make working expired listings your way of business life.

You can tighten up your geographic range or price range to throttle back your opportunities and better meet your time constraints. The most common mistake is working too many prospects and spreading yourself too thin. You're better off doing fewer listings well rather than many poorly.

Terri's experience with working expired and withdrawn listings turned out to be the pivotal point of her career. After six years of successful listing and selling with her initial agency, she changed agencies and moved into an inner-city area in Brisbane, where her competition was primarily from very well known and experienced area experts. However, this proved to be an asset, not a liability for her career! The 'big name' agents were far too busy and had no need to put in the huge effort required to chase expired, withdrawn and FSBO opportunities. As well-known and very successful agents, the bigger agents' brand recognition and huge marketing budgets resulted in the majority of their new listings coming from referral and repeat sources.

So, as the 'newbie', Terri went to her new principal and asked for the list of all the agency expired and withdrawn listings for the past 12 months. She then methodically called each seller, with the intention of updating the database. Her main goal, however, was to ascertain whether the sellers had any interest in putting their properties back to market again — this time with a different agent and a different marketing strategy. She then asked about setting up a face-to-face meeting and from there moved to requalify the seller and list the property.

This was a very successful strategy for her — resulting in many listings, many open houses and many more opportunities to meet even more potential sellers!

Today, your schedule is dictated by limitations stipulated by national Do Not Call registries. For more information, see the sidebar 'Keep it legal! Following the rules of the relevant national Do Not Call registry'. If you can't secure the phone number because of the Do Not Call registry, or if you simply can't find the number, go directly to the homeowner's front door and use the scripts, dialogues and surveys in this chapter. You'll reach fewer people, but you'll be more effective because you're face to face (and many people prefer talking face to face).

You should always aim to be the first agent to get through to the owner of every expired listing, but obviously that isn't always possible. However, as soon as you do make contact, schedule an appointment, and establish a good connection and sense of trust.

See the section 'Calling the seller: What to say and how to say it' for more info about contacting owners of expired listings.

The key to success with expired listings is to work them consistently and with commitment. Most agents who claim to work expired listings do so only at the end of the month and, even then, only sporadically. Only a small group of agents work expired listings as a way of life, but we can vouch for the fact that those who do build great businesses.

Keep it legal! Following the rules of the relevant national Do Not Call registry

Many agents cheered when the relevant national Do Not Call registries took effect in Australia and New Zealand. (In Australia, the registry is managed by the Australian Communications and Media Authority (the ACMA); in New Zealand, the Marketing Association manages the Do Not Call list.) With the creation of these registries, agents were handed an excuse for not picking up the phone.

In our experience, the effect of such registries has been negligible; a high percentage of agents don't prospect anyway, so the new restrictions affected only a tiny segment of agents. Consumers are delighted with the registry, but most salespeople are even happier with the built-in excuse.

Agents must face the fact that the Do Not Call registers are here to stay, and they must become more creative at sourcing leads than relying on the phone book! (All Australian agents also need to be aware of the new privacy rules that apply to all businesses and came into effect on 12 March 2014. The new laws apply to an array of areas, including direct marketing, the disclosure of personal information, and the requesting of personal information to be held by an organisation or a third party. To learn more detailed information about these rules, check out the website `www.oaic.gov.au/privacy/privacy-act/privacy-law-reform`.)

However, within the law, you can still prospect. You just have to follow the rules:

- **You can turn your call into a survey.** You can collect information on home-buying trends, real estate services, consumer expectations of real estate agents, or a million other aspects of the industry.
- **You can gain advance permission, preferably in writing, to place calls.** For example, at the bottom of your open house sign-in sheet, buyer interview data form or email newsletter subscriber form, include a permission statement. By signing, prospects grant you permission to call them with updates on market activity and their equity position. With this signed statement in hand, you have carte blanche permission to call the prospects until they tell you to stop, at which time you must stop immediately.

Note: Even with permission, you can only make calls between 9 am and 8 pm on weekdays and between 9 am and 5 pm on Saturdays. Unless consent has been given in advance from the call recipient, unsolicited telemarketing or prospecting calls are not allowed on Sundays or public holidays.

You or your agency must also wash your contact lists regularly. (*Washing* your contact list involves you going through the list and removing anyone who has now registered with the Do Not Call list or requested specifically to be removed from your list.) To neglect this is to invite trouble from disgruntled consumers.

Qualifying expired listings

When working expired listings, get ready to work with owners who are frustrated that their homes didn't sell and who, in most cases, blame their agent and, by association, all agents in their real estate market. Many also blame the marketing strategy, the marketplace and the lack of effort put forth by the real estate community. They're not happy campers.

In most cases, the blame is misplaced. The real culprit is usually the price the owners expected to reap from their property sale. If you help them dive back into the market with the same unrealistic price expectations, you'll set yourself up for another unhappy ending — and that's not good risk management for you or for your career!

Your ability to gauge the owner's level of motivation to sell at this time, along with the current market conditions, will determine your likelihood of receiving a commission cheque. To help qualify your clients, find out the following:

- Are they determined to seek a buyer at their current inflated sale price?
- Do they have a time frame for the sale? What happens if this time frame isn't met?

  If the sellers have no time frame for the sale, taking the listing is probably not a good idea. You may waste your time bringing good buyers to an overpriced, unsaleable property.
- Which is more important: Obtaining their desired price or securing a sale?
- Are they open to your bringing along evidence in order to discuss the true market value of their home?

What you're trying to find out with these questions is whether the owners *have* to sell or just *want* to sell. Someone who's forced to sell is a higher-grade prospect and is more likely to result in a sale — and a commission cheque — than someone who's just testing the market. Sellers who are being transferred to another part of the state or country, who have financial difficulties, who are expecting a child and living in a home that's too small or who are going through a divorce usually have to sell. While some of these situations are uncomfortable and unfortunate, they create opportunity for an agent who can help them come to a successful conclusion.

Take time to ask questions and probe the answers to find out the prospect's situation. Many prospects are reluctant to reveal the reasons behind their decision to sell. Some feel that an agent may try to take advantage of them — and unfortunately in a few select cases, they may be right. The vast majority of agents we've ever met, however, want to help people achieve their dreams and desires.

The best way to extract the information you need from prospects is to keep asking questions. If you don't manage to get the answers but you feel that the prospect has motivation, ask for a quick appointment to preview the home. By getting in the door and meeting face to face with a seller, you have a better chance to get your questions answered while also having a look around the property.

Calling the seller: What to say and how to say it

When you call the owner of a home with an expired listing, you have one objective: Securing an appointment for a face-to-face meeting. Ideally that's for a listing presentation, but if you can gain only the opportunity to preview or appraise the home, take it. Remember, the owners will likely be contacted by dozens of other agents, so you need to move quickly and skilfully by following this advice:

- **Address their situation.** Quickly convince the owners that if they choose to work with you, the outcome will be different than the last time. Explain why working with you provides them a higher probability of sales success than they'll receive by working with any other agent. (Turn to Chapter 13 for help defining and concisely explaining your unique and strong competitive position.)

- **Be proactive.** The most serious sellers will re-list their home within a couple of days of a listing expiration. To land the listing, you can't be low key with your dialogue and delivery. These owners are ready for action. You must convey power, conviction and belief in your ability to achieve success.

- **Leave yourself wiggle room.** At this stage in the game, you may not be aware of all the factors. You don't know the condition of the home, the neighbourhood layout, the level of access the owners are granting to potential buyers, the price and time frame they're trying to achieve, the probability that their expectations can be met, and what the previous agent really did over the course of the listing term.

  Because so much is up in the air, you have to leave yourself a little wiggle room by not overcommitting to what you can and can't do for the client. You also don't want to commit to what you will charge in terms of commission. You need to be flexible, depending on the market and motivation of the prospect.

- **Turn the most frequently asked questions to your advantage.** Be ready to answer the questions, 'What will you do differently?' and 'Why did my home not sell?' by saying that you don't have enough information to give an accurate answer. You can say something like, 'Are you asking me to guess, or do you really want to know for sure?' When they say, 'I want to know for sure,' you book an appointment to see the house and have a friendly discussion. With that helpful move, you get your foot in the door.
- **Gain information.** The owners need to understand clearly that, without firsthand knowledge of their situation, it's impossible for you to determine which specific approaches will achieve their desired outcome. You need to see their home in order to review its features, benefits, condition and street appeal.

  You also need to figure out the previous agent's marketing strategy. Ask the seller what the other agent did to market the property. If you can, get the previous agent's flyers, ads and brochures. Taking a look at the previous agent's website may also help. Finally, you need to gain an understanding of the owners' expectations regarding time frame, listing price, sale price and access for showings, as well as their interest in your evaluation of the competition they face in the current marketplace.
- **Differentiate yourself.** Use your track record (or your agency's track record if you're new in the business) to gain credibility with the owners. (See Chapter 13 for tonnes of advice on how to use the Big Three Statistics to differentiate and position your service.) As you present your success story, do so stressing that your success is based on your outcomes with clients who sought your guidance, accepted your recommendations and implemented your advice. Tell the owners that you want to contribute to a similarly successful outcome on their behalf. You may even want to supply references of satisfied clients — especially those clients whose listings were also expired before you began working with them.

- **Provide the option of an easy exit.** The seller with an expired listing most likely wanted to fire the agent long before the listing term was up but, in most cases, was bound by the contract terms to wait out the agreement. Acknowledge your understanding that the owners feel cautious about tying their home up for another long period of time. To put the owners at ease, offer them a shortened listing time — perhaps 30 days to prove to them that your service and your expertise is indeed different to what they had previously experienced. If your agency guidelines allow (and your principal agrees), you can also offer a *no-risk guarantee*. This can be terminated at any time if they're not happy with your service. Either approach allows the owner to sever the agreement any time before it expires, which greatly reduces the perception of risk they may have about committing to another agent.

Sales skills

Winning expired listings is the result of superb sales skills, including the following:

- Daily prospecting
- Focused dialogue
- Strong delivery
- Solid ability to handle objections
- Compelling description of the unique benefits you offer
- Ability to win appointments that end in listing agreements

As you initiate contact after the previous listing has expired, your first objective isn't to convince the owners to re-list with you. Instead, your initial aim is to pique their interest and make a compelling argument regarding why they should take the time to see your presentation. The sample scripts in the following section can help you plan your approach.

Sample scripts

Following are some sample scripts that you can build on when making initial contact with the owner of an expired listing. No matter which script you follow, remember this: Don't get sidetracked. Stay focused on your single objective, which is to secure an appointment with the owner.

Script for an expired listing when making first contact and building rapport:

> *Hi, I'm looking for _________. This is _________ from _________.*
>
> *I was just wondering — is your home still available for sale?*
>
> *OR*
>
> *I noticed that your home has been taken off the market. Is that right? If you don't mind me asking, have you decided not to sell or .... If you're still interested in a sale, I would very much like the opportunity to meet with you — would that be okay?*
>
> *OR*
>
> *I noticed that your home was no longer on the market. I was calling to see if you still were interested in a sale — obviously at the right price?*

The following questions are for when you actually get inside the home. These examples help you make conversation but be careful not to overdo it or be 'smarmy'.

Questions for your first meeting:

- *When you sell this home, where are you hoping to move to?*
- *Do you have a time frame to get there?*
- *What do you think caused your home not to sell?*
- *How did you select your previous agent?*
- *What are your expectations of the next agent you choose?*
- *Has anyone shared with you the real reason your home failed to sell?*
- *Homes fail to sell for only a few reasons: Lack of exposure, changes in market competition and price. One you control, one the agent controls, and one no-one controls. Which do you think it is?*
- *Let me ask you . . . do you want to know which one for sure?*

Response to the objection that all agents are alike:

> *I can sure understand where you get that impression and feeling. And I know the kind of frustration you feel because I've felt it myself when I've taken over listings like yours only to find poorly written and prepared offers. Mr and Ms Seller, there really is a difference in agents. If there weren't, we would all be doing the same level of business in terms of listings, sales, time on the market and list-to-sale price. And we'd all have the same level of client satisfaction. Wouldn't you agree?*
>
> *So the real question is what's the difference, right? I would be delighted to spend just a few minutes with you to help you understand the differences. Would __________ or __________ be better for you this week?*

Response to the question 'Why are you calling me now?':

> *It must seem like a lot of people are calling. The reason is that your home's listing came up as expired, so I'm calling to see if I can be of service. In order for me to accurately assess my ability to help, I need just a few minutes of your time and to see your home. Would ____________ or ___________ be better for you this week?*

Response to the question 'Where were you when my home was listed?':

> *That's a great question, and I'm sure this is a source of frustration for you right now. I can assure you that I personally take the responsibility of selling someone's home very seriously. In many cases, my clients have entrusted their largest asset to me.*
>
> *Because of that trust, I work almost exclusively to ensure their sale. With a 98 per cent success rate against the market average of 68 per cent, I must be doing something right. Wouldn't you agree? When would be the best time for us to meet to evaluate your situation? Would _________ or _________ be better for you this week?*

Using technology to gauge your expired efforts

Several major technological advancements in the past few years have made it easier to work expired listings.

The most important thing you can focus on is doing the leg work in your own area — you should be keeping an eye on all the listings and diarising when their listing authority expires and contacting them then. FSBO listings have no listing authority because the sellers have chosen not to use an agent: These sellers are best identified by you driving your area regularly and looking for their signs, checking out one or more of the private sale websites or monitoring the classified ads in your local paper — particularly the city newspapers.

To use technology to your advantage, first keep an eye on the relevant websites and monitor when listings first appear. No formal notice that the listing has expired or been withdrawn will appear, but you can use your CRM to set up reminders for yourself.

You can set a reminder to check back on the property straight after its auction, or perhaps 30 days after first listing if a private sale. Using these reminders helps you monitor properties and identify the ones that haven't sold or have been withdrawn.

Refer to the section 'Three Reasons to Work Expired, Withdrawn and FSBO Listings', earlier in this chapter, for details of sale-by-owner and property listing websites.

Withdrawn Listings

Withdrawn listings are another lucrative source of listings for a committed and patient agent. As with expired listings (refer to preceding sections), you know that the sellers did have a strong interest in selling — otherwise, they wouldn't have listed the property in the first place. Your job is to discover why the property was withdrawn, out of the possible three main reasons.

Chances are, the property was withdrawn because

- **The property was overpriced and the agent not skilled enough to educate the seller on the current market conditions.** This likely meant few inspections took place and any offers that were received were rejected as far below seller expectations.

  If the property was listed above market price, ask to see the original comparative market analysis (CMA), if possible. You can then present a new, more up-to-date CMA with extensive research on current sale prices. (Refer to Chapter 3 for more on CMAs.)

- **The marketing was inadequate or targeted the wrong buyer.** Here you need to look at the marketing that was done (if any) and convince the seller that with a new improved strategy you could easily revamp and reignite buyer interest.

- **The agent performed badly.** Perhaps the agent provided inadequate follow up or feedback on campaign progress. Perhaps the agent was sloppy, turned up late to open homes, forgot to lock the house or didn't respond swiftly and adequately to new inquiries. The agent could have been sacked for any number of reasons. Here you need to demonstrate your own service guarantee and assure sellers of your focus and attention to every detail.

When contacting sellers with withdrawn listings, you can use similar scripts as when contacting sellers with expired listings and handling their objections (refer to the section 'Sample scripts', earlier in this chapter, for more information).

Once you have earned the seller's trust and checked motivation, you can discuss selling the property with a new strategy, new photos, new text and a whole new campaign.

The For-Sale-by-Owner World

Converting FSBO listings involves a process that in a number of ways is similar to working with expired or withdrawn listings. However, the key differences between the areas are:

- **Timing:** If you contact the owners of a FSBO (usually referred to as *private* sellers in Australia and New Zealand), you can usually expect them to take at least a few weeks to try to sell on their own before they commit the listing to you. For most private sellers, four to five weeks is the norm for them to realise that selling their own property is not all that it's cracked up to be!
- **Sales approach:** When working to convert an expired listing, you need to take control in order to prevail over a bunch of other unknown agents who are vying for the same listing. The owners of the expired listing rarely have an agent preference at this point. Their 'first-choice' agent was the one whose sign just came down. This isn't always the case with FSBO sellers, who sometimes have an agent in the wings just in case they don't have success on their own. For this reason, you need to take a lower-key approach and work to build a relationship in order to win over the FSBO listing.

Understanding why to pursue FSBO listings

When the marketplace is active and everything in sight seems to be selling, as has been the case recently, FSBO listings abound and FSBO sellers achieve a reasonable sales success rate without the services of an agent. So, you may be wondering why an agent would even spend time trying to convert FSBOs to agent-represented listings. Here are just a few good reasons:

- **FSBOs are simply too tempting and attractive a market segment not to work.** You know who these owners are because they're actively marketing their presence in the marketplace. They want to sell their property! You know they have motivation or they wouldn't be spending the money to advertise their home for sale. It doesn't make sense to ignore this great market segment, though most agents do.

- **Owners of FSBOs are qualified client targets.** Unlike other prospective clients, you don't have to wonder whether they own their home or whether they're serious about selling it. However, you do still need to keep in mind that their sale price can be influenced by emotional reasons and so way over market value. You can be certain that they have the authority and ability to conduct the deal.

- **Owners of FSBOs are easy to find and reach.** One of the most difficult steps in the sales process is locating prospects in need of your service. With FSBOs, like expired listings, you know who your prospects are, and you know how to get in touch with them. Reaching FSBOs is easier than reaching expired listings because FSBO sellers want to be found. Just look at the local paper or search the many private sale websites (see the following section for details) — easy!
- **The vast majority of FSBOs fail to sell without an agent.** Even in a robust market, only a very low percentage of FSBOs sell themselves. This means that the vast majority of the owners, if they want to sell, eventually enlist the services of a real estate agent. Sellers get tired of the work involved in attracting buyers, don't know how to effectively follow up with those who do come through their home and, because of the emotion involved, aren't usually able to negotiate effectively.
- **FSBO sellers often net lower prices than those achieved by agent-represented sellers.** Among the FSBO homes that result in a sale, most are priced right at or below fair market value. The only reason buyers take the additional risk of working with a FSBO is that they're trying to buy a home for less money than they'd spend on a traditional transaction. The problem is that low price is exactly the opposite of what the homeowner is trying to achieve. In fact, with FSBO sellers, price is the primary marketing ammunition. Sellers are focused on saving money on commission and don't see the value in employing an agent. With good market research, you can convince them otherwise.

In general, more than eight out of ten serious FSBOs end up as agent listings within a reasonable period of time — usually four to five weeks. Owners set out to sell their own homes for one reason: They want to save money by not paying the agent commission. They view the real estate commission that an agent earns as too much pay for what they mistakenly think is 'such an easy job'! They ask themselves, 'How hard can it be?' as they pound the FSBO sign into their front yard and post their home on one or more of the private seller websites. In the back of their minds, many think, 'Let's give it a go. We'll probably meet a few agents along the way, so we can always change our minds'. And most do. After a month of the hassle, time, energy, emotion and stress of trying to sell their own home — after running ads, fielding phone calls, holding open houses and showing people through their home (think of the security risk this poses for the inexperienced) — 90 per cent of homeowners rethink their situation. Fortunately for agents, selling a home isn't all that easy.

Using technology to find FSBO listings

FSBO owners want to be found by buyers — not by an agent (at least not initially). However, the exposure makes your search much easier — you don't have to look far to find them. You just need to check the private sale sites (refer to the section 'Three Reasons to Work Expired, Withdrawn and FSBO Listings', earlier in this chapter, for details). Another option is to simply do an online search for private real estate sales in your area — chances are you'll find heaps of leads!

The private seller websites make it easy for you to find homeowners and contact them. Some sellers don't put their phone numbers on the sites. They want prospective buyers to contact them via private message on the site. This gives you a less direct way to reach them. However, face to face contact is always good so, if you don't have a phone number, you can still reach sellers by personally making a visit to their home. This way they can see that you're a professional offering help.

The truth is, many FSBOs don't actively market their home, or they market it badly. They don't know how to market their home in a way that attracts the best buyers and are unaware that their home being a FSBO listing attracts the bargain hunters every time!

Converting FSBO listings: The successful agent's approach

Plan to take a patient approach to FSBOs. Realise that you can't do or say anything — short of offering to give your services away — that will rush the owners' decisions to abandon the idea of selling their own homes. Basically, you're playing a waiting game that you can't win in a hurry, but that you can quickly lose if you're pushy or confrontational.

Agents who go on about themselves and their service, or who try to tell owners that FSBOs fail to sell themselves, use the wrong tactic. Owners don't want overly confident agents making them feel like idiots for trying to sell on their own — even if they are! These sellers have their pride — plus, they're actively trying to avoid paying your commission so why would they welcome you with open arms? Just be patient and don't expect too much too soon.

The best approach is to dial back your sales pitch and enhance your emphasis on service. Focus on helping the owners in their effort. Always encourage them and wish them success, but don't give away all your valuable services without a signed contract.

Organising your plan of attack

Confine your efforts to a concise geographic area that enables you to stop by the FSBOs and see the owners as regularly as once every two weeks. When it comes time for them to convert to an agent listing, they'll find it harder to reject you or choose not to interview you if they've met you and know you personally.

The easiest way to organise your opportunities is to track each home by the owners' phone numbers. Owners will change their ads and their asking prices, but they'll rarely change their phone numbers. Organising each home under its phone number eliminates the risk of duplication.

All you're trying to do is gain a commitment that if and when the owners decide to turn the job of selling their home over to an agent, they'll interview you for the job.

Targeting your prospects

In targeting FSBOs for conversion, use the following selection criteria:

- Clear motivation to sell
- A short selling time frame
- A specific place they need to be by a certain date
- The capacity to sell at fair market value with a commission
- Owners who don't have a best friend or relative who is a real estate agent

You need to ask owners these questions to understand how they fit into your criteria. By asking, you know which prospects to invest your time in.

The best approach to target FSBOs for conversion is to create a top 10 list. When you're starting to target these sellers, if you try to work much beyond ten FSBOs, excellent service becomes a difficult proposition. If you pursue the best ten FSBOs, knowing that 80 per cent — or eight of the ten — are likely to list in the next 60 days, you have eight solid prospects. This is an amount you can handle well and is a good start — you can always increase your numbers as you gain experience.

If you provide solid advice, service and care, you can get 30 to 50 per cent of those ten FSBOs to interview with you. Depending on your skill in the interview, you may convert two to five prospects into listings each month. Think about it: A business source that generates this many listings is a great source of business. And even if it delivers only two a month, that's still 24 listings a year. Not bad!

Making the initial contact

Making initial contact with owners of FSBO homes is the toughest step for most agents, so we recommend that you make calls as soon as you see a FSBO come onto the market. By doing this, you can call owners of new listings to have a professional conversation before the onslaught of calls from other agents begins to come through.

If you're the first agent to place a call or attend a FSBO open house, you'll find some owners more open to dialogue. You'll also find it easier to distinguish yourself when you're the first to get through, rather than after 20 other agents have already done so. Some FSBOs are 'die-hard' and will be dismissive in needing your assistance. This attitude may come from a previous negative experience or from overconfidence. Don't be bothered by this because most of these FSBOs will soften over time.

Don't take rejection personally — except perhaps by reputation, the FSBO sellers are unlikely to even know you — but they're most likely judging you from every bad agent they have ever met or even read about!

One benefit to calling FSBO owners early on a Saturday (remembering the Do Not Call requirements — refer to the sidebar 'Keep it legal! Following the rules of the relevant national Do Not Call registry' for more) is that you leave your afternoons free to drop in on some FSBO open houses. Meeting owners face to face in their own homes presents an effective way to establish contact. The owners are sure to be home, they're expecting visitors, and they're ready to make contact and discuss the sale of their home.

Putting the post to work

Because of the four-to-five week sales cycle involved in converting FSBOs to listings, you can use mail-outs more effectively with them than you can when dealing with expired listings. By mailing (or letterbox dropping) helpful items once or twice a week, you give yourself a reason to make follow-up phone calls on a regular basis.

After every face-to-face or phone contact, follow up with a handwritten thank-you note. The owners are likely getting mail from many other real estate agents, so to avoid the round file (also known as the rubbish bin), personalise your notes with handwritten addresses.

Also, use your mail-outs to send useful information that sellers may need. Too often, agents act like the adversaries of FSBO sellers. Take a different and better approach by helping them out. Most have no idea what they really need to do to complete the sale. For example, if they receive helpful advice from you every five days, when it comes time to sign their home over to a listing agent, they're more likely to think favourably of your interview invitation.

To use mail-outs or letterbox drops effectively, follow these suggestions:

- Send the owners a sample contract and any other forms required by legislation in your area (check with your principal). Advise them that buyers can back out even at the last minute if the owners don't handle legal details on the contract properly (highlighting the seriousness of this area also means they'll appreciate your advice more). If solicitors commonly draw up the contracts for sales in your area, advise the owners to work closely with their solicitor and make sure they complete the buyer details correctly with signatures and initials wherever indicated.
- Explain that very rarely does anything get agreed upon in the first contract, and provide some details on how they must document counteroffers.
- Send numerous other items to service FSBO sellers and create a connection, including
    - Sample walk-through inspection forms
    - Updated market analysis reports of comparable properties
    - Sample brochures or photos of the owners' home
    - Guest registers (with privacy statement) for use at showings
    - Lead tracking forms to log information on people who call about the home
    - Lists of homes that would meet the owners' needs if they're looking to purchase a new home in the area
    - Free tips about selling their home

Free tips on selling their home are an effective device because they enable owners to educate themselves and increase their likelihood of success, while simultaneously positioning you as the expert. By sending these tips, you establish yourself as a strong resource to help them succeed. Then, when they don't succeed, you'll be there to pick up the pieces and list and sell their home.

Dialling for dollars

As you work your high-priority FSBO homeowners, make phone or in-person contact at least once a week. Use these communications to see how sales activity has been, whether a weekend open house is scheduled, whether they received your latest mailing and, most important, whether they got the home sold.

A portion of FSBOs sell on their own, but a big difference lies between getting a purchase offer, negotiating the sale and closing the deal. The fact that the owners achieved an offer doesn't mean that they'll get their money. Don't forget 'it's not over till it's over!' Even if FSBO sellers report that they've sold their home, keep following up. A large number of these sales fall apart before actually getting to unconditional status. When that happens, sellers who thought they were on the downhill slope wave a white flag and call in a real estate agent. Make sure that you're still in touch when that moment of frustration arrives.

Overcoming rejection and staying resilient

FSBO sellers will reject you because they prefer not to use your services: They're wary and don't want to outlay on good marketing or commission. But if you maintain a steady, professional relationship, offering help and staying in contact for four to five weeks, you'll usually be able to win an interview. From there, if you have excellent presentation skills, a listing follows.

Increase your odds of success by taking these two precautions:

- **Limit the number of FSBOs you cultivate.** Remember, ten is a good number to start with. As your confidence and skill in this area increases, you can up this number. Focus only on the best potential clients, as described in the section 'Targeting your prospects,' earlier in this chapter.
- **Avoid prospects with low motivation or unrealistically high price expectations.** These sellers are usually the most toxic, and too often they'll try to take their frustrations out on you.

Playing the game of lead follow-up

Working FSBOs fundamentally turns into a game of lead follow-up. You need to personally and regularly contact your FSBO leads to discover their motivation and qualifications, book face-to-face meetings, disqualify prospects as necessary, provide regular service and communication, and schedule presentation appointments. Then you need to repeat the service and communication steps several times weekly until the listing is in hand.

Coming face to face

To make personal contact, begin by asking the FSBO seller if you can come by and see the home. You can ask in a few different ways. You can explain that you want to stay informed of the market in your area — both listings and sales. Or you can say that you're working with buyers who may be interested (just make sure, however, that you can deliver on this promise if the seller calls you on it). When you can, you can use the *reverse-no technique*. The idea of this technique is to get the prospect to say 'no', which you end up reversing into a 'yes' for business. For example, you can ask your client the following: 'Would you mind if I came by to take a look at your home?' 'No' is what she really wants to say, but you end up turning her 'no' reply to this question into a 'yes' to your real request to see the home. Following are sample scripts for each approach.

Script for keeping up with the inventory:

> *Mr Seller, your home is located in my core area. My goal is to keep as up to date with everything as possible. I am lucky to be able to attract many good buyers — maybe even one for your own property. Because your home is in my area, I'd like to come by and preview your home. Would there be a time on _________ or _________ to do that this week?*

Script for FSBO that you're working with a prospective buyer:

> *Ms Seller, I understand you're selling your home on your own. Let me ask you this: Are you open to talking with real estate agents? What I mean is, if a real estate agent brought you a qualified buyer at an agreeable price to you, would you be willing to allow them to show your home?*
>
> *We're working with a few buyers for your area that we haven't been able to place yet. May I come by on _________ or _________ later this week to see your home?*

When you use the script for the prospective buyer approach, understand that you're not interested in reducing your commission. What you're really trying to do is achieve a face-to-face appointment to collect more information on the sellers' motivation in order to determine the probability of securing a listing in the future.

Script for a potential investor:

> *Mr Seller, your home is located in a solid area for real estate investment. I was wondering if I could come by to see your home as a possible investment purchase, to see if it's a property that would meet my own investment needs. Would _________ or _________ be better for you?*

In using this approach, realise that the key phrase is 'investment needs'. You'll rarely find a FSBO that meets your investment needs. My personal investment need is a home that can be acquired at a 70 per cent discount below fair market value, whereas most FSBOs are trying to sell their homes at 110 per cent of fair market value. However, this technique gets you in the door to see the home and talk with the sellers.

Script for a reverse-no:

> *Ms Seller, would you mind if I came by to take a quick look at your home?*

The reverse-no technique can be used with any script. It capitalises on the normal reflexive human reaction of 'no' in order to achieve a positive response. It opens the door and allows you to then set an appointment.

FSBO survey script:

> *Hi, this is ________ from ________. I'm looking for the owner of the home for sale.*
>
> *Your home is in my core area. I'm doing a quick survey of the FSBOs in this area. May I take a few minutes to ask you some questions?*

If the seller agrees to answer your questions, make sure you've already done your homework. Driving by the home is a good idea — this shows that it is indeed in your core area and gives credibility to your questions.

Try the following questions:

- *The ad in the paper said that you had _____ bedrooms and _____ bathrooms. Is that correct?*
- *Do you have a two-level or one-level home?*
- *Are all the bedrooms on the same floor?*
- *Are they good-sized rooms?*
- *How is the condition of the kitchen?*
- *Are the bathrooms in good condition?*
- *Can you describe your yard for me?*
- *Is there anything else you feel I should know?*
- *It sounds like you have a great home; how long have you lived there?*
- *Why are you selling at this time?*
- *Where are you hoping to move to now?*
- *What is your time frame to get there?*
- *How did you happen to select that area to move to?*
- *How did you determine your initial asking price for the home?*

- *What techniques are you using for exposure and marketing of your home?*
- *Are you aware that more than 86 per cent of home buyers begin their search on the internet now?*
- *If there was a clear advantage for you in using me to market and expose your home, and it cost you very little, would you consider it?*
- *Could we set a time to get together for 15 to 20 minutes, so I can see your home and understand your objectives? I have time available ________, or would ________ be better for you?*

Building relationships

FSBO relationships are built over time. By introducing yourself to the owners the first weekend their FSBO is announced, before the masses start calling on Monday, you create a good connection. By sending tools, educational materials, free reports and forms, you become an ally. By taking a personal interest in them and their situation, you create a solid connection that, in many cases, pays off when the owners decide to go with an agent they know and trust — preferably you.

FSBO owners unwittingly let buyers basically steal the 'saved' commission through under-priced offers. People don't shop FSBOs because it's the cool thing to do. They do so because they know they can secure a low price and the owner is not usually a good negotiator.

By building a relationship over time, you demonstrate your value to the FSBO seller. Whether you're working with FSBOs, withdrawn or expired listings, your goal is simply to be one of the two, three or four agents whom the owner interviews when the time comes. You just want the opportunity to compete and make your presentation.

Chapter 8

Using an Open House as a Prospecting Tool

In This Chapter

- Working out the benefits of hosting open houses
- Using open houses to meet prospects
- Preparing for an open house and boosting numbers
- Improving your hosting skills and managing prospects

If you're one of the many real estate agents who think open houses are only good for selling the home being shown — or if you judge success by the number of sales you generate as a result of your open houses — expect this chapter to redirect your thinking.

For many agents, open homes are *the* preferred method to attract lots of buyers, and the upside is that you get to meet many prospective sellers also! These potentials are visiting open homes in your area, checking you out and deciding whether they will put you on their short list for a listing agent interview when they're ready to sell.

Open houses give you a setting to show your marketplace what a great agent you are, ultimately providing a terrific opportunity to generate prospects. And all savvy agents know that prospects are the lifeblood of real estate business success. You can also demonstrate firsthand your market knowledge and command of technology because of the portability of an agent's office in today's world.

Even though today's buyers do much of their upfront shopping via the internet, open houses continue to draw do-it-yourselfers and provide a valuable avenue to get face to face with these buyer types. In addition, they are an easier way for a buyer to start getting an idea of the marketplace without feeling the pressure of going through an agent for personal inspections.

Count on this chapter to help you plan, stage and host open houses that generate buyer prospects, listing prospects, and — if the stars align just right — perhaps even a buyer for the home you're showing. The focus in this chapter is on using an open house to generate prospects — for more on getting the house ready for inspection and creating the 'wow' factor, see Chapter 10.

Understanding Why to Host an Open House

Two categories of buyers operate in the marketplace. The first are the 'active buyers' — this group has set up email alerts from real estate websites, and spends hours in front of the computer screen and scrolling through the media ads. You may be surprised to know that this group comprises around 3 per cent of the marketplace.

That leaves 97 per cent of potential buyers who don't even know they're buyers — until they 'accidentally' come across a property they love, either for investment or to move into. This is the group who are not serious enough to arrange a private showing through an agent, but who will come along to a non-threatening open house inspection out of curiosity.

Funnily enough, because this group isn't researching the market like the committed 'active' buyers, they will often pay top price! And this can be a real benefit to your sales totals.

But, along with catching the 'accidental' buyers, open houses are hugely important for another reason: As mentioned earlier, open houses are a great means for prospecting.

An open house can provide a real estate agent with a neighbourhood storefront from which to meet potential clients. Each time you host an open house, you open the doors to the opportunity to meet prospects, establish relationships and expand your real estate clientele.

If your real estate business could benefit from an influx of buyer or seller prospects, start staging more open houses. You can hardly find a more effective way to generate leads face to face. And, as a bonus, your efforts could very well end in a sale. Not a bad bonus for a solid prospecting tool.

Think of the open house as the real estate agent's equivalent to the retailer's *loss leader,* which is something that creates the initial opening for a sale. In the same way that a grocery store manager offers milk at a discounted price to draw shoppers into the store, a real estate agent invests time and money in an open house to build traffic, attract prospects, hand out business cards, and cultivate future listings or sales.

Buyers often want to search for homes on their own before committing to a real estate agent. Many prefer to not reveal their phone numbers, email addresses or intentions at the onset of their search. They feel that by attending an open house, they may get to view a home they're interested in without having to commit to an agent.

The privacy laws in both Australia and New Zealand mean that you must always provide a privacy statement for your buyers if you're asking for personal details on entry to the home. This statement can be displayed on the buyer registry table or on the bottom of the separate pages where you're recording details. (***Note:*** Don't record buyers' personal details on a common sheet — this is against the privacy rules.)

Most agents now also display a sign saying that they have instructions from the seller not to admit anyone who is not willing to provide personal details. This is for security purposes in case anything does go missing — the authorities can check these names and details.

A great percentage of internet home searchers drive by a home they're interested in, checking out the neighbourhood, the condition of the home and the street appeal. Buyers then take action when they're interested in a home.

For interested buyers, the next step is walking through the home that caught their eye online and during the drive-by. The largest portion of this group accesses the home during an open house — where they can remain anonymous. Doing an open house helps you tap into the 'avoid the agent' mentality of today's buyer.

Always keep in mind that your first loyalty at an open house is to your current seller. Rather than persuading buyers to inspect other properties while they're at your open house, simply start relationships and gain details for follow-up later. Keep in mind your current seller could be watching from afar or even could have sent through a 'spy' to check up on you!

Meeting potential clients face to face

The explosion of online real estate marketing and shopping has led to a dramatic drop in the number of phone-to-phone and face-to-face meetings between real estate agents and their prospects. The open house is a proven way to gain clear and easy real-time access to prospects who are ready to buy or sell homes.

In addition to giving you the opportunity to meet home shoppers who drop in, an open house gives you the opportunity to meet the neighbours and friends of the sellers — all of whom may end up in the real estate buyer or seller market in the future. Take time to figure out the needs, wants, time frames and motivations behind each person's home-shopping experience. Form a connection with the shoppers. After they meet and visit with you, home shoppers find rejecting you as 'just a salesperson' much more difficult, especially if you have made an impression with your personal presentation and your service.

Catering to 'avoid the agent' home buyers

Many buyers believe that, at some stage in their real estate dealings, they have been let down by the mediocre service of agents. In some markets, frustrated buyers are taking matters into their own hands by actively searching listings online, spending their weekends doing home-shopping 'legwork,' and attending open houses in droves. These buyers are trying to do as much as they can themselves, avoiding agents for as long as possible.

When do-it-yourself home shoppers drop into your open house, you're safe to bet on two things:

- They're pretty serious about finding a home for sale, and have started their own market research or checked out agents to potentially list their own home.
- They usually aren't represented by an agent.

In other words, they're great buyer prospects.

The pros and cons of open houses

Whether you can conduct open houses may depend on the franchise or brand you choose to work with, either in Australia or New Zealand. Specific agencies have different policies in this area, each presenting their own reasons for being for or against open houses.

Those in favour of holding open houses to attract buyers say that the advantages far outweigh any negatives. They feel that many more buyers attend the inspections (because they can skip the step of calling the agent, making a personal appointment and then being hounded by the agent for the future). Those in favour also say it creates a sense of excitement and urgency for buyers when they see their direct competition for the property as they watch many other buyers inspect. Finally, many agents also say that an open house is an invaluable opportunity to meet buyers and potential sellers face to face, build rapport and demonstrate their professionalism and expertise.

Those not in favour often quote statistics of loss — the risk of theft being the biggie. They also feel that unqualified buyers will just be stickybeaking, which is a waste of both the sellers' and the agents' time.

Many agents now adopt a compromise — they hold open houses at designated times and then if a buyer expresses interest, they set up further private inspections, which allow the buyer to view the property with no rush. This also allows the agent to build rapport and invite written expressions of interest or offers on the property.

Creating a high-touch opportunity in a high-tech world

One of the big challenges facing real estate agents in today's wired world is discovering the identities of their prospective clients. Buyers cruise and click their way around real estate websites, requesting information via email from numerous agents without ever revealing more than an email address.

As an agent, you can respond with an email that provides the requested information, but it hardly allows you the chance to provide your professional counsel and to establish a professional relationship.

For one thing, it's almost impossible to distinguish yourself from other agents via email. Also, while email enables you to communicate promptly, it doesn't enable you to easily determine the desire, need, ability and buying authority of the prospect. Communicating via email also stops you from determining the prospect's motivation and time frame and from customising your advice to the prospect's unique situation.

How many open houses should I host?

Real estate agents always seek a magic formula that defines how many open houses to host and when to host them. We have found no magic formula exists; however, here are a few good guidelines to follow:

- **If you're a new agent** trying to build a clientele and get your business off the ground, host open houses weekly, or at least frequently. Volunteer to hold open houses for the listings of other agents in your company. (You may need to offer your services for free — think of it as great 'work experience!')
- **If you're an established agent** working to increase your business and win market share (see Chapter 13 for more on the topic of market share), add up how many open houses you've hosted during recent months and aim to increase that figure at least proportionately to the amount you're working to increase your business.

Increasing your contact with potential buyers is where open houses come to your rescue. Open houses cut through the electronic interface and put you right in front of prospective buyers and sellers. From there, you can distinguish yourself, define your prospect's interests and begin the professional relationship that leads to real estate success.

Setting Your Prospecting Objectives

The main purpose of an open house is to attract solid buyer and seller prospects. So, when setting your objectives for each open house, don't just focus on selling the featured home. Be aware of this opportunity to acquire prospects. You're 'on show' — never forget that potential sellers could be taking note of you!

Before each open house, set your prospecting objectives for the number of visitors you hope to meet and greet and the number of contacts you hope to collect contact information from.

For success when asking for contact information from visitors to the open house, follow these tips:

- Have a sign-in sheet (one sheet per person for privacy requirements) and tell guests that you've been asked by the seller to ask for names and contact details. (Some agents also ask for photo ID and have a notice to inform visitors of this request at the door.)

At the bottom of the sign-in sheet, be sure to state that by signing this sheet they're agreeing to allow you to contact them in the future with real estate information. This helps you stay legal with the national Do Not Call registries.

- Have your brochure and home information ready to hand to people who walk in. As you hand it to them, ask for contact details. If someone refuses, you can make it obvious that your seller has asked that this is the requirement of entry. Because you're representing the seller, you are quite within your rights to be assertive at this stage. Your seller will likely find it difficult to trust someone who can't negotiate right to refuse entry to their home. Very rarely will anyone cause a scene — if they do, allow access but take down details of car number plates or similar sort of identification.

Following up with all your open house visitors as soon as possible is a good idea for two reasons. The first is that you need to check whether any of your visitors have interest in the property. You could suggest a second inspection, or you could suggest other properties which may suit them better.

To suggest a meeting to discuss other properties, you can use a script like this:

> *Bob and Mary, so that I can help you to find a new home for your family, let's meet for a coffee. Would __________ or __________ be better for you this week?*

Your seller is also depending on you to provide feedback, particularly about price expectations, and checking in with visitors about their interest in the property allows you to do this. No feedback from you means a very unhappy seller. Even if no-one turns up for the open house, you need to relay this to your seller — this may indicate that a review of strategy is needed.

The second reason to follow up all the visitors to your open house is that you need to ascertain whether you have any potential sellers in the group. If so, you might use a script such as:

> *Bob and Mary, how would it be if I came by to take a look at your home? Would __________ or __________ be better for you this week?*

If you can't secure a face-to-face appointment, aim to at least set a specific time that you can contact attendees by phone. Then you can work to acquire an over-the-phone appointment for a specific day and specific time to speak next. Simply agreeing to call them later in the week is not good enough.

Check out the upcoming section, 'Being the Host with the Most: Effectively Managing the Open House,' for help planning the strategy to achieve your attendance, lead-generation and prospecting objectives.

Planning Your Open Houses to Gain Maximum Exposure

To achieve success with an open house, follow four clear rules to ensure the greatest return on your investment of time, money and resources. If one of your current listings doesn't meet the following four criteria, consider skipping the open house for that listing:

- **Rule 1:** Feature an attractive home in a high-demand area, or a home with renovation potential.
- **Rule 2:** Choose a home with great street appeal.
- **Rule 3:** Market to the neighbours (they could have friends or family who may buy, or could be potential sellers).
- **Rule 4:** Lead prospects to the home with easy-to-follow signage (as long as local council rules allow for this).

The following sections provide advice on how to achieve each of these four success factors.

Featuring a high-appeal home

Here's a hard truth to swallow: No-one comes to an open house to meet the agent. They come to see the home and, unless you have a home that clearly needs renovating on your hands, your role as the hosting agent is to make that house shine. Your reward is the list of prospects you amass and, sometimes, a home sale to boot.

As you prepare for an open house, think of the home you're featuring as the headliner of the show. Choose a home with star power by following these points:

- **Choose a home that's one of a kind.** Scarcity is a well-proven marketing strategy. People line up to get into crowded restaurants. They respond enthusiastically when told they're limited to 'one per customer'. And they'll show up at your open house in flocks if the home you're showing is one of a kind in your neighbourhood.

- **Do your homework before making your selection final.** Study the inventory levels in the neighbourhood you're considering for your open house. Obtain the prices of recent sales to be sure that your home is within the acceptable range. Research the number of days that recent sales and current listings have been on the market. Then compare your findings with research on nearby neighbourhoods to be sure that the home you're considering competes well.

  The statistics you compile provide you with information you should be tracking anyway, so even if you rule out the home you're studying, the time you spend on the effort is worthwhile.

Open house selection isn't a time for guesswork. Use your market knowledge to choose a home with high appeal and demand. Rely on gut instinct only when you're deciding between two homes with equal market appeal.

Looking good: Leveraging the power of street appeal

All agents have seen it happen: A prospect pulls up alongside an open house, touches the brakes, takes a careful look and then drives off without ever going inside. Nine times out of ten, the house failed the drive-by test. It lacked street appeal.

It's your job as an agent to counsel the sellers to turn the house exterior into a perfect ten (or as close to as possible without breaking their budget). This is also where your 'For Sale' picture board comes in — you can showcase home features not visible from the street, and ones that may cause the drive-by prospect to stop, look closer and attend the open house (or schedule a time to inspect).

In preparation for an open house, work with the sellers on at least the two areas that most significantly affect the home shopper's first impression: Landscaping and paint colour and quality.

Typical landscaping reaches maturity after about six to eight years, and after that it needs to be thinned and reshaped.

If the home you're showing is in a mature neighbourhood and the landscaping is overgrown, convince the owner to enhance street appeal by following these steps:

- **Spend a day trimming and removing overgrown and excessive plants.** Hosting an open house in a home blocked from the street by a jungle is a formula for disappointment. Your drive-by prospect will see only untended bushes and trees — hardly a great first impression.

- **Plant or place seasonal flowers that add colour, warmth and an inviting first glance.** A few hundred dollars of seasonal flowers can dramatically change the appearance of a 'plain-Jane' house.

Exterior paint colour and condition is often the first thing a prospective buyer notices about a home. To make the first impression a good one, you may need to urge your seller to consider replacing shutters or sidings, or even repainting the facade of the house in a more neutral colour. You may even advise calling in a home styling specialist to help with improving the street appeal of the house. For complete information on getting the house ready for showing, including increasing street appeal through landscaping and painting, flip to Chapter 10.

Inviting the neighbours

Many agents achieve greater open house results from neighbourhood marketing efforts than from general public exposure. As you plan your open house announcement strategy, pay special attention to your nearest prospects by marketing to those who live right around the house you're showing. Follow these steps:

- **Consider a neighbourhood 'sneak preview'.** Invite neighbours into the house an hour before the home opens to the general public.
- **Send at least 25 invitations to generate an adequate neighbourhood response.** Better yet, hand-deliver 25 invitations. Before you allow yourself to assume that door-to-door delivery is too time consuming, realise that this simple touch will increase your invitation response rate dramatically.

- **Use neighbourhood events to gain access to prospects in restricted-access neighbourhoods.** Restricted-access neighbourhoods include gated communities or complexes that require the public — including real estate agents — to gain permission before entering. This entry barrier makes prospecting in these areas difficult at best. So whenever you achieve a listing in a restricted-access neighbourhood, leverage the opportunity to stage an open house neighbourhood preview that enables you to meet and establish relationships with surrounding homeowners.

Showing the way: Leading prospects to the open house

Open house advertising is important, but it pales in comparison to the importance of a well-selected open house site and a signage strategy that leads prospects to your open house front door.

In choosing your open house site, if possible make sure that you do the following:

- **Select a home near a well-travelled street to gain exposure from the traffic volume.** More prospects will pass by and hopefully stop to inspect!

  Be careful that the home isn't too close to the traffic or you'll get traffic *by* the home but not *to* the home. Remember that many buyers are reluctant to live too close to a thoroughfare or busy street.

- **Use good signage.** Make sure your directional signage is clear and you take it down after the open house.

  Make sure you check with your local council regulations as to how many signs you're allowed to put up, and exactly where and for long they can be placed.

Being the Host with the Most: Effectively Managing the Open House

A successful open house requires a well-chosen and presentable home, a well-organised host, and an impeccable follow-up plan so that no prospect gets lost in the post-event period. Use the following information to guide your planning.

In addition, you may want to use the worksheet featured in Figure 8-1 to be sure that you cover all the planning bases and arrive ready to open the doors to a successful event.

OPEN HOUSE PLANNING WORKSHEET		
	Planning Step	Notes
	ADVANCE PLANNING Select the right property/Factors to consider High-demand area Attractiveness of home Street appeal Proximity to major street Set open house objectives Number of visitors Number of leads Number of buyer interviews Set the open house hours Plan neighborhood events, including: Sneak peak event Establish date/time Determine number of invitations Decide whether to mail or hand deliver Other neighborhood events Plan directional sign strategy; choose sign locations Plan advertising and write ads Assess street appeal; advise seller re: suggested improvements	
	DAYS BEFORE THE OPEN HOUSE Place open house ads Prepare and produce flyers or home feature sheets Research up to six similar properties to share with prospects Advise seller of hour to depart prior to open house	
	OPEN HOUSE DAY Prepare house by opening blinds, turning on lights, and arranging music, candles, and so on Place guest book or sign-in sheet and pen in entry area Put out flyers or home feature sheets Put out and carry a supply of business cards	
	FOLLOWING THE OPEN HOUSE Send hand-written note to each attendee Send requested or promised material to prospects Make phone calls to set appointments	

Figure 8-1: Use this worksheet to standardise your open house planning.

Doing your homework before prospects arrive

Before you open the doors to open house guests, be sure that the home is clean, bright and welcoming — and be sure that you're ready to present not only the home you're showing but also other homes that may better fit the interests of your prospects.

Presenting the home you're featuring

Arrive at the open house at least ten minutes before the advertised time armed with flyers or brochures presenting the property you're showing. Bring enough copies of your brochures to provide one to each visitor as a way of reminding the prospect of the home and, especially, of you. A few tips:

- Make sure your brochures are full colour.
- Include a picture of the home and information about bedrooms, bathrooms, area in square metres and amenities. Providing a floor plan is also handy for helping buyers remember the home and start imagining themselves within it.
- Include your picture and contact information at bottom of brochure.
- Include some testimonials on the reverse side of brochure (useful for impressing potential sellers).

Research proves that, although most visitors won't buy the home you're showing, they may very well buy into the idea of working with you on their future home sale or purchase. The brochure provides prospects with information on how to contact you.

Discussing other available properties

Before the open house, arm yourself with information on about a half dozen other homes that are similar in price, amenities, neighbourhood status and geography to the one you're showing. Then when an open house guest indicates a lack of interest in the home you're showing, you're prepared to quickly and easily shift the discussion to another possibility. Load the listings onto your tablet so you can quickly access them to show buyer prospects. You can also prepare and preview properties in a price range just below and just above the price range of the home you're in and have that information loaded as well. Come armed with your tablet and prepared to show your market knowledge and expert command of the inventory.

Be careful not to obviously be using this home as a way to sell other properties — you never know who is taking note of this and reporting to your seller!

The best research approach is to personally look at comparison homes on your list. At a minimum, take a few minutes to review the pictures and virtual tours of each home that is similar to your open house. This allows you to explain the house more fully to the prospective buyer and handle any initial objections. It will also establish you as an area expert.

Shooing the homeowners out the door

Having the seller underfoot during an open house only causes barriers between you and the potential prospects. You must make arrangements for the seller to be away during open house hours, and here's why:

- Without intending to do so, the owner may convey to the prospect a strong desire to move, causing the prospect to believe that the owner is anxious to sell, which may prompt a lower initial offer.
- The seller may say something that raises a red flag about the condition of the property.
- The seller may describe his or her favourite things about the house. If these features are ones the buyer dislikes and is thinking about changing, the seller's input may simply shut down interest in the home.

Most sellers want to help you sell their homes and, the truth is, the best help they can provide is being absent during the open house.

Setting the mood with last-minute touches

Right before opening the doors to your open house, take a few moments to enhance the warm, welcoming feeling attendees want to feel upon arrival. Consider the following:

- Throw open blinds to expose nice views.
- Turn on lights to brighten corners.
- Burn candles and plug in air fresheners to scent the air.
- Play soft music.
- Set out simple but tasteful refreshments to encourage attendees to linger.

- If you don't plan to write down contact details as people enter, or have another agent do this for you, place a sign-in sheet, along with a pen, in the entryway or at a point where guests gather. Still make sure you greet each visitor in person.
- Keep a stack of business cards and house flyers in a visible location.

Wallflower or social butterfly: Meeting and greeting during the open house

Your primary objective during the open house is to meet guests and sell guests on meeting with you. Your measurement for success is how many appointments you book for after-the-open-house buyer or seller interviews, which are meetings during which you determine the prospect's motivation, time frame, wants and needs, and the prospect learns how you work and what services you provide.

The single best way to obtain a buyer or a seller interview is to convince the prospect when you're face to face at the open house that you're the best real estate resource, based on:

- Your superb knowledge of the marketplace
- Your high level of professional service
- Your ability to deliver an advantage in the marketplace
- Your commitment to delivering the quality representation and service that the prospect truly deserves

Most agents who host open houses are too interested in obtaining contact information so they can initiate rounds of mailings and follow-up activity. Don't let your objective get off-track. Your aim is to get an appointment (not just contact info) so that you can make a personal presentation.

The big difference between highly and marginally successful agents can be measured by the number of appointments they schedule and conduct daily, weekly, monthly and annually. When you host an open house, keep your eye on the prize, which is the chance to sit down following the event in a quality one-to-one appointment with the most valuable asset your business can acquire: a quality prospect. If multiple prospects are at the open home and you can't spend enough time with them to secure an appointment, ask permission to contact them with a follow up call and secure the appointment during this call.

As you work to develop prospects, consider these tips:

- **Ask attendees to sign the open house guest book or sign-in sheet.** Many guests may be reluctant, at first, to provide you with the information you want and need — which includes their names, addresses, email addresses, and work, home and mobile numbers. However, you owe it to your seller to ensure the security of the home by getting visitor contact details.
- **Present your flyer to introduce yourself and create a professional impression.** Depending on how many visitors to the house, you may be able to begin getting the information that you can use as you convert the visitor to a buyer or seller prospect. Keep in mind that the visitor may be on a tight time schedule with a list of homes to see and may resent being asked personal questions at the inspection. If you feel the time is right, the following questions can be asked at the open inspection, or during the follow-up call if necessary:
  - **Ask the prospect a time frame question.** How long have you been looking? Have you seen anything you've liked? How soon are you hoping to be into a new home? The answers tell you not only about the prospect's time frame but also about his motivation. If a couple says that they've been looking for six months, you know that they're not very motivated buyers or that they're slow to make a decision. Either one is not a good answer.
  - **Ask the prospect a dream question.** What are you looking for in your new home over your present home? What features do you want in your new home? Describe your perfect new home for me. By getting the prospects to share what they want, you open up the dialogue. You also show that you care and are there to help them.
  - **Don't be a tree.** In other words, don't be rooted in the kitchen or family room. Wander the house and stay close to the prospects without hovering around them. You have a secondary responsibility to protect the home and the property of the seller. If the open house guests are in the master bedroom and you're in the kitchen, they could be in the jewellery box and you wouldn't even know it. Make sure that you're in the general area of your guests at all times. If the bedrooms are at one end, meander down the hallway and ask a question, simultaneously checking on the whereabouts and interests of your guests.
  - **Ask the prospect to buy.** Before open house guests leave, ask them whether they could see themselves living in the home (or, for an investor, they could see themselves adding this one to their property portfolio). If you've not yet secured their information, you have nothing to lose. If they're not interested, ask them what about the

home causes them to feel it's not right for them. Doing so opens up the opportunity for you to share information on other listings (and provide feedback to the seller).

Securing the deal by following up after the open house

Promptly after the open house, send handwritten thank-you notes or an SMS message to every single person who provided you with contact information. In today's world of email and computer-generated correspondence, the power of a handwritten note or personalised message is multiplied many times over.

When following up, don't assume that your event was the only open house your prospect attended. We guarantee you that this isn't the case. Realise that you're in a competition with other agents, and one way to prevail is to prove that you're the one most skilled at lead follow-up.

When following up with potential buyers, take the following steps:

- **If the prospect requested additional information, send it promptly.** This request identifies them as a prospective buyer.
- **On the afternoon or evening of the day your note arrives, place a phone call to the prospect.** If the open house was on a Saturday, your note should be texted within hours or in the mail on Monday, and you should make your phone call the next day, usually on Tuesday. The objective of the call is to book a buyer presentation appointment in your office or at the local coffee shop (with you buying the coffee). At this meeting, take a notebook and take the time to ask lots of questions about your prospects needs and wants. If they're a motivated buyer, emphasise that you're committed to helping with their purchase.
- **Later that same week, probably on Thursday or Friday, phone again.** This time, tell the buyer prospect that you've found a property that is similar to what he or she is looking for in a home. Send an email with links to suitable properties and offer to organise inspections at a suitable time.
- **Repeat the previous step weekly for a few weeks, until you find a property that suits their needs.** If they keep rejecting your choices, it's probably time to cut them loose and move on to more motivated buyers.

If you suspect a prospect at the open house is more interested in selling their own house, when you contact them ask for feedback on the home, telling them the information is for your seller so that they can make decisions about the sale. If the contact isn't interested in the house and doesn't want to know about other offerings, you can usually safely assume that they're a prospective seller. Your job then is to build rapport and endeavour to make a time to come and view their property.

When you prospect at open houses, among the leads you acquire are people who hope to move but never will. I call these *hope-to prospects* rather than *have-to prospects*, and it's your job as an agent to determine which prospects fall into which category. That way you can turn your time, attention and talent to the needs of the more motivated prospect group.

Overall, most agents see open homes as win–win — they either sell the house, or they find prospects for their database and opportunities for future business.

Part III

Developing a Winning Sales Strategy

Five Tips to Help Your Sales Strategy

- **Be prepared.** The first and most important sale is of *yourself*! Before every appraisal, every listing presentation, and every sales negotiation, do your research, look great and sound great.
- **Be confident.** If necessary, 'fake it till you make it'. Your clients will be expecting an expert in the marketplace — be that person.
- **Be knowledgeable.** Take time to do your research. Know your area, new listings, recent sale prices and local facilities. This will impress both buyers and sellers.
- **Be skillful.** Train and keep training. Seek out coaches, mentors, colleagues; everyone who can help you learn the skills you need for success.
- **Be resilient.** Things won't always go right. Be prepared for the knocks, learn from your mistakes, keep your goals strong and clear, and always remember 'tomorrow is another day!'.

Visit `www.dummies.com/extras/successrealestateagentau` to discover more tips to help you develop a winning sales strategy.

In this part ...

- We share all the secrets about real estate sales and client services, starting with perfecting your skills at the listing presentation.
- Get tips and tricks for preparing a house for buyer inspections. From virtual tours to perfect property photos to counselling owners on improvements, we guide you through all the components necessary to give properties that 'wow' factor!
- We show you how to find effective tools for marketing your listings and marketing yourself.
- Seal the deal! The part ends with an important chapter on how to negotiate contracts and close deals.

Chapter 9

Conducting a Quality Listing Presentation

In This Chapter

- Sorting out prospects based on their desire, need, ability and authority
- Perfecting your presentation and delivery skills
- Overcoming objections
- Bringing presentations to a successful close

Prospects are potential clients who are interested in considering the service options you provide. That's the good news. The not-so-good news is that prospects seem to assume that all agents are cut from the same mould — that all agents do the same things in the same ways. This is especially true with tech-savvy consumers who are empowered by broader access to information about real estate. That access is now as close as their smartphone or tablet. Your consumers are so immersed in technology that you have to drive home your value and difference to them — otherwise, they don't see the value in hiring you. Technology accentuates the sameness of real estate agents. You can sometimes hide your lack of sales skills, experience and knowledge behind the flash of technology. But, you know what? Consumers are truly unaware of the different skills, systems and philosophies various agents bring to the job — and the huge difference in results they achieve. It's up to you to change this perception!

Too often, real estate agents are viewed as a bunch of bananas — the product is the same, so why not shop around on price? Most listing presentations sound about the same, so it's no big surprise that prospects frequently make their selection based on highest listing price and lowest commission rate. This chapter helps you set yourself apart. It provides the steps to follow as you convey your differences, distinctions and competitive advantages in presentations that are planned, practiced, rehearsed and perfected. No more winging it! You're about to move into the league of the best, most preferred real estate agents.

Qualifying Your Prospects

The success of a listing presentation is determined by what you do before you even walk through the door. Mediocre agents enter the meeting flying blind, ill prepared and oblivious to the needs, wants, desires and expectations of the prospect — they expect to win the listing solely with charm and personality. This doesn't work. Today's consumers are savvy, and only willing to part with their money for an agent who convinces them of his or her value.

Early in her career, Terri had an experience where lack of preparation was the sole reason for an embarrassing loss of a top listing. She answered a request to meet about potentially listing a beautiful Queenslander in a desirable inner-city Brisbane suburb. Out she rushed, with no preparation but confident in her ability to impress! Her listing presentation went brilliantly — right up to the point when it was time to price the property. Not being familiar with the suburb, Terri based her appraisal figure on similar properties in her own area. This was a big mistake — not only was she wrong in her appraisal price but she was also wrong to the tune of more than $200,000! Needless to say, she was shown the door by some very disappointed sellers. From then on, she never went to an appraisal or a listing presentation unprepared and hoping to 'wing it'.

Never just roll up to a listing presentation or an appraisal hoping to make it up as you go. Preparation is vital — and being underprepared can cost you tens of thousands of dollars in lost commission. Never just drop everything and rush out when someone calls to ask for an appraisal. Do you want to be seen as the agent who's sitting there bored with nothing to do? Always say something like, 'Mrs Jones, I would love to come out to meet you at your property. Let me check my diary and give you a choice of times that could work for us both. Is that okay?'

Before you go to another appraisal or a listing presentation, you must gather as much information as you can.

Using questions to gather information

Asking questions helps you start to determine the seller's motivations and expectations, and helps you tailor your presentations to the seller's needs.

Working out motivations and price expectations

The first question you should ask is the important qualifier, aimed at working out whether the person is genuinely interested in selling or just after an appraisal. You can ask something like:

> *Mrs Jones, are you thinking of selling, or would you just like an appraisal to give you an idea of the value of your property? Either way, I am more than happy to come out to meet with you. An appraisal takes around 15 minutes usually but if you would like a more in depth conversation, could we say around 45 minutes?*

The aspect in the forefront of people's minds when thinking of selling or asking for an appraisal is the price! They will be expecting you to be the price guru. Tell them that before you come out you will be doing some research in order to give them as much information as possible. Then, in a conversational voice, you can ask, 'To help me with this, could you give me an idea of the range you are thinking — around $400,000, $500,000, or more?' Of course, you should be making it your business to know your areas and markets so you don't insult anyone by quoting silly figures.

Finding out a prospect's purpose and thoughts on sales price will arm you with vital information and put you miles ahead of the average agent who will rock up with a big smile and not much else. You will know the motivation (if not the actual reason for the sale) and will have an idea of the price they want so you won't shoot yourself in the foot when you get there.

You're not the guardian of price; the market is. You can only give an opinion based on your research. The market determines what people are prepared to pay for a house — your job is to market the property well, get lots of buyers in the door and then negotiate the best price possible.

Asking more detailed questions

Detailed information about time frame, motivation, previous experience with selling and/or agents can be asked in the conversation you have when you meet face to face. You also need to allow time to deliver your pre-listing kit, which should contain information about yourself, your agency, the different methods of sale, and even a questionnaire about the property — for example, what they love most about it and what attracted them to this property and the area in the first place.

If you're just starting out with an agency, your office should already have a pre-listing kit, containing information about your agency and the team, different methods of sale, testimonials from past clients — everything you need to pave your way when you're at the appointment. Ask for a copy of this kit, and then personalise it with a covering letter to your potential seller, thanking them for the opportunity to visit and confirming the appointment.

Also ask sellers how they found the property — this then leads into the importance of good marketing to find that one best buyer!

Many salespeople, especially in real estate sales, think they'll offend the customer if they ask questions. Here's an analogy that should put your mind at ease. Imagine you're sick and schedule a doctor's appointment. You arrive, the doctor calls you into their office, and you say, 'Guess what sickness I have today?' From across the room, the doctor is supposed to assess your symptoms, diagnose your ailment and prescribe a cure — without checking your ears or throat, listening to your lungs and heart, or, most importantly, asking you questions about what's wrong and how you feel. It sounds ridiculous, yet it's what real estate agents do when they try to serve clients without first asking questions to determine their wants, needs and expectations.

Without good client information, a listing presentation becomes an explanation of your services and service delivery system. But what if the prospect sitting in front of you wants to be served differently? Then what? To be honest, they're probably not that interested in you or your company. They really don't care how many homes your company sells worldwide. Their only concern is, 'What can you do for me?' If you can't answer this question (even if it remains unsaid), you'll most likely never secure the listing.

The customer ultimately determines whether your service is outstanding, fair or poor. Because the customer judges the quality of service received, the only way to start the service process is to learn what customers want, rather than trying to guess their desires and expectations. Additionally, your level of service satisfaction determines the level of referral volume you receive from that client in the future.

Knowing when and how to question listing prospects

Learn to use conversational questions as opposed to interrogation. Never make the prospect feel pushed into a corner. Space your questions into the conversation but listen intently to the answers to pick up what you need to know.

Question prospects for two main reasons:

- **Making the best use of your time.** By questioning prospects before you meet with them, you find out the two most important bits of information: Whether they're actually prospective sellers and the general price they have in their mind. This lets you assess the odds that talking with the prospect will result in income-producing activity. The questioning process increases your probability of sales success by determining which prospects are likely to result in commission revenue and which are likely to consume hours without results. This is a *qualifying* process, and following it is what will stop you wasting time and money with no chance of a profitable return for you. Keep in mind that this is your business and, unless you're on a salary, you don't receive any money until you have a sale.
- **Determining their service expectations.** What kind of service do they expect from you? What might they have experienced previously? Is there a match between your philosophy and theirs? If not, can you convince them that your approach is better than their preconceived notion of what and how you should represent their interests? If not, are you willing to turn down the business? The only way to address these issues is to learn what your prospects are thinking before you make your presentation.

If you wait until you're face to face with the prospect to begin collecting vital information, it may be too late. By then you want to be offering a tailored presentation, not acquiring baseline information.

To build valuable rapport, ask permission before you start asking questions — for example, say something like, 'Would you mind if I asked . . . ?' When you meet face to face, focus your questions around the following four topics:

1. **Motivation and time frame.** Ask questions that reveal how urgently the prospect needs to buy or sell, and in what time frame. Sample questions include:
    - Where are you hoping to move?
    - How soon do you need to be there?
    - Tell me about your perfect time frame. When do you want this move to happen?
    - If we don't find that perfect buyer in this time frame, do you have a fallback position or a back-up plan?

2. **Experience.** A prospect's view of the real estate profession is filtered through personal experience and experiences related by friends and family members. Here are some good questions to help you understand your prospect's real estate background and preconceptions:
   - Have you sold any properties in the past?
   - When was your last sales experience?
   - What happened? Were you happy with the outcome?
   - How did you choose the agent you worked with?
   - If you don't mind, what did you like best and least about what that agent did?
3. **Pricing.** The following questions help you gauge the prospect's motivation or desire to sell. They'll also help you determine whether the prospect is realistic about current real estate values.

   Listen carefully to the answers to the following three questions. They'll reveal whether your prospect is ready to sell or just fishing for a price:
   - Have you thought about what you would like to list your home for?
   - Do you mind if I ask how you arrived at that value for your home? (Ask this regardless of what the answer to the preceding question was.)
   - If a buyer came in today, what would you consider to be an acceptable offer for your home?

   If you want to approach the seller with a softer series of questions in the pricing area, you might try these:
   - Most people do a little research on real estate values before they sell their home. What have you found?
   - Most people have a general idea of what they want for their home. What are you thinking?
   - Compared to what you have seen so far, what price range do you think your home is in?

This could be a time when you can begin to talk about the current market and determine how much research the sellers have themselves done to this point. Keep in mind that this is mainly a time to ask questions of your seller. Save the more detailed comparative market analysis (CMA) for your full listing presentation. (See the section 'Presenting prices', later in this chapter, for more detail.)

4. **Service expectations.** Learning your prospect's service expectations is absolutely essential to a good working relationship. If your prospect has never met an agent concerned enough to ask what she wants, values and expects, asking questions here can build trust and open up a more detailed conversation. (Of course, you don't need to ask questions in this area if purely visiting the house to provide an appraisal.)

   Here are some possible questions for you to ask your prospective seller:

   - What do you expect from the real estate agent you choose to work with?
   - What are the top three things you're looking for from an agent?
   - What will it take for you to be confident that my service will meet your requirements?

Deciding on a one-step or two-step listing presentation

When we say one-step or two-step, we're not talking about dancing, although many agents feel that is what they're doing with some sellers. Our goal has always been to help agents fill their dance cards. The real problems arise when you're doing the cha-cha and the seller wants to waltz.

What we're referring to is whether you meet once or twice with a seller before you secure agreement or commitment. This decision of whether to pursue a one-step or two-step presentation is important.

One-step presentations

A one-step presentation requires you to ask more questions in advance of meeting with the seller. You can do that when you set the appointment or about 24 hours in advance when confirming your appointment. The one-step means you need to craft a solid CMA without seeing the home in advance. This can be done if your market knowledge is up to date.

At a one-step presentation, you must be prepared to present yourself as the 'area expert'. You must be sure of your facts and very confident that your research is spot-on. Your goal is to leave with a signed listing agreement. You may like to advise your prospect of your time frame for this meeting and get their agreement to spend this amount of time with you — otherwise, they may cut your presentation short!

Two-step presentations

If you feel you must see the home before you can complete your CMA accurately and express the value of the home confidently, you'll need to do a two-step process. In the two-step, you conduct two appointments:

- **The first appointment:** You ask the more detailed questions about time frame and expectations at the first appointment with the seller; it's more of a meet-and-greet type of appointment. You don't provide any specifics about the value of the home — if you haven't done your research properly and just take a guess, you may very well shoot yourself in the foot and not be invited back!

  Although the price question is usually the 'elephant in the room', the purpose of the first appointment is to see the home layout, the condition of the home, the amenities of the property and the feel of the neighbourhood, and to build a connection with the seller and ask your pre-listing questions. In most cases, the seller will want you to provide an expected selling price straightaway. Get in first here! Say something like, 'I know the most important question you want answered is the price. Now that I have seen your home in detail, let me go back to the office, do some thorough research and bring this back so we can decide what we think it could sell for — is that okay? What time tomorrow is good for you?'

- **The second appointment:** This step is really about explaining why the prospect should hire you, getting the listing price agreed on and the listing authority signed. Even the marketing budget can wait — secure the listing first, keeping in mind that if the sellers have only just met you for the first or second time, you may still need to prove that you can be trusted with their marketing investment.

  While this appointment doesn't need to take place at the seller's home, the majority of times this is the best option, because you need to have all the decision-makers present. Doing your presentation for one person is pointless if they have to pass on your words to another decision-maker before the agreement is signed. With people's busy schedules, holding the second appointment in the home usually makes getting everyone together easier. People are also likely to be more at ease, and you get another chance to get the feeling of the property.

One mistake agents can make in two-step listing presentations is what we call the one-and-a-half-step presentation. This happens when, either because your presentation structure isn't set or the seller leads you, you start to give information about what you'll do or the value of the prospect's home in step one of the two-step.

If you choose to do a two-step presentation, don't give the sellers the impression that they've already gotten all the information they need. Doing so gives them an excuse to cancel the second presentation before you give it. Structure your research and when you will present it, and leave the second meeting with the listing secured.

Checking your prospect's 'DNA'

Based on your qualifying efforts, determine the likelihood that your prospect will convert into a good client for your business by conducting what we call your DNA analysis. This involves measuring the prospect's level of desire, need to take action, and ability and authority to make a purchase or selling decision.

D for Desire

Desire or motivation is the strongest indicator of a successful outcome. A prospect's burning desire can overcome all other deficiencies, including a lack of financial capacity. If they want something badly enough, most sellers will make the adjustments they need to create the sale.

Desire isn't the same as interest. Anyone can have interest. Interest doesn't reflect intent, and it doesn't indicate a high probability of action. If a prospect says 'I have an interest in selling,' probe deeper to see whether the prospect has real desire to sell, or just interest.

N for Need

A need is a specific and identifiable problem that your service can help a prospect overcome.

The need may be a lifestyle change — a family may be expecting another child and so needs a larger home. Empty nesters tired of yard work and home upkeep may want to move to a maintenance-free apartment or townhouse. A divorce requires one household to become two households, forcing the home sale and several purchases in the aftermath.

One of the reasons we suggest working with expired listings is that the owners' level of need is so apparent. After sitting with an unsold home for months or longer, the sellers' need to find an agent who could solve the problem is pretty clear. Your job is to convince them that by working with you their problem would be solved — that you have a strategy to deliver a different and more positive outcome. (Refer to Chapter 7 for more on working with expired listings.)

A for Ability and Authority

Clients need both the ability and the authority to sell the property. Ability relates to the financial capacity of your prospects. Do they have access to funds for the marketing investment? What if the selling price does not allow them to move on? Do they have a Plan B? Authority means the prospect has the power to make the decision — to say yes or no to the deal. Find out: Are you working with the ultimate decision-maker or decision-makers, or is someone else also involved? Will the prospects decide autonomously, or will they seek the guidance or advice of others as they make their decision?

Agents make a huge mistake when they make listing presentations without both spouses or significant others in attendance. Check the names on the title deed — if at all possible, you must be sure that each of the people listed are present to sign the listing authority. Otherwise, you must get the remaining signature(s) as soon as possible, because legally you can't begin to market or show the property unless the listing authority is correctly completed with signatures from all parties. This also makes sense from a practical viewpoint — why would you tell a prospective buyer details of a property when you don't have an exclusive listing authority? This is asking for trouble because the buyer is quite within their rights at this stage to approach the seller personally and negotiate a private sale.

Presenting to Qualified Prospects

A quality listing presentation involves considerable advance planning, careful research and analysis, and highly developed presentation and sales skills. These enable you to derive maximum impact from the minimal time you have to present yourself and your recommendations, close the deal and obtain signatures on a listing agreement.

Your advance planning takes two forms: First you need to ask those important pre-listing questions of your prospects, determining not only their desires and expectations but also their ability to make the selling decision and complete the transaction. The previous portion of this chapter provides prospect-qualifying advice. The other essential ingredient in a listing presentation is a comparative market analysis, or CMA.

The following section guides you as you prepare a presentation that displays the full complement of your sales skills and abilities and helps you win your prospects' confidence and secure their listing.

Knowing the purpose of your presentation

Be crystal clear on this point: The objective of a listing presentation is to secure a signed listing agreement before the meeting ends. If you've decided the two-step is the right approach (refer to the section 'Deciding on a one-step or two-step listing presentation', earlier in this chapter), then in that second step you're securing the signature before you leave the property. You're not paving the way for returning at a later date to handle paperwork and secure final prospect approval. Your purpose is to make your case, close the deal and get ink on the paper right then and there while you're face to face with your prospects. If you don't, the odds of securing the listing start to swing away from you. Some other agent with better negotiating skills is likely to beat you to the punch!

If you let even a few days or a week slip by, your prospects will have a hard time separating your presentation from the presentations of other agents they meet in the meantime. And the moment they lose sight of your distinguishing attributes, they'll revert to a commodity mindset, focusing on price and selecting an agent based on who offered the lowest commission or highest list price.

These are two reasons you need to get the listing agreement signed during the presentation:

- **The moment you leave the appointment, anything can happen.** A buyer can appear out of nowhere, knocking on your prospects' door with a direct offer. An agent who interviewed your prospects a few days ago may be desperate enough to call with an offer to cut her fee by another per cent. Or the sellers may begin to confuse you for a different agent whose presentation they didn't like at all. The list goes on and on. The only thing you know for sure is that when you don't get the signed listing agreement at the appointment, you leave it up for grabs.
- **You need to feel the win.** The win in the listing game is when the contract is signed. Don't underestimate the power of that personal victory. Selling involves the risk of rejection. If it didn't, it would be called order taking, and you wouldn't be paid so well because it would be so easy. A listing presentation gives you the chance to go for the win, perfect your close and attain the victory. Give yourself the satisfaction and adrenaline rush of walking out of the home with a signed listing authority. Your drive home will be the shortest ever known. However, if you don't get the listing signed up, it will be the longest few minutes you've ever known.

Nothing is more disappointing than losing a listing to a rival agent. Especially after you've spent hours with potential sellers who seem to love what you say, love your marketing campaign strategy and are happy about every single thing. But when you call the next morning to confirm the appointment to sign up the paperwork, you're told that they're so sorry but they've given the listing to your rival agent. This exact scenario happened to Terri. Hours of rapport building and what seemed like a perfect presentation were blown out the window when the sellers called the next morning to say that they had decided to list with another agent who was 'more aggressive and could likely be tougher with the buyers'! From then on, she very rarely left without that signed authority in her hands. To leave a presentation knowing 100 per cent that you have the job is an incredible feeling and sets you up for the next step — which is a well-deserved pat on the back! Anything less seems like a rehearsal for the real thing — so make every opportunity count.

Making a quality presentation

A quality presentation follows these four steps: You begin by building trust, move into a demonstration of the benefits and advantages that you bring to the prospects, present your pricing recommendation and rationale, and move to close the deal by presenting a listing agreement and getting the prospects to sign on the proverbial dotted line.

The appointment itself usually takes under an hour, so allow for at least 45 minutes and warn your sellers that you will need this time frame to go over all the information and answer all their questions or concerns. The preparation involves a good deal more. The upcoming sections guide you through the preparations that go into each segment of the presentation.

Getting off to a good start

Paving the way for a good listing presentation involves only three steps, but you can't afford to skip a single one:

1. **Be sure all decision-makers are present.**

   This is also an overarching rule, but particularly important for the listing presentation. If one decision-maker can't attend because an emergency arises, reschedule for another time. If a decision-maker is absent, you'll have to rely on the other party to relay your presentation, complete with paraphrasing, misinterpretations, abbreviated points and omissions. Not a good option for you.

2. **Based on your pre-appointment calls and visit, enter the meeting with a presentation that incorporates your prospects' needs, desires and expectations.**

   The next section in this chapter guides you through the steps to follow.

3. **Open the presentation by building trust with your prospects.**

   Forget about finding common ground or seeking to establish rapport by talking about your common interest in fishing, hunting, water skiing or horses. Prospects see right through this disingenuous effort to establish a pseudo-friendship. They're looking for business associates. Be real and sincere and get to the point.

   To build trust, summarise what the prospects have told you about their values, their goals for this move, the motivations behind the move and what they hope to accomplish. Refer to your pre-listing questions and confirm the answers they shared with you. Confirm that you got their input right and communicate that what is important to them is also important to you.

This introductory and trust-building segment should take 10 to 15 minutes, max, at the beginning of your presentation.

The success or failure of your presentation can usually be traced back to this initial segment. If prospects don't feel that you understand and relate to their needs, wants and desires, they'll tune you out after just the first few minutes, long before you get to the part where you tell them how great you and your company are and how you can get their home sold.

Setting yourself apart from the real estate agent pack

In this part of the presentation, you demonstrate the benefits and advantages prospects can count on when they're with you. Talk about what you do and end each point by emphasising how this benefits the seller.

Most agents make a big mistake by either omitting this segment or using it to present features of their business rather than benefits derived by clients. There's a big difference between the two. An example of a *feature* is air conditioning in a home, or anti-lock brakes on a car. The *benefits* of air conditioning include comfort, coolness and ease of sleep at night. The benefits of anti-lock brakes are safety, protection and faster stopping.

Selling benefits, not features

The vast majority of salespeople, and especially real estate agents, sell features. Look at image ads for agents or listen to listing presentations, and all you'll see and hear are features:

- I sold 150 homes last year.
- I've been in the business for 20 years.
- I work for the #1 company in the marketplace.
- I'm a member of the million-dollar club.
- I put my clients first.
- I'm honest and have integrity.
- Blah, blah, blah!

In these feature-dump presentations, prospects don't hear anything about what's in it for them — what advantages they reap as a result of the agent's attributes. As a result, they tune out a good deal of the presentation, and the rest sounds just like what they hear from other agents. No wonder clients tend to make decisions based on list price and commission.

If you want prospects to listen and care, don't talk about *you*; talk about what you offer to *them*, and how you can help them achieve their goals. Turn every feature of your business into a benefit for the customer. For example, 'I sold 150 homes last year' can become 'I sold 150 homes last year, and what really matters to you is that nearly 80 per cent were on the market for far fewer days than the regional average.' See the difference? Or 'Our office has a huge database of buyers, and the benefit of this to you is that we may very well find that perfect buyer in a very short space of time!'

Proving your competitive edge

As you prepare to present your distinct competitive edge, ask yourself:

- What makes you different? You need to be able to answer this question with something that speaks to the clients' needs, so spend time alone getting this bit right before the question is asked of you.
- Why should someone hire you?
- What are your strengths? And how do these benefit your clients?

While you don't need to share your findings with your seller, spend time assessing any weaknesses in your service and ways you can compensate for your shortcomings. For instance, if you're a new agent with few past individual triumphs, highlight the success of your agency and the strength of the team. For example, you could say, 'One of the reasons I chose to work with XYZ real estate company is its long and widely recognised success helping their clients achieve their goals and dreams.'

Using the power of your strongest statistics

Here are some very important points for you to weave into your presentation:

- **Start by acknowledging what your prospect already knows: Agents all provide a similar service.** You could say something like, 'As you know, every agent will put your home on the internet and in their agency window.' Then you can add, 'If that's all it took to achieve success, then every agent would sell hundreds of homes and we both know that doesn't happen!' With this introduction, you admit that agents all do basically the same thing, yet they achieve vastly different results.

- **Then set yourself apart**. You could say something like, 'Do you know what really creates the difference for my sellers compared to clients of other agents? It's the power of the Big 3: Sales skills, conversion ability and conversion of leads into customers.' And you need to show how your personal results or that of your team illustrates these important points.

  To underscore the point, you can present this logic:

  - Increased inquiries = Increased inspections
  - Increased inspections = Increased competition for the sellers' home
  - Increased competition = Higher probability of sale, higher sale price, or both

  As a newer agent, you may not be able to show your own strong numbers, but you can present your company's Big 3 instead. For instance, you can perhaps focus on the fact that your company sells more properties than its competitors do, that your company has more agents to help create more exposure, and that your company has high market share, which leads to increased ad calls and sales calls — or work out whatever fits your own situation. Then present this logic:

  - Increased market exposure for your seller = Increased number and quality of leads
  - Increased number and quality of leads = Increased inspections
  - Increased inspections = Higher probability of sale, higher sale price, or both

Your use of technology may be awesome but this is merely a feature of the service you and your company provide. The question is still, what's the benefit to the client? To be successful, you must show the benefits you offer.

Gaining confirmation

After you've conveyed your benefits to the sellers, pause to confirm that they understand and agree with the points you've made. Do this through a *confirmation close* or *trial close*, using the following scripts as a guide but personalising your delivery:

- *Do you see how our company delivers the benefit of greater exposure and higher probability of sale for our clients?*
- *Do you see why we have such a large market share, and does it make sense how our market dominance benefits you?*
- *Do you see the advantages our sellers have in today's market because of the increased exposure we provide through our technology platform?*

If you're from a more boutique agency, try something like, 'Do you see how the benefit to you of us being a small boutique agency is that we are free to focus our attention on just a few properties — you will love our service and we won't stop until we get the result for you.'

Presenting prices

The moment you receive confirmation that the prospect understands the unique benefits you deliver, move into the pricing segment of your presentation, during which you share your CMA — your research and your findings regarding the value of the property, based on the current state of the market and on prices that comparable houses have recently sold for in the area or are currently being advertised at. (Refer to Chapter 3 for more on CMAs.)

You're not a qualified valuer — you're only able to give an 'appraisal', which is an opinion of market value based on evidence. Keep in mind that comparable houses may be on the market that are listed too high, so you need to highlight this. If they've been on the market for a while, also point this out, emphasising that the reason they've been around for so long is that they're not priced to meet the current market and already have the dreaded 'lemon' tag.

This portion of the presentation should take as long as it needs. If you get this bit right, your whole campaign should go smoothly. Get it wrong and your campaign could be a nightmare of negotiation to get your seller thinking realistically about price.

The best way is to tackle the price issue head on. You could say something like, 'Now we come to price — the question that has probably been on your mind from the moment I got here!' If you can lighten the conversation at this point it will help your sellers relax.

Next you can lay all your research on the table and invite your sellers to participate in deciding the listing price. As with most things, a collaborative agreement is what you want. If you present yourself as the expert arbitrator of price, you will be the first one the sellers blame if this price is not achieved. Instead, work towards the seller coming up with a realistic price based on the market evidence you've provided. (***Note:*** If the sale is via auction, don't set a reserve figure at this early stage — wait until you have more buyer feedback.)

Present your evidence as you have a general discussion about where the sellers think their own property could sit in comparison with the competition. You could say something like, 'Just for a moment, can we pretend you're the buyer? In light of these comparative properties, where do you think your own property might sit?' If the sellers feel their property should sit higher than the comparisons you've gathered, ask them to list the features that lead them to this conclusion.

Usually a motivated seller will place their own property exactly in the range it should be listed. If not, you can ask the reasons that they think their property is worth more than the competition. This is a very sensitive part of the conversation, so don't be argumentative or dogmatic, but do be direct regarding your own thoughts on the price range.

If your seller doesn't offer a figure, provide a small range — giving a specific figure means that this is the figure the seller will remember, and may discount other offers even if they're close. Always keep in mind that you're not the arbitrator of price — the market is. You are just the guide. Your role is to attract the greatest number of potential buyers to the property and then negotiate the highest price possible.

Once you've presented and discussed comparisons, prices, time on market, and differences between initial listing price and actual selling price, it's time to stop and listen to your seller's thoughts. Allow time for any objections, concerns or frustrations to be aired.

If the sellers agree with you on the listing price (when listing as a private treaty sale), you can do an *assumptive* close. Ask if they need you to explain anything further or if they still have any questions or concerns. If the answer is 'no', move to your close, saying something easy like, 'Okay then — how about we get the paperwork out of the way so I can get to work for you!'

If your sellers don't agree to move onto the listing agreement, are not happy or want to negotiate commission or any other issue, take the time to address their concerns before asking for signatures. If they say they want to sleep on it and call you in a day or so, most likely this means that they're planning to not list with you, but are too polite to say so to your face. In this case, it's even more important not to leave until you address their concerns and hopefully reassure the sellers that you are the right agent for the job.

Sometimes you may find that you can't agree on price but, nevertheless, they are very motivated sellers. In this case, don't walk away too quickly! As long as you have qualified well, the seller has every right to start above what you might think is the market feedback. However, if you do take this overpriced listing, ask for a guarantee that you can come back within two weeks to discuss the buyer feedback and review the strategy, including the listing price.

Going for the close

As soon as you have agreement on what you have explained, start to close and get a signed listing authority.

You may be thinking, 'When do I tell them about the marketing plan?' You don't need to do this at this early stage. They may very well ask you about marketing or ask if your firm offers free advertising like the one up the road. It's immaterial to the discussion if you've done a good job of explaining the benefits of engaging you. The days of 'I do this and this and this' are long over. You can integrate your marketing info and connect prospects to the related benefits, but just doing 15 minutes on your marketing plan is ineffective. This will be part of your campaign strategy and the details can be decided on later. If they insist on a marketing budget from you, just say that this is something that is flexible and decided later in collaboration with them. At this later stage, you can gain their commitment to a realistic marketing budget.

The listing presentation is about the results you achieve. If your key statistics and the benefits of doing business with you aren't strong enough, no marketing plan will fill the gap. As they say, the first sale you have to make is to sell yourself (figuratively speaking!).

Prove that you and your company are the best. Convince the sellers of their home's value. Know their expectations of service and results and guarantee that you'll meet and exceed them. Then ask for (or assume) their business and get the signatures.

Closing is the natural ending to a great presentation.

Making your presentation useful and interesting

In the past, some agent presentations put sellers to sleep, mainly because most presentations lack interest, usefulness and structure. They were long and boring and not structured to clearly answer the seller's two burning questions: How much will I get and how much will it cost?

The presentation advice in the preceding section provides all you need to know to overcome the structure and usefulness issues. To increase the interest quotient, you can try this advice:

- **Use presentation technology.** Wow the seller with your presentation on your iPad or with PowerPoint or Keynote — whichever you are familiar with. This engages the seller in a selling experience that's not exclusively dependent on your words. The slides should be graphically appealing and contain more than just words. You need images, too. For example, if you're using testimonials from former clients, use an image of them in their new home (with their permission). Or better yet, use a video of them expressing how well you performed. The former clients will connect with your prospect. The seller will think, Hey, we're just like them. The testimonial video will sell you better than you can sell yourself.
- **Share market knowledge.** Become a student of the local marketplace and share meaningful statistics. Also track trends in the national marketplace, both to enlighten your prospects and distinguish yourself as a well-read, well-connected and well-informed agent.

- **Ask questions.** Listen in on typical listing presentations, and you'll hear the agent talking 80 per cent of the time, with the prospect hardly getting a word in edgewise. The seller finds that monologue uninteresting. The rule is you talk around 20 per cent and listen around 80 per cent of the time.
- **Watch the clock.** Don't let your presentation run too long, and don't save the information the seller most wants to receive until the very end. Set an agenda that you run through with the seller before you even start. You could joke that it keeps you on track, but in reality it reassures your seller that you will indeed be covering all the important points. If you put your price recommendation at the very end of a 90-minute presentation during which you did 80 per cent of the talking, you can pretty well predict that your seller will be tuned out.

What the prospect has to say is more important than what you have to say. Great salespeople do less than 25 per cent of the talking. You already know all that you need to know about what you're thinking. You need to learn what your prospects think, know and desire so you can match your service to their wants and needs.

Keeping it short and sweet

Let's get right to the point: A 90-minute presentation is neither short nor sweet. Sellers don't want to sit through a 90-minute appointment, and they most certainly don't want to listen to an agent for that long.

Within the first few minutes of the appointment, inform your sellers that your listing presentation will take no more than 45 minutes. More than half of the serious sellers will thank you when you tell them that your presentation will be brief. Sending a pre-listing information kit prior to your face-to-face meeting also helps with time management, because you can cover many of the salient points before you even arrive — for example, methods of sale, your service guarantee, testimonials and more. A good, brief presentation results from a proper structure, a clear presentation plan, and a knowledge of what to say and how to convey it.

Many agents translate the terms *structure* and *plan* to mean 'canned presentation'. They say, 'I don't want to sound mechanical and scripted.' People sound mechanical and scripted for lack of practice, not because they have a pattern or process to follow. Be well prepared and the right words will come out — simple as that. Otherwise, it's easy to waffle and bore your seller into submission.

You need to have a framework that you're comfortable with, that allows you to deliver key facts, findings and segments, using key phrases and dialogues, every time you present. However, better to err on the side of 'canned' than just 'wing it' — and this is exactly why an agenda will work until you are so experienced that you don't need it.

The previous section provides the structure to follow as you prepare a great presentation. Additionally, follow this advice:

- **Know your prospects.** If you aren't completely clear on your prospects' interests and needs, flip back to the first pages of this chapter. One of the reasons we constructed the opening section on qualifying prospects so meticulously is that acquiring prospect knowledge is truly the key to a good presentation. You absolutely have to secure the right information before going into the appointment.
- **Set a goal to keep your presentation to 45 minutes or less.** Look at every piece of sales material you present. Does it demonstrate clear benefits to the seller? Does it need to be used? Does the seller understand it? Does it create differentiation between you and other agents? As the saying goes, 'When in doubt, leave it out.'

- **Be sure that your PowerPoint or Keynote slides convey a clear and powerful message.** An abundance of slides can eat up your presentation time and your chance to dialogue with the sellers. Typically, each slide in your presentation represents two to four minutes of presentation time by the time you advance it, talk about it, emphasise key points and ask for questions to confirm your prospect understands. Do the maths: 30 slides eat up at least an hour, putting you well over your time limit before you even get to the contract.

Four steps to a great delivery

Research shows that your body language and tonality account for more than 90 per cent of your presentation's effectiveness. What you actually say accounts for less than 10 per cent of the delivery. If you're scrambling to find the right words, as most salespeople are, you're spending your energy in inverse proportion to what impacts your effectiveness.

The solution is to plan what you're going to say beforehand, so that during the presentation you can focus on language, tonality and the following four steps to a great delivery.

Conviction

The Macquarie Dictionary defines conviction as a fixed or firm belief. To that we can add that nothing is more compelling than conviction.

Your belief that you can get the job done draws clients to you. Your belief in the value of their home or how their home should be sold earns their trust. Your firm belief about where the marketplace is headed, backed by statistics that prove your point, sells you and your recommendations.

Before you go face to face with sellers, determine three things that you're going to express with absolute conviction. If your sellers share your views (you'll know based on your pre-listing questions), that's a bonus. If their views are opposite to yours, be doubly persuasive and resolute in order to win them over to your point of view. Then, confirm that their view has in fact shifted. It's easy to forget this important step.

Enthusiasm

Enthusiasm sells in spades. People want to work with those who are enthusiastic about their home and the market. If the market is tough, you have to be frank and honest; you can't just hide market realities. But you can still be enthusiastic and show that you're excited about the opportunity to 'beat the odds' of the marketplace.

Your listing presentation is more interesting if you're enthusiastic about your career, your business, the home and the sellers. As the old sales adage says, 'Enthusiasm is to selling as yeast is to bread. It makes the dough rise!'

Confidence

Where have you experienced victories? Tap into those experiences as you pump up your confidence in preparation for prospect presentations.

If you lack confidence, determine what you need to do to increase your belief in yourself and your ability to achieve success. What activities may help increase your confidence? What skills do you need to master to dramatically affect your confidence? What one thing, if you do it with excellence, will change your self-confidence?

The Macquarie Dictionary defines confidence as 'full trust; belief in the trustworthiness or reliability of a person or thing'. The great motivator Napoleon Hill says, 'What the mind can conceive and believe, it can achieve.'

When Terri moved to a new agency, her intent was to gain auction listings with full marketing. However, she had no experience in this area — she hadn't used this tactic at her previous agency. She found reaching her goal tough — not because of her lack of skill as an agent, but because of her lack of confidence in her knowledge of the options she was offering. The only answer was to increase this confidence, which she did successfully through training and mentoring. The end result was that Terri soon became one of the top auction agents in her agency — proving everything comes back to your confidence in what you're selling your clients, which is both yourself and your skills.

Assertiveness

Agents don't want to come off as pushy or aggressive in their sales approach, and by mistake they shy away from assertiveness as well.

Our definition of a great salesperson is 'a person who convinces someone to do something that is beneficial to them or convinces them to do it faster.'

Going for the close or asking for the order isn't pushy. It's assertive. As a real estate agent, your job is to persuade prospects that you have the best service, the best value and the highest probability of success. You must convince them to sign up for the benefits you provide, now!

One of the easiest ways to exert your assertiveness is to say something like the following: 'At the end of my presentation tonight, provided we're all in agreement, we can get the paperwork out of the way and I can start working on your property right away.'

Being assertive in selling is a good thing.

Staying in control

Agents lose control of the listing presentation when they allow the sellers' agenda to take over the discussion. Some agents can lose control to the seller in the first five minutes. The problem for most agents is that if they lose control, they don't have the skill to wrestle it back.

The sellers' agenda is simple. They want to know what their home is worth. They want to know what you can do to sell it and what you charge for your service. And for sure they want to know how much they'll pocket when the deal is done. If the order of your presentation doesn't address their issues, you won't walk out with the listing.

However, if you talk about the listing price of the home and your fee structure before you've built trust, credibility and value for your service, you'll lose every time. Don't ever follow the seller's agenda!

Setting the agenda early on

The most powerful technique is to have an actual order or agenda you follow. You can introduce this agenda by saying something like the following:

> *Mr and Mrs Seller, I've found this presentation order to be most effective for my clients. It allows me to present to you the important facts, marketplace strategies and benefits you receive as my clients. In addition, we'll have plenty of time to answer all your questions so you're completely comfortable with your decision. Would it be all right with you if we follow this agenda for our meeting?*

You can put your agenda on one of the first slides in your presentation, and also have it printed on high-quality paper. This enables you to hand it to the sellers as well. It gives them something tactile to hold. When you ask them to approve it, it's in their hands.

The agenda also tells them clearly:

- You are organised and professional.
- You have thought this through.
- You aren't making it up as you go.
- You have a plan.

Keeping on track

When the seller brings up a point that may cause you to abandon your presentation plan, pick up the agenda sheet and ask:

> *Would it be all right to discuss that when we get to this point in the presentation?*

Your agenda may look like this:

1. Review agenda for the meeting
2. Do visual inspection of the property
3. Discuss clients' goals, needs and expectations of me
4. Discuss my professional credentials
5. Determine listing price
6. Complete the paperwork so I can begin work to sell your property

The last item needs to be on your agenda. It alerts the clients in advance that you're going to close. In fact, etch all six items in stone; don't move them or rearrange them. You have to build trust, credibility and value in that order, or you lose.

Dealing with Sales Objections

Sales objections are part of selling. For most people in sales, they present an immovable object in the road to your success. Real estate agents often freeze when presented with a sales objection. They don't know what to do or say in the face of this perceived danger.

Consider this radical concept: Sales objections are actually good. You can't sell anything significant without sales objections. Sales objections indicate an elevated level of interest, desire or motivation to buy what you're offering. Think of them as requests for more information.

The prospect is saying, 'I need more information. If I like the information you give me, I'll do business with you.' What could be better than that?

Delaying objections

One of the best ways to delay objections is to refer to your approved agenda (refer to the section 'Keeping on track', earlier in this chapter), saying:

> *Mr and Mrs Seller, would it be all right if I answered your question when we get to item number five on our agenda? That's where we discuss _____.*

Better than 40 per cent of the time, the sellers won't bring up the sales objection again. You handle the sales objection by delaying its arrival.

Using your agenda to delay objections is particularly important when the concern deals with the recommended list price or the cost of your service. Don't ever respond to pricing concerns until you've determined the sellers' wants, needs and expectations, and established the value of your service.

Handling objections in four easy steps

Objections are inevitable, so be ready to deal with them following this four-step system.

Pausing

When an objection arises, hear the client out completely. Then pause to collect your thoughts and, for many salespeople, to lower what may feel like rising blood pressure. Pause to ensure that you heard the objection completely. Don't try to cut the person off. Often salespeople interrupt, as if they're hoping to stuff the words back into the client's mouth before they're even out. This is the biggest mistake you can make. It demonstrates rudeness and insensitivity.

Acknowledging concerns

After hearing the objection and pausing to consider it, acknowledge the concern. This confirms that you understand what the client said, and it also gives you a few moments to consider and prepare your response.

Notice, nothing in the previous paragraph advises you to agree with the client. You can acknowledge the concern and thank the client for bringing it up without saying that it's right.

You can acknowledge by using any of these phrases:

I understand your concern in this area.

That's a really terrific question. I'm glad you asked it.

I can see where that might cause you concern.

A great technique is to follow acknowledgement of a concern with a question or comment that probes for more information. The following responses give you an opportunity to learn more while also buying a few moments to develop a response:

I understand your concern in this area. Why do you feel that way?

I can see where that might cause you concern. Tell me more.

Isolating concerns

By now you may be ready to pounce on the objection with your best answers. Hold off, if you can, while you isolate the concern. Isolation at its fundamental level, asks: 'If it weren't for this concern, we'd be working together, right?'

By isolating, you cause the prospects to lay all their concerns on the table. Through this one step you learn everything that is standing between you and a signed listing contract.

Use any of these isolation scripts as you help sellers get their concerns out into the open:

Is that the only concern that holds you back from moving forward with me?

Suppose we could find a satisfactory solution to this important concern of yours. Would you give me the go-ahead?

If this problem didn't exist, would you be ready to go ahead right now?

By isolating the concern, you learn exactly what you're up against. You may surface another objection in the process — which is why many agents shrink away from this step — but you would have heard it later anyway.

Responding with confidence

By now you've heard the objection, paused, acknowledged and isolated. Now is the time to respond.

The most commonly stated objections centre on the agent's commission, the recommended list price of the home, the length of the listing term and the need for extra time to make the listing decision. More than 80 per cent of the objections you'll hear over the course of your career stem from these key concerns. Prepare yourself by outlining and mastering responses that convince sellers you're able to handle the concern more effectively than other agents.

Ask your principal for scripts the agency recommends for handling sales objections. If the company doesn't have them, make an investment in your career and source them from an expert.

Asking for the Order

After you've overcome seller concerns or objections, ask for the order. In sales terms, this means asking the prospects to do business with you.

At the end of a presentation, a typical salesperson's close is something like, 'Well, what do you think?' It's obvious to me why the typical salesperson sells very little. Winding up with a question like 'What do you think?' is hardly asking for the order or closing.

Closing is making a definitive statement about your conviction that you're the right person for the job and that the sellers should take action now. A good closing statement goes like this:

> *Mr and Mrs Seller, based on your goals, needs and expectations, I'm confident that I'm the right person to handle the sale for you. Let's get started now!*

As you say 'Let's get started,' slide the listing agreement in front of them. Hand them a pen and smile. Most importantly, shut up! Don't utter a word.

Bringing the Presentation to a Natural Conclusion

Following any major sales transaction, people feel a bit of uncertainty, a feeling of 'What did I just do?' Pre-empt that fear by addressing and controlling your clients' concerns.

Before you leave the meeting, recap what steps will happen next and what you'll be doing for your clients in the next 24 to 48 hours. Then reassure them that they made a great decision, that you look forward to serving them and working with them, that the goals they set will be achieved, and that they selected the right agent for the job.

Chapter 10

Getting the House Ready for Showing

In This Chapter

- Preparing a property for online viewing
- Advising clients on what to do and what to skip
- Helping a home make a great first impression — inside and out

Getting a home ready for the big show is necessary to achieve a sale. The more competitively the home is priced and prepared, the sooner the rigour of showing will end. And the sooner the sale takes place, the sooner your clients can return to their normal routines — except for that little challenge of packing and moving. This chapter helps you guide clients as they transform their homes from how they look most of the time to how they need to look to win attention and positive decisions from prospective buyers.

Getting the Home Ready for Virtual Tours First

Most buyers use the internet to search and review homes, and to access real estate properties and information, so visual information is essential to selling homes. The vast majority initially find the home online — according to `realestate.com.au`, over 90 per cent of people looking to buy, rent or sell use the internet to search for property. People then either drive by, come to an open for inspection or contact the listing agent for a private showing.

Today's consumers want to understand a home's features and benefits, and want to feel and experience the home online before they take time to visit the home in person. For a large number, the next step is to drive by the home. Potential buyers frequently check out the neighbourhood, street appeal and condition of the property before even contacting an agent. This means that by the time they actually walk in the door they're half convinced that this could be the one!

Presenting the right image online

The first rule of online property marketing is pictures, pictures, pictures. A recent study comparing the average number of pictures per listing found that the average listing has fewer than five photos. Buyers are cluey and when they come across property listings with few photos, or photos mainly showing shots of the local area, they reach one of several conclusions, covered in the following sections.

The most commonly used websites for agent listings in Australia are `www.realestate.com.au` and `www.domain.com.au`, and in New Zealand the most preferred is `www.realestate.co.nz`. Each of these companies has pricing structures that differ according to the number of images allowed or positioning in searches. Check this pricing in detail for yourself or ask for advice from your agency.

They don't want to waste their time

If potential buyers can't align their wants and needs with the visual images of the property, they quickly cross it off the list for lack of information. Many buyers think properties are like buses; another one will be along in a few minutes or days. 'I'll wait,' they say. They don't have time to look through every property so they are looking to eliminate rather than add to the list of potentials.

The property barks at cars

In other words, the property is a dog! If the property was a quality one, buyers think, the agent would have taken more pictures of it. Their mindset is that something must be wrong. Even if you overcome that hurdle and buyers do come to inspect, you now have buyers on your hands who are focused on finding something wrong with the property. You've dug yourself into a hole.

The agent is unskilled

Many buyers who search the internet are just beginning their research. They're researching properties for sale while formulating ideas for their move. They may start the search process six months, one year or even two years before they actually move. A large number must sell a home to buy their next home, and they will need an agent. But you've demonstrated to them a lack of basic marketing skills. Their thinking is that if they can't easily get a basic understanding of this property, everyone else who finds this home online will have the same issues. You have little chance of securing their business in the future.

Unlocking secrets to perfect property pics

You don't have to use a professional photographer for all your listings; however, some listings benefit from the expertise that a professional can offer. You will be surprised at how little this will cost your seller — usually less than $500! However, if you secure a luxury property, the golden rule is to always invest in a professional. Other properties that warrant an investment include those with unique architectural attributes, enhanced amenities, objectionable characteristics or challenging furnishings. A professional can capture just the right image of a positive feature and downplay something that might turn off a buyer in an online search. Remember, buyers are likely to be looking for ways to cross a property off a list rather than adding it to their list.

If the seller's marketing budget is tight, you could do the shots yourself. When you're tackling the role of photographer, the right props can really enhance a shot. The goal is to make whatever space you're photographing warm and inviting to the viewer. Placing wine and cheese in a kitchen, for example, can say to the buyer, 'Welcome; come relax.' Avoid props like magazines, fruit and towels that give the home the 'lived in' look. Clearing away any mess will make the rooms look more inviting and spacious.

The laws of lighting

In most cases, the more light, whether natural or artificial, the better. The only exception is light that creates a glare in your lens. Turn on the lights and, if you have dark or shadowy areas and angles, fill in with work lights. Because lighting is different in each room, consider shooting different rooms at different times throughout the day. This takes extra work, time and effort, but it can improve the pictures and balance the lighting. Think about lighting when taking exterior pictures, as well. Most exterior shots of homes look better from an angle rather than dead on. Additionally, you don't want the home to be backlit because of glare in the lens. Ideally, the sun should be behind you, shining on the home. If the entry is shaded, you can take the shot on an overcast day to reduce the shade in the shot. Or you can turn on the outside lights and take the shot at night, with the front door open to look more inviting.

The right angles

Your goal is to create interesting and inviting shots and angles. Try to avoid shooting more than two walls in a given room. If you shoot three walls, you create a box. When photographing an empty home or room, be sure to combine rooms in a shot or capture the spaciousness of the environment. Because you don't have furniture, you're selling the size and openness of the space. Shoot at chest level or even on a stepping stool to show less ceiling in the shot.

Creating the right images is an art, not a science. You have to play with the shots on each home you list. Thanks to digital photography, you can take countless photos and easily disregard the ones you don't like. You can never have too many to choose from.

See Chapter 11 for more tips on taking digital photos.

Talking with Clients on Home Improvements

Before you advise owners about home improvements, remember these two rules:

- **First and foremost, never advise before you're hired.** This step happens after a client relationship is established. Attorneys don't offer legal advice before their services have been officially retained. Doctors don't diagnose without assurance of compensation. Real estate agents should follow suit. Wait until the listing agreement is signed. After it's signed, begin giving advice regarding how the owner can achieve a quicker sale or higher price by making recommended home improvements and implementing staging advice. This may involve recommending a home staging professional, who can be worth their weight in gold — often adding tens of thousands to the final sale price.

Terri has put many of her own properties up for sale, always with another experienced agent who has no emotion around the property — except for the determination to do a great job and get the best price. She hires a home stylist and never ceases to be amazed at the result.

Too frequently, agents give away their expert advice during listing presentations in hopes of proving their ability and expertise to sellers. More often than not, though, the sellers simply take the tips with them when they link up with an agent who is less skilful but promises a cheaper fee.

- **Second, tell the truth.** If the sellers need to clean the home, tell them. If they're smokers and the house reeks from cigarettes, or if their pets are causing odour problems, tell them. Just make sure you do it in a tactful way, highlighting the fact that you don't want anything to give the wrong impression for the buyer.

  Likewise, appearances can kill buyer interest. If the home is crowded with too much stuff, say so. If the pink exterior colour may cause people to click next on their browser or drive right on by, speak up. Holding your tongue only delays the day of reckoning. What's more, it's easier to be totally frank when you first notice the problem — though only after the listing contract is signed. If you advise before you gain commitment, your advice may offend the sellers and cost you the listing. This is another reason to follow Rule #1 and get a signature before offering suggestions for change.

Improvements that contribute to the sale price

When it comes to preparing a home for sale, worthwhile and necessary improvements fall into three categories:

- Improvements that bring a home back to standard
- Improvements that correct defects
- Improvements that enhance street appeal or first impressions

The following sections provide guidelines for each area.

Bringing a home back to standard

Before you present a home with horribly dated decor, suggest to the sellers to modernise the interior look to align it with the expectations of current buyers, because this will almost certainly result in a higher sale price.

Sellers don't have to go overboard; they just need to use a reasonable colour scheme and provide enough of an update so that new owners feel they can move in without having to undertake an immediate facelift. Share the following advice with sellers:

- **Keep improvements simple.** A total redecoration isn't necessary or even advisable. The objective is to arrive at a widely acceptable and reasonably current colour scheme with paint, counters and floor coverings. The colour palette tends to shift, so picking something too trendy can be problematic if you're on the tail end of the latest trend . . . think avocado appliances in the '70s or black glass in the '90s. Advise your clients to create a warm, blank canvas that any prospective buyer can work with.
- **Don't aim to create a design showpiece.** Realise that after the purchase, buyers often change a home significantly to make it their own. The sellers' objective is to allow prospective buyers to feel that their changes can happen over the next few years — that they're not glaringly and immediately necessary.

- **Focus on the big stuff.** If the interior of a home looks current and the landscaping, yard, decks and patios are well kept and serviceable, the buyers' need to make significant, immediate changes lowers greatly. As a result, they're more likely to buy the home. They may also make a more competitive initial offer than would be the case if the home presented obvious exterior or interior colour or repair issues. If buyers have to make changes to a home, they have to pay for them with their own personal funds, not with money they borrow in their mortgage payments (unless they take out a separate loan for this purpose). Many buyers consider this fact when deciding which home they should buy.
- **A little paint makes a huge difference.** Repainting is one of the most cost-effective ways to freshen the look of a home. It can even disguise design shortcomings.

Correcting defects

If a home has defects, the seller has two choices: Fix them or provide equal monetary compensation to the buyers.

For example, if a roof needs repair or replacement, the improvement will be expected by both the bank and the buyer. The seller can offer one of the following two remedies:

- **Handle and pay for the repair or replacement.**
- **Provide the buyers with sufficient compensation to cover the cost and hassle of correcting the defect themselves.** This compensation

comes in the form of a reduction in the sale price. In most cases, if buyers have to decide between contractor bids, arrange for repairs and check the work of the contractor, they'll also want some compensation for their time and effort.

Other items that may need to be addressed are excessively worn carpet or windows with broken seals, especially when condensation has built up around the panes.

Enhancing first impressions

Any cost-effective improvement that adds street appeal or enhances first impressions can increase the sale price. Here are a few improvements the seller can make:

- You may advise sellers to select a better colour palette for the home's facade or spend a few hundred dollars to plant flowering plants to brighten the exterior walkways. The effect will increase the probability of a sale and positively influence the sale price.
- Inside the house, after improving the home's colour scheme, advise sellers to assess the quality of the home's surfaces, including carpet, floorboards, tiles, vinyl and countertops. Advise them to look for simple fixes, like replacing a few chipped tiles. If they are considering replacing floor coverings, remind them that neutral, widely accepted colour tones are best, and that light colours can create the feeling of a larger, brighter room. Some older homes have floorboards covered with worn carpet — you can suggest taking up the carpet and polishing the floorboards for a more modern and appealing look. Also ask sellers to look at how rooms are being used. Perhaps a room has been used as a small bedroom, but could be converted into a study. Alternatively, if a bigger room has been used for a study, perhaps it would add more value as an additional bedroom.

- Kitchens and bathrooms sell homes. Advise your seller to purchase some brand new towels and keep them only for times of buyer inspections. Suggest they remove all tea towels, kitchen knives and utensils from the kitchen benches, and have everything sparkling clean.

If you're not an expert, be careful what home improvements you recommend to sellers. Some improvements could end up costing the seller a large investment in terms of time and money, and result in a sales price that's not significantly greater, or perhaps even less, than what they would have received without the improvements. If you're not confident advising in this area, a home stylist can advise sellers in a really practical way and, coming from an independent third party, this advice can defuse the seller's possible emotions around change.

Improvements to skip

As a general rule, advise sellers to skip any improvement that isn't simple or reasonably priced or which doesn't affect street appeal. Don't, for example, tell sellers to landscape extensively, because the cost of this may not be recovered. Just bring in some colour and cover gardens with brand new bark — this smells and looks amazing. Perhaps a newly painted front fence will create a good first impression, but advise sellers to not go overboard with a style that may not appeal to the next buyer. A kitchen renovation may seem like a great idea but unless the sellers are talented in this area, it could look shoddy — better to clean thoroughly and accept that you may need to compensate for this in the sale price.

Focus on quick, cheap improvements. Even older bathrooms look fresh if you take out the bath mat, bring in new towels, and add soaps and candles. Potted plants can also give an old bathroom a lift with minimal cost. Whatever you do, be careful not to advise the seller to spend money that may or may not be realised in a higher sale price. Let it be their decision as to what to spend — just offer advice and be careful not to guarantee anything as far as return on investment or you could be in trouble come sale day!

The general rule is: The more money spent, the higher the risk for the seller and the lower the chance of making a return or even breaking even.

Passing the Street Appeal Test

As a listing agent, one of the first rules of real estate you need to remember is that you have to get prospective buyers into the house that's for sale. They won't buy it if they don't step inside to see it. The technological world we live in makes this even tougher. With the majority of buyers driving by a home which they saw online, you won't get a showing if the home doesn't pass the street-appeal test. We believe this first impression is more important today because so many buyers are do-it-yourself types in their home-search process. They've already said, 'Next!' Real estate investors are the only exception to this rule: They'll often buy a house without ever looking at it. However, most sellers don't want to settle for the price a shrewd investor will pay. To get top dollar, you must win the street-appeal game.

You can also use your pictorial sign outside the house to improve your chances of getting buyers inside the house and perhaps counteract a street appeal that's not so great. Use your sign to show inviting images of the home's interior or backyard — anything not visible from the outside.

As an agent, nothing is more discouraging than seeing potential buyers at your open house drive off without even coming inside. This is where your pictorial sign is your silent salesperson, promoting the property's hidden appeal 24 hours a day.

Landscaping

If the property's gardens and landscaping aren't well presented, particularly from the street, you can advise your seller to make some quick improvements, such as the following:

- **Trim trees to create openness in the yard area.** Once larger trees are established, usually after about six to eight years, they can usually do with some trimming and shaping, particularly if branches hang low to the ground or partially block walkways. Keep in mind, however, that established trees can create the impression of privacy, secluded space and shade so don't let your sellers hack too much away — they could totally change the wonderful energy that the established trees bring to the home.
- **Use the space opened by tree trimming to plant colourful plants, which will brighten up the yard.** You should also use plants to brighten any sidewalks or paths to and around the front door. You can also quickly freshen up the yard through adding new bark.
- **If the seller's yard features grass, make sure it's healthy and green.** Sellers may need to put down extra seed or even replace turf in trouble spots. (Turf can purchased in small quantities from home improvement stores such as Bunnings Warehouse — `www.bunnings.com.au` in Australia or `www.bunnings.co.nz` in New Zealand.)
- **Create dimension through colour.** The landscaping can look pretty monochromatic if you're presenting a home in a season other than spring. Colourful plants go a long way toward adding visual interest and strengthening street appeal.

If the seller doesn't have the time or inclination to improve the property's landscaping, a good investment for the seller could be engaging the services of a professional — this is often cheaper than sellers think and could be the best investment they can make.

Exterior paint condition and colour

In a split second, the colour and condition of a home's exterior paint can either attract or repel a prospective buyer.

- **Paint colour.** Just as with hard surfaces on the inside, the exterior of a home for sale should ideally be painted in classic, muted tones, such as cream or beige, with a soft accent colour that is slightly darker than the body of the home.

  The architecture of the home can contribute to the decision regarding what colours are appropriate. For example, in Australia, federation colours work well on homes from that era, but may look too busy on an Art Deco home. White paint on a colonial-style home can enhance the property's visual impression from the street. However, the same white paint on a 1950s home may result in a house that looks like a plain little box with no character.

- **Paint condition.** Buyers are quick to cross homes in need of new paint off their lists, whether the chipped paint is on the body or trim of the home or on fences or railings.

  The worst outcome is when prospective buyers drive by but don't stop. However, even if they decide to stop and look at the house, trouble still lurks. If the exterior paint condition is poor and buyers consider the home anyway, you may wish they hadn't, and here's why: When buyers notice that paint is peeling, cracking, chipping or stripped down to bare wood, they go into high-scrutiny mode and begin to pick the home apart. Rather than looking for wonderful things about the home, they fixate on what they think is wrong. They assume that because something as obvious as the paint is in poor condition, other aspects of the home have also been neglected. A buyer determined to find faults will succeed. No home can withstand a microscopic fault-finding inspection.

  Even if the home passes the inaugural buyer examination, the sellers aren't out of the woods. If the buyer decides to make an offer, almost certainly it will be accompanied by an extensive repair list and the request that every minor offense be rectified before the closing. Then a building inspector will enter the picture, providing a more extensive report and the chance for the buyer to hit the seller up all over again. All this happens because of a little chipping paint that could (and should) have been fixed before buyers ever drove by to view the home in the first place.

One of Terri's secrets to getting high prices for sellers was to encourage them to have a professional building inspection report done prior to any buyer inspection. The purpose of this was twofold: It firstly gave the seller a chance to fix any minor defects that may have caused anxiety and low offers from buyers and, secondly, it meant buyers could be reassured that there were no major structural issues in case they did not want to pay for their own independent report.

Prepping the Interior of the Home

After prospective buyers are through the door, you need them to be greeted by a good first impression. Help sellers achieve the lightest, brightest and largest interior possible by taking the following advice to heart.

Ask your seller to accompany you through the door as if they're a buyer (not the seller). Ask them to take note of first impressions — is the home light, airy and inviting, or cluttered, dark and messy? How does the bathroom appear — is it sparkling clean with all shampoos, soaps, makeup and so on removed and clean new towels on the racks? What about the kitchen? Are the benches clean and uncluttered? Is the bin out of sight? Are all tea towels and dishcloths removed? And how about the bedrooms — are the bedcovers clean and straightened, and do the pillows have fresh slips? Are all clothes picked up and out of sight, and personal photos removed? You're likely getting the picture — asking your seller to walk through every room, even taking notes as they do so, is a great way to get ready for the buyer showings.

To help sellers prepare their home interiors for showing, you could suggest that they take two initial steps:

- **Get them to throw away or donate anything they haven't used in a while.** Most people have too much stuff, and the longer people have lived in a house, the more stuff they accumulate. And you know the old saying: Stuff always accumulates to fill the space allocated to it.
- **Suggest the sellers rent a storage unit just for the short term.** After filling a skip bin to overflowing and dropping off car loads at the local op shop, they may still have things that should be moved out of the house — if not out of their lives. A storage unit provides an inexpensive, readily available solution.

After these initial steps are taken, you and the sellers can focus on other ways to make the home more appealing to potential buyers.

Staging a home

The term *staging* describes the process of rearranging and decorating a home's interior in an effort to downplay deficiencies and accent strengths. In its simplest form, staging involves adding specialty accessories like towels, candles, throw rugs, bedding, cushions, dishes and napkins. Staging at its most extensive level involves rearranging or replacing furniture or even adding specialty furniture pieces to create a feeling of comfort and liveability.

Some agents pride themselves on their interior decorating skills but this talent is definitely not shared by everyone. You could research trends and ideas but personally we have found that the less risky option is to turn to pros for help. In most real estate markets you'll find people who specialise in staging homes for sale. Many interior decorators offer hourly consultations. Others offer, for a fee, full-service staging, where they work up a design plan, bring in the furniture and accessories, handle the installation and dismantle it all after the sale. Just do an online search for **home stylist** in your particular area and you will find any number of suggestions.

Better yet, find out the names and experience levels of staging or interior design specialists in your market area and buy them a coffee. Tell them that you are looking to promote their services to your sellers but need some testimonials and examples of their work. If they are any good, they will be only too happy to share this with you. Then be ready to suggest to your sellers that it's in their best interest (to attract the highest price) to invest in their home's interior look. Remind them that well-staged homes attract many more buyer prospects. In most cases, the investment pays off in two ways: A faster sale and a higher price.

Terri has many examples of how home styling can result in higher prices. In one case, she had listed two identical ground floor units in an inner-city complex. While one seller saw the value of investing in a stylist, the other couple did not — they thought their unit was already well presented. They were both great units, so the stylist actually didn't need to do much. She introduced some modern art works and lush plants, changed the lounge room rug to a bright (but inoffensive) colour and used different bedroom furnishings. She then de-cluttered the kitchen and bathroom completely and brought in some vibrant colour with towels and a few classy knickknacks.

The cost of the stylist was around $1200 — but the sale price was $28,000 more than the neighbours who had decided not to engage the stylist. This decision turned into an expensive mistake!

Clearing the clutter

When buyers are house shopping, they're given the challenge of mentally removing the seller's stuff before deciding whether they actually want to move in. This type of mental gymnastics helps buyers assess how well the home they're viewing will accommodate their own possessions. (In the section 'Helping the buyer "move in"', later in this chapter, we offer tips to help buyers with these mental gymnastics.)

Some sellers' homes are so full of garage-sale and flea-market finds that the buyers honestly can't see the home through the clutter. They can't 'move in' because they can't see anywhere for their own things to go. So what do they do? They leave without making an offer.

If you're working with sellers who are surrounded by clutter, do the following:

- **Advise them to remove excessive amounts of accessories and knickknacks.** Do this in the context of making more money for them, to make sure they don't refuse because it seems like too much effort — and, besides, they love their clutter! Whether they get rid of them altogether or pack them up in preparation for their anticipated move, get them out of sight. The result can do wonders for a home's interior appearance.
- **Dismantle the 'family and friends wall'.** A wall of pictures of children, grandchildren, nieces, nephews, friends, acquaintances and snapshots of every experience the owners fondly remember adds clutter with little to no buyer appeal. Buyers feel they are intruding into someone else's private space — not a great inducement to stay around too long.
- **Follow the design rule 'When in doubt, take it out'.** Advise sellers to keep clutter, wall decor, and placement of figurines and mementos to a bare minimum. Make it as much like a display home as possible — you want the buyers to notice the home, not the sellers' ornaments!

Knowing what to keep and what to remove

The point of showing a home is to allow prospective buyers to mentally move in and assess how well the home fits with their lives and possessions. Real estate agents know to listen and watch for buying signals, and one of the clearest and best signs is when buyers discuss how their own belongings may fit in various rooms.

Buyers can hardly think about where their piano, china cabinet or most-treasured family heirloom will go when they can't get their eyes past the visual onslaught of the furnishings, accessories and clutter of the current owners. Use the following information to guide your recommendations regarding what sellers should leave in place and what they should move out prior to the home presentation.

- **Pictures:** Suggest that the owners pack up all but a few of the personal photos in the home. If they have a wall covered with pictures, advise them to pare down to just a few.
- **Appliances:** Except the ones that get used daily, store all small kitchen appliances. Leave the coffeemaker on the counter (and perhaps have fresh coffee smells wafting through the house), but lose the blender and maybe even the toaster.
- **Bathroom items:** Remove everything on the bathroom vanity, including decorations and toiletries. A collection of items draws attention to a small vanity size.
- **Closets:** Thin clothes out of closets to create the illusion of greater space. Even a good-sized closet that is crammed with clothes looks undersized and inadequate.
- **The garage:** Too often, what gets removed from the home goes into the garage. Don't let your sellers make this mistake. Ask them to move household items into a rented storage unit instead. While they're at it, they can move garage items — from extra sets of tires to out-of-season recreation equipment — to the storage unit. Then advise them to organise what's left. Suggest that they can hang bicycles from the ceiling and install a few inexpensive pre-made cabinets to hold paint cans, tape, shop rags, toolboxes and the rest of the amazing collection of stuff that ends up in most garages. The objective is to end up with a clean, spacious garage that adds openness and perceived square footage to the home — and dollars to the final sale price.

If you encounter seller resistance, remind your clients that not only are they likely to get a higher price for their home, but they're also going to have to pack their stuff up anyway. By preparing their home for presentation, they eliminate visual clutter and get a leap on the packing process at the same time.

Simplifying traffic flow

The design rule 'When in doubt, take it out' applies to furniture as well. Rooms that feel cramped and hard to move through usually have too much furniture in too little space.

To make a diagnosis and suggest recommendations, do the following:

- **Walk through the home with your seller to find the spots that feel cramped.** Where do transition areas from room to room, or from one part of a room to another, feel restricted?
- **Make recommendations to improve traffic flow.** The sellers can't move walls (without great expense), but they can move furniture that restricts movement.
- **Evaluate the number of pieces of furniture in each room and note the sizes of each piece.** Ask yourself the following questions:
  - Are too many pieces of furniture crowded into one room?
  - Are furnishings too large and beefy for the room?
  - Does the furniture arrangement work in terms of space and flow?
- **Be on the lookout for small, decorative pieces of furniture.** These pieces are often the biggest culprits when it comes to restricting walkways and creating a crowded feeling.

Most people have too much furniture in too small of a space. Be ready to recommend that the sellers remove furniture to create more open spaces, which makes the home appear larger and more comfortable.

Your furniture-removal recommendations will most likely be met by owner resistance. Sellers will resist because they think that people won't have any place to sit. Stick to your story: Tell them a home with too little furniture almost always shows better than a home with too much.

Toning it down

Themed bedrooms — those with wallpaper, wallpaper borders, sheets, pillows, comforters and wall hangings that all match — are very popular for children today. The problem is that buyers walk in and can't see an alternate use for the room. What if the bedroom is themed for a little princess with pink everywhere? Could they really imagine their lively little boy in there? And if they *can* actually see an alternate use, they may also see the considerable expense and effort it will take to get the room from where it is to where they'd like it to be in terms of decoration and usability. As a result, the buyers will likely offer a lower price, if they make an offer at all, in order to cover the costs they anticipate when replacing the theme with a more neutral design.

Be on the lookout for the following red flags:

- Loud or outlandish paint colours or wall coverings.
- Immediately visible and highly personalised themes. A vibrant pink bedroom with lots of stuffed animals may be off-putting to empty nesters or a family that has only boys.

Explain to the sellers that some buyers may be design-challenged and may have little sense of how to redecorate or of how much it costs to paint or wallpaper a room. Tell them that a more neutral design will attract more buyer interest and command a higher price.

Making a clean-up checklist

Don't assume that sellers understand what needs to be done before a showing, even if they've bought and sold a home before. Take a proactive stance by providing a detailed step-by-step checklist of the steps they need to take before the first buyer presentation. Figure 10-1 is a good sample to follow as you provide your clients with valuable counsel and help them ready their home for presentation.

House Clean-Up and Presentation Preparation Checklist		
Task		Recommendation
Cleaning	☐	Hire professional cleaners to eliminate odours from pets or smoking, clean carpets, polish wood floors
	☐	Other:
Interior Walls	☐	Repaint to achieve a neutral, broadly accepted, contemporary color scheme; tone down bold colours
	☐	Repaper or repaint to eliminate themed rooms that limit usability
	☐	Other:
Interior Hard Surfaces	☐	Replace dated carpets
	☐	Replace dated counters with light, bright surfaces, focusing efforts on key areas in which owners spend the most time
	☐	Other:
Exterior Paint	☐	Repaint to eliminate chipping, blistering, or peeling and to achieve a neutral, contemporary colour scheme
	☐	Repaint fences and railings if necessary
	☐	Other:
Landscaping	☐	Thin or limb large trees on mature lots
	☐	Plant annuals to add spot colour
	☐	Reseed or resod lawn
	☐	Add dimension to flat lots with plants and rocks
	☐	Other:
Clutter Removal	☐	Rent skip bin or dumpster
	☐	Rent storage unit
	☐	Clear out old, unused, outdated belongings
	☐	Pack up and store accessories and knickknacks
	☐	Dismantle walls of photos, leaving only a few good-quality framed pictures as decoration
	☐	Remove most small appliances from countertops, leaving only ones you use on a daily basis
	☐	Remove items from bathroom vanity
	☐	Remove items to open space in closets
	☐	Other:

Figure 10-1: House clean-up and presentation checklist.

Traffic Flow	☐	Remove small pieces of furniture that restrict walkways
	☐	Remove large pieces of furniture that crowd spaces
	☐	Other:
Home Defects	☐	Repair defects or be prepared to provide compensation to buyers
Garage	☐	Move storage and out-of-season items to a storage facility
	☐	Hang bikes and other equipment from walls or ceiling
	☐	Install storage cabinets

Figure 10-1: *Continued.*

Making a Great First Impression: Final Ways

For most buyers, selecting a home isn't a logical undertaking. Instead, it's more of an emotional upheaval. Most buyers are swayed by the initial emotions they feel when they first walk through the door of a potential new home. Almost instantly, the home either feels right or feels wrong.

Rarely do people warm up to a home after an initial bad impression. After buyers receive a first impression, they soon figure out whether a home is 'the one'. That first impression can be the beginning of a sales success, or it can be a prohibitive factor that will be difficult to overcome.

Terri is one of those buyers who make up their mind the minute they walk in the door. Her first purchase in Brisbane was an unfinished project house but the minute she walked in the door she saw it as perfect for her. She immediately started planning the finishing touches that would make it into her own. The property had structural problems and design issues that made furniture placement a challenge but the house had the right feel! She bought it immediately without doing any research into comparables. Crazy — even stupid — you may say, but as a seller's agent you need to keep in mind that many buyers are exactly like Terri. They buy purely on emotion, usually paying a premium price — a seller's dream!

Good first impressions, feelings and emotions control the sale, and logic takes a distant second place in the decision process. For this reason, you want to ensure that your seller's home makes a good first impression with potential buyers. In the following sections, we share a few finishing touches that can make all the difference.

Enhancing the first glance

A home has ten seconds to make a good first impression. All the senses are in play, and a home either passes or fails the initial test.

Use this advice to positively engage all the senses in the first moments of the buying experience:

- **Scent:** Fill the home with smells that invoke feelings of comfort, warmth and calmness. Sellers don't need to bake bread or cookies, but can create a positive aroma with mild air freshener, potpourri or a gentle incense.

  Don't overdo it with the scents. A scent that is too strong can drive buyers out of the home before they even get a good look.

- **Sound:** Play soft, soothing music that is universally acceptable, such as classical pieces with limited instruments or even just piano music. Gangster rap or loud rock is inadvisable.

  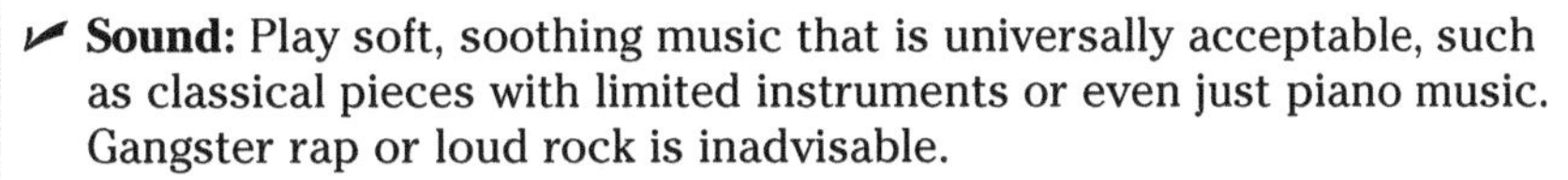

  If the home has a sound system wired throughout each room, your music selections also give you an opportunity to demonstrate this feature of the home.

- **Ambience:** Ask the sellers to create a visually inviting environment by preparing a nicely set dining room table. Suggest that they place small flower arrangements in various rooms. You may even recommend that they build a fire in the fireplace if the home is for sale during the autumn or winter months.
- **Brightness:** Open all the blinds and curtains to let in natural light and make the home appear larger. Also turn on lights in corner areas to pull the eye to the perimeter of the room and provide a sense of expanded space.

Helping the buyer 'move in'

When showing a property to buyers, your job is to help clients imagine living in the home. The more quickly you can get them thinking about actually moving into the house, the more quickly you'll help them make their decision.

The way to help the buyer mentally move in is to ask questions like these:

- *Susan, would you arrange your furniture this way?*
- *Which of these bedrooms would be best for Bobby?*
- *Where would you place the swing set?*
- *How would your oval table fit in this dining area?*
- *Where in the garage would you put your workbench?*
- *Where do you think the big-screen TV could go?*
- *What do you feel is the best location for your piano?*

Any question that engages the buyer's imagination is a good question. If the answers convey negative feedback, the home is probably not the right one for the buyer. After you realise this fact, you can cross it off the list and move on to another home.

Too many agents walk buyers through a home making absurd comments like, 'This is the family room,' as if the clients may have mistaken it for a kitchen! Assume, quite safely, that buyers know which rooms are living rooms, kitchens and bedrooms. They don't need an agent to tell them what's what. But they may need you to help them trigger their imaginations so they can decide if the rooms are right for them.

Chapter 11

Marketing Yourself and Your Properties

In This Chapter

- Targeting the market you want to reach
- Getting prospects on board with your vision
- Figuring out how to position each property
- Writing and producing real estate ads and flyers
- Putting the internet to work in your promotional program
- Making the best use of pictures for your listing

Marketing is the one topic that gets all agents to stop and listen. It's a big field that takes time, money and an almost bewildering number of decisions. Marketing, as it should be, is high on the to-do list of anyone trying to make a sale.

You have many marketing options for yourself and your properties but the most important thing is to *focus.* Focus on what you want to accomplish, what you want to communicate and who you want to reach with your message.

At its core, real estate marketing is simply a matter of communicating a message about what you have to an audience that may or may not want what you're offering. If that sounds like a simple definition, it's because marketing real estate services and products is really not all that complex, as long as you take a focused approach. In this chapter, we share some advice on how to proceed.

Shifting from Print to Online

The biggest shift in real estate marketing in the past five years has been from print marketing to online marketing — both for listed properties and for agent services in general.

Your most important decision is where to invest your marketing dollars, and your focus should be on what is going to result in the best return on investment (ROI).

Setting up a monitoring system

Before you invest a single dollar, set up a system to monitor returns or results. It makes little sense to throw money at something without being able to measure and monitor whether your marketing strategy is creating real dollars in your pocket.

What many agents fail to understand is that sellers are really hiring them to generate buyer leads for their property. That is really the first step in marketing their home. If you do that well, you increase the odds of closing the deal. You also benefit from the many new leads you create when you discover that some buyers don't want this seller's home but need help finding something else. The marketing you do for a property can generate a broader lead opportunity.

Set up a spreadsheet to monitor lead sources from all of your marketing efforts, both online and offline. Potential buyers come from dedicated property websites, email alerts, signs, media advertising, local paper ads and more. Simply ask people when they contact you how they heard about the property, or include this question on the sign-in sheet at the open house for the property. Before you start throwing money at different marketing tools, you need to know which are creating the best leads and, ultimately, results.

Focusing your marketing dollars online

As a new agent, the first, second and third place to invest your marketing dollars is online.

The two main issues you face with the internet are quality and quantity. You want to increase the odds of generating leads. You also want to increase the quality of the prospects so you can separate the really good buyers and sellers from all the rest. You want to achieve a reasonable conversion rate, preferably much higher than the 0.5 to 1 per cent many agents now experience with web leads.

You have to do a delicate balancing act in terms of quality and quantity. If you had to choose one, which would you choose to do first — quality or quantity? Before you select, let us tell you the truth of the internet. The volume of traffic is important. At the end of the day, the one who has the most visitors usually wins. You may build a beautiful website or online listing, but you have to drive traffic to make money with the internet.

When you get the traffic, you have to convince people to stay and leave a trail of contact information. You need them to at least leave bread crumbs: Their first name and email address. You can bring a couple of thousand people to your site monthly and end up with two or three prospects. We're not talking about clients; we're talking only about prospects. You now have to do the work of moving them up the loyalty ladder to becoming a client by converting them from web visitors to buyers or sellers.

You can do this by offering a free report, a newsletter, or something that a potential buyer or seller deems valuable enough to give you at least their first name and email address (see the later section 'Converting ad interest to action' for more details on tracking prospects). You need to walk them up each step of the conversion track. With each level or step they take, your probability of earning a commission check grows. The object is to move the visitors to prospects, prospects to clients, and clients to referral sources. (See Figure 11-1 for this conversion track.)

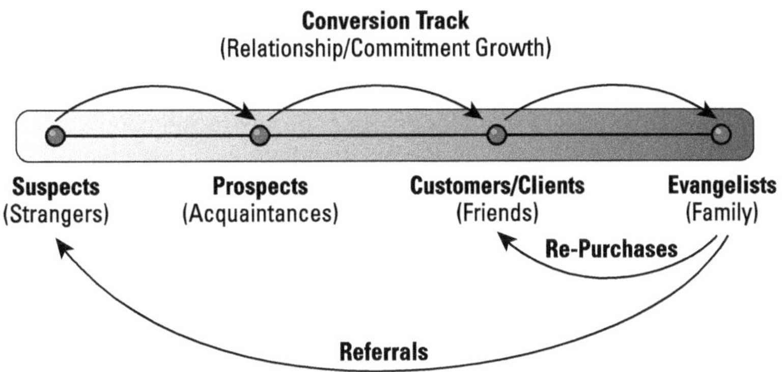

Figure 11-1: This conversion chart illustrates how prospects can turn into referral sources.

The more complete the contact information you can get people to leave, the higher the probability you can move them up to the client stage. More information increases the opportunity to move them to a fundamental sales channel of send, call, see.

Getting prospects to reveal their full contact information when they make their inquiries is paramount. For example, too many internet leads come in without phone numbers. Getting a prospect's phone number enables you to call them back, which also raises the conversion ratio substantially. Most agents are chasing a lot of low-probability prospects through the internet. They have an email address and are sending property-match searches daily. They have the prospects on an electronic newsletter list. These agents start the prospecting process but often let it stall at this stage. All of those methods are automated, so agents invest limited time — but also reap limited rewards.

Choosing Internet Strategies that Work

The first step to finding an internet strategy that works for you is to establish which strategies you have at your disposal. As mentioned earlier in this chapter, with any strategy you need to monitor and measure the results. This helps you discover which strategies are most effective and which need more work.

Company websites

An easy way to make your presence known on the internet is through your real estate company's website. It can be the most cost-effective way, as well. Most companies set up basic agent webpages within their site, so make sure you keep yours current. If a prospect comes to the company website, clicks on your tab, and sees just a blank template, you lose credibility.

You can have a website up and running within days or even minutes for the cost of a nice dinner, and it gives you all kinds of data about your visitors. Basic requirements for this type of site are a professional look, your company logo, professional photos of agents, bios of agents, and several means of contact for the visitor. (If you're with an agency, it will no doubt have its own website you can refer to.) The main purpose of this type of website is to make it easy to reach you. Visitors to this site will likely be people who have your marketing pieces and want to contact you. You should send a lot of traffic to this site because its sole purpose is to show that you're legitimate and help the prospect or customer get in contact with you.

Branding isn't for everyone

Branding is a fairly standard term to marketers of all types. It basically means that you want to establish a memorable professional identity for your potential prospects and customers. Ideally, you want all of the people in your market to think about you when they think about buying or selling a home. Branding could involve putting your name and picture on billboards, at bus stops and other forms of public transport, or in public phone boxes.

However, a few factors associated with branding don't make it the best solution for 99.99 per cent of real estate agents. First of all, it's *very* expensive. Second, it takes a very, *very* long time to establish a brand. Finally, it's almost impossible to quantify the effectiveness of branding. All three of these difficulties are contrary to what most people think the internet is all about — and rightly so. On several fronts, therefore, branding isn't a very good choice for real estate agents. It may work for an already established agent, but rarely for a 'newbie'.

Property information websites

These special sites are focused solely on one property and can be very effective in systematising the sales process of individual properties. The sites allow you to showcase one specific property, promoting the property, but also promoting you as an agent using a variety of tools. The sites are competitively priced and can help you win listings and attract new buyers.

You can add the website address for a particular property — for example, `www.120BrownStMainville.com` — at the very top of your pictorial board outside the property. This helps buyers go straight to the property online for their virtual tour.

Listing a property on one of these websites enables you to include a virtual tour of the home, all the particulars about the home, all of your contact information, and many more details. The site, by itself, really has no value, but if you run a marketing campaign talking about the home and include the URL (domain address) of the site, now you've gotten somewhere.

An Australian website that offers this service is `www.homewebsites.com.au`; unfortunately, no sites are yet available in New Zealand.

The problem with these sites is that prospects may make negative decisions based on a bad photo on the virtual tour or a paint colour they don't like. You can't answer a prospect's objections, and you may never have the opportunity to even know his or her name. However this could be true for photos on any website — another reason to use professional photos if at all possible.

So, these sites can be a valuable way for you to gain exposure for your properties, but the lead volume will likely be small — although the leads will likely be good ones. Use this type of site as *part* of your arsenal, to gain exposure for specific properties.

Lead-generation websites

The sole purpose of this type of site is to generate a large volume of a specific type of lead, whether for buyers or sellers.

This website is designed for a very targeted audience. This may be buyers or sellers of homes in a specific area or of a specific type, or it may just be buyers or sellers in general. The narrower your focus, and the more targeted your niche, the better.

For example, if you decide to target only buyers, you need to create a site loaded with content that is valuable to your target prospects. Let's say your site is geared toward buyers in your own city or town. The website must be focused solely on topics that (1) are valuable to buyers in your market area, including specific school districts or neighbourhoods, and (2) help buyers accomplish their objective, which is to buy a home in the area.

You may want to include a section of community events and a list of key community facts and dates. Consider providing market statistics and featuring listings for prospective buyers to view. Also valuable is information about mortgages and home-design trends. You have endless options to create value for your prospects.

Buyers can also register on the major real estate sites (such as `www.realestate.com.au` or `www.domain.com.au`) to get alerts when properties that fit their requirements come up. However, individual agents don't receive lead information from these alerts, just for inquiries related to their own listed properties.

The Art of Persuasion: Getting Prospects to Buy Into You

Your online marketing must include an element of persuasion. Having high-value content for a targeted audience isn't enough by itself. You must, through persuasive sales copy, persuade those who visit your website to become prospects.

Something you can do is to connect with a good copywriter — preferably one who has website experience. You can find them online at very reasonable rates at such websites as `www.elance.com` (where you can access freelancers based in Australia or New Zealand, or even use someone based in another country to your own). A great copywriter can earn you hundreds or thousands of dollars for every dollar you spend.

Check out the next sections to find persuasive ways to get prospects to buy into you and what you can offer.

Get the customer to interact

The goal of a website is to interact with visitors and have them leave a trail. You also want them to come back to your site again and again. They become more valuable with each return visit and are more likely to leave a recognisable trail.

Here are three ways to interact via your website with potential customers:

- **Offer free reports.** Get potential clients to take information that is valuable by offering free reports. Offer access to information (for example, 'The 10 Mistakes Sellers Make When Selling a Home'). Such a report lists both mistakes and solutions. Someone who requests that type of report is at least considering a sale. Another report (for example, 'How to Guarantee You Get Your Home Sold and for the Highest Price Possible') can lead seller prospects through the steps to ensure the sale at a top-dollar sale price. Only potential sellers will apply for these kinds of reports! You can develop similar reports for buyers.

  At this point, you're trying to generate a volume of leads. Free reports are a good first point of contact. Thousands of reports have already been produced, so don't sit down to write one. You can search the web for reports of this type that are free or practically so.

- **Offer free newsletters and blogs.** Free newsletters and blogs are also an effective means of communication. Having an email or blog list of people who read your material regularly is immensely powerful. Your job is to provide value in that newsletter or blog. Start by doing a newsletter monthly and a blog post a couple of times a week. Start with a generic or template version and then move on to a more customised approach when you get a feel for what prospects are looking for.
- **Offer a consistent message.** The ability to consistently communicate with an audience is extremely valuable. The best marketing results usually come from the consistency of the message delivery, as well as the message that's delivered. It's easier for an agent to be consistent if he or she starts with a template newsletter. Test it: Evaluate how much or how little work it is, and see whether your contacts like it and read it. Then work up to a hybrid or combination newsletter, in which some material is your own and some is from a template. If that goes well, create your own newsletter. One of the keys to marketing is consistency.

Expand your reach in cyberspace

We may be getting a bit technical here, but another lead-generation strategy is to link to other sites and sources to increase your search-engine ranking. Be careful, though, with this strategy, because search engines give weight to the relevancy of a link. If you go out and link to anyone and everyone, your search-engine ranking probably won't improve that much. Instead, your links should be focused on real estate and/or your specific market area.

Following are two ways to gain presence on the web:

- **Search engine optimisation (SEO):** The goal for every agent should be to have a website that is optimised for search engines. The value of being ranked highly in search engines continues to grow. SEO means that your website, because of its design, keywords and links, comes up higher on the list when someone does a search for real estate in your area. Because you have higher positioning, you're more likely to create traffic to your site and, in turn, leads.

  Major search engines like Google, Yahoo! and Bing represent about 90 per cent of all internet search traffic. If you aren't ranked with them, you won't be found. If you're not on the front page, you won't be found. Most people don't go beyond the first page when they type in a particular search. If you're number one on a search engine, you can expect about 40 per cent of searchers to click your link. If you're number two through number five, you can expect to share the next 40 per cent. The rest go to the remainder of the first page. It pays to be number one. The next four ranked sites have to share the same traffic that the top-ranked site gets all to itself.

Before you run out and hire someone to implement SEO strategy for your website, be careful! SEO strategy is a tricky business. You need to make sure you're working with a reputable firm that stands behind its work. You also can't have the philosophy of once and done. Effective SEO strategy is never-ending. Everyone is fighting for that front-page position. It changes each day, so you have to work to maintain your ranking.

If you're uncertain about how to use links to increase your search-engine ranking, you may need to source someone with this specific expertise — otherwise, you could waste a lot of time for very little return.

- **Pay per click, not pay per prospect:** More and more agents are getting into pay-per-click advertising as an answer to their online marketing. Pay-per-click advertising on search engines and other sites can be effective, or it can be a bust. Most search engines have pay-per-click areas on the right side of the website. People bid for the spots on a pay-per-click basis, which can range from a few cents to a few dollars each. The truth is, only about 10 per cent of searchers go to the pay-per-click section. The vast majority of people use a search engine to search a specific phrase and then select the top-ranked sites to click on.

You're not paying per prospect but *per click*. A click doesn't mean that you're going to get anything. Pay-per-click can be used effectively if you know the conversion numbers of your website, meaning you know how many people take a free report, sign up for your newsletter, ask for more information, identify themselves as a lead, or book an appointment with you after they get to the website. You have to watch the analytics of your site. Only use website hosting services that enable you to review your traffic. To make pay-per-click advertising profitable, you need to know your numbers, both online and through your standard sales process. Until then, you're only guessing whether it works and is profitable.

Using technology to market yourself and your properties

The information in this section comes courtesy of Peter Hutton — a great friend and colleague of Terri's, and an experienced agent, principal, coach and mentor. Peter's passion is looking at ways for agents to set themselves apart with cutting-edge branding. His success in this field has been proved many times over, so here are his tips that can be applied anywhere, in any location and in any market!

Changes in the technology available to agents have helped smart real estate agents create more meaningful conversations with their target audience. But this isn't just about pushing you and what you're selling. Used right, technology enhances engagement, leads to a greater connection with your prospects and helps you build trust.

So technology should be looked upon as providing 'trust-building' communication tools. These tools include mobile phones, tablet computers, email, websites, CRM systems, email 'auto-responders', text messaging apps, social media, video, QR Codes, ebooks, podcasts and webinar software.

Here's how to use technology to your advantage:

- Use text messages, emails and your website for the timely delivery of quality information that your prospects value. This is called *outbound marketing*.
- Offer an email newsletter subscription to build your prospect list. This is known as *inbound marketing*.
- Offer a free home-selling guide in the form of an emailable PDF and in return for their name and email. This is known as *direct response marketing*.
- Use a customer relationship management (CRM) software system to stay in regular contact with your database.
- Use an auto-responder email system (which needs to be part of your CRM) to automate regular contact using an email nurture trail.
- Use text messaging templates (you can access an app for your smart phone) to ensure quick messaging. For example, you can adapt a template to send a pre-formatted text message to a seller with feedback about their open home.
- Use videos for marketing properties and for blogging.
- Use an iPad at open homes to showcase information about the property, and to register buyers and add new prospects to your CRM.
- Use QR codes on signage and business cards to connect prospects to your website and to your listings.
- Use Facebook, LinkedIn, Twitter and Pinterest (just to name a few) to engage and interact with your community. Use social media to build a tribe. (Refer to Chapter 5 for more on social media.)
- Invite property owners to live online events using Google Hangouts, or webinar software.
- Create your own YouTube channel and build an audience based on the sharing of quality information.
- Record podcasts about helpful tips and information for home owners as a way to build an audience.

Targeting Your Marketing Message

Just as important as where you put your marketing dollars is how strong your message is. Agents turn off on the wrong marketing road when they try to take communication short cuts by blitzing the market with their ad messages. This route leads to a dead end for two reasons:

- You don't have the budget of a major national corporation, so you can't compete well in the mass-media environment.
- Your prospective customer is already drowning in marketing messages. Simply lobbing another ad missile into the general market arena is hardly the way to target the person you're trying to reach.

Because of the successful efforts of media salespeople, agents get roped into spending huge sums of money on image- or brand-building marketing campaigns that reach large, untargeted groups of consumers and that produce zero sales results. You have to establish a name and presence before this type of marketing works.

Agents at the top of their games may want to reinforce their dominant market positions and enhance their strong reputations by shifting some of their marketing dollars into image advertising. But if you're an agent just beginning to ascend the ladder of real estate success, image advertising isn't what you need, so leave the billboards to the established agents. At this point in your career, you need to reach highly targeted prospects with messages about specific offerings that align perfectly with their interests and needs.

As you plan your marketing communications, think in terms of who, what, and why: Marketing communications is anything that you mail or email to the general public, your sphere of influence, or current and past clients. You must have a plan and an objective before you slap on that stamp or hit 'send'.

Think about

- **Who** is your target audience?
- **What** are you offering to your target audience?
- **Why** is the product you're offering a good fit for the wants, needs and purchase abilities of your target audience?

In this section, we help you target your marketing audience, define your product and determine the position your product fills in the marketplace.

Defining your target audience

Before you can choose how you're going to communicate your message and what you're going to say, you need to know who you're trying to talk to.

The single biggest mistake in advertising — not just real estate advertising, but in all advertising — is that marketers create ads without a clear concept of the people they're trying to influence. As a result, they use the wrong media, say the wrong things and fail to inspire the right outcome.

Before you risk a similar mistake, begin by answering these questions:

- **Who are you trying to reach with this particular message?** Be specific: What age are your target prospects? How much money do they make? Where do members of this group currently live?
- **Will this message be going to people you know?** If so, it can (and should) be more personal than an ad reaching brand-new prospects. People who already know you will most likely be the ones to consider doing business with you. Move them toward action by stressing your results and professional credentials while also conveying the benefits and features of the offer you're presenting.
- **Is this marketing message targeted to specific buyer groups, such as first-home buyers, empty nesters, second-home purchasers or investors?** If so, you need to focus your message toward the interests, needs and motivations of that specific group.
- **Is the market for this message comprised largely of consumers in a specific age group or generational demographic?** If so, decide whether the offering you're promoting is of primary interest to one of the following groups of consumers:
  - The senior generation, whose members are 65 years old and over
  - Baby boomers born between 1946 and 1964
  - The post-baby boom generation born between the mid-1960s and early 1980s, who are sometimes referred to as generation X or generation next
  - People born between the mid-1980s and mid-1990s, labelled by marketers as generation Y, the echo boom or the millennial group

Prospects in the older generation still love the face-to-face personal touch. You may like to sponsor trophies at the local bowling club or other places this generation is likely to hang out. Often this age group is very wary of the 'smooth-talking salesman' so your communication could include testimonials and photos of previous satisfied clients who they may identify with. You may also try a message in the local paper, because the older generation are more likely to see this than receive an email alert.

Baby boomers are usually either still in the work force or just about to retire. They are tech-savvy and don't appreciate being talked down to. They like to see their agents as human but professional. You reach this segment of the population with good marketing that encourages them to meet you at open houses where you can begin to build trust and let them see you as a 'real person', not the slick salesman. They like to be treated with respect and are happy to receive your marketing via email as long as they're not hounded.

Lastly, people in the age group roughly between 18 and 35 are also happy to receive your messages via email but are also very familiar with text messaging SMS, and you can easily set this up as a way to keep in touch. Once you discover what type of properties they're after, you can send them quick alerts via SMS.

Positioning your offering

In today's cluttered marketing environment, consumers are trained to tune out messages that don't seem to address their real and unfulfilled wants and needs. In other words, if your message doesn't clearly deliver a solution to your prospect's exact problem — if it doesn't position itself into an open slot in your prospect's mind — then your efforts, dollars and time will go down the marketing drain.

Positioning is the marketing art of knowing what available space or position you and your offering fill in the market and then getting that message to exactly the people who want what you're offering.

By first figuring out the position your offering fills, you can easily decide who you want to talk to, what you want to say and what marketing vehicles — from advertising to direct mail to online to personal calls — you need to use to reach the people you're targeting.

Positioning the property you're selling

Understanding your product position can make the difference between reaching your prospect and not, between motivating interest and action and not, and between making a sale and not.

In real estate, price is the cornerstone of positioning. In our experience, 85 per cent of your marketing strategy is set during the listing presentation when you and the seller agree on the right price and, therefore, the right market position for their home (refer to Chapter 9 for more on this).

After you've worked with a seller to agree on the right listing price, your marketing strategy unfolds naturally, following these steps:

- Creating a description of the home's likely buyer
- Listing the home's benefits and the reasons likely buyers won't want to let the home go to anyone else
- Selecting media channels or communications approaches that are most apt to get your marketing message in front of your target audience of likely buyers

Knowing your product position and the nature of your likely buyer puts you in a better position to select the right media vehicles to carry your message to your market. Consider the following generalities in your planning:

- **If you're marketing a lower-end home in your marketplace, some of your prospects may not be technologically savvy.** With limited resources, they probably haven't invested in the latest technology. They may have standard mobile phones rather than smartphones. Their internet connection may be slow. Print media advertising in local papers can work more effectively here.

Using positioning to your competitive sales advantage

Take time to look inside some of the other homes that compete for the same product position as your listing in terms of price and location. See how their features and benefits compare. Especially when handling ad and sign calls, this comparative information is valuable in two ways:

- By expressing with certainty your listing's benefits compared to the benefits of other available properties, you convince callers that they must see and consider the home.
- By offering information on other homes in addition to the one you've listed, you increase the odds of converting callers into buyer clients by establishing yourself as a skilled agent and valuable home-buying resource.

One segment of these buyers that is tech savvy is the first-home-buyer category. Young buyers may have limited funds, but they spend those funds on gadgetry. They may be eating instant noodles morning, noon and night, but they have the latest smartphone that came out last week.

- **If you're marketing a home in the mid-price range, you can be fairly confident that your prospects are somewhat internet savvy.** Studies show that more than 90 per cent of middle-income home shoppers have internet access and that most make the internet their home-shopping starting point. To reach this audience, an effective internet marketing strategy is essential.
- **If you're marketing a high-priced home, one-to-one communications may be the most effective tactic.** Sometimes because of time constraints these buyers are using technology effectively but aren't on the cutting edge. In some cases, they have people who do that for them. With one-of-a-kind, top-priced properties, you may find that mailing a high-quality brochure to carefully selected prospects nets greater success than your internet marketing. Buyers for a property in this market position are likely too busy to spend hours on the internet poring through properties. Additionally, many are connected with agents, so your other approach may be to market to agents directly.

Product positioning only works if the home you're selling is priced appropriately. If you give in to a seller's desire to set an unreasonably high listing price, your marketing task is vastly more difficult because

- **You'll be forced to market to the wrong audience.** In order to reach buyers who can afford the price the seller is asking, you'll be talking to people seeking a higher-level home than the property you're offering.
- **Your product will lose in competitive comparisons.** It won't take long for buyers to realise that the home you're offering is inferior to others they can buy with the same amount of money.

When you list an overpriced property, you have only two hopes for success: The marketplace will heat up dramatically and lead to escalating prices, which brings your listing price in line with others, or your seller will agree to a rapid price reduction.

Positioning yourself

Contrary to the opinions of consumers and a good many agents, not all agents offer the same or even similar services. It's safe to say that all agents work to bring real estate transactions to successful closings, but from there the differences in approach, style and effectiveness vary wildly.

As the owner of a real estate business, you must help prospects and clients realise the unique and beneficial position you hold in the marketplace. People need to know clearly why they should hire you. Chapter 13 is full of information that helps you define and claim your market position. As you communicate your position through your marketing efforts, remember these three points:

- **Tell and remind people that you're in real estate sales.** After your business achieves a high level of success, people will contact you based on your reputation. As a newer agent, however, you must notify everyone you know that you're in real estate sales, and then you must keep reminding them at regular intervals.
- **Say and prove that you're good at what you do.** In a service business where all choices cost basically the same amount of money, as is the case in real estate sales, agents must differentiate themselves based on the expertise and service quality they provide. Client success stories, references from past clients, presentation of statistical advantages, results of satisfaction surveys and glowing testimonials break you free from the crowd. You can include one or more client testimonials on the reverse of every property brochure to speak to the potential sellers inspecting your properties. They may not buy the property, but they could very well 'buy' you.
- **Remind consumers that their choice of agent matters.** Agents need to band together to get this message into the minds of all real estate buyers and sellers. Agents as a whole haven't convinced clients that the right agent makes a difference in terms of deposit, sale price, net return on settlement, ease of transaction, level of satisfaction, after-sale service and countless other benefits. Make it your job to convey to the public that the right agent makes a difference and that you're the best agent to make a difference in their deal.

Creating and Placing High-Impact Ads

When you're marketing, whether offline or online, the copy you write creates a powerful connection and engagement. You want prospects to experience the property. This section covers all the ins and outs of ad placement, paying special attention to what to say, where to say it and how to achieve action.

Emphasising benefits versus features

A large kitchen, a spacious backyard, a three-car garage and air conditioning are all descriptions of a home's features. Not one of these descriptions tells buyers what's in it for them. Not one conveys a benefit that the buyer gets from the feature. However, these terms fill most real estate marketing communications.

Add impact to your marketing by converting features to benefits. Follow these examples:

- Instead of simply announcing the feature of a three-car garage, advertise a three-bay garage with abundant storage space and think of a benefit that goes with this feature. For example, the space could provide a workshop where the owner can fix the kids' bikes or work at their carpentry or mechanical skills.
- Translate the feature of air conditioning into the benefits of comfort, coolness and the restful feeling that results from a good night's sleep in an air-conditioned home.

Staying legal

Whether you're using offline or online strategies, certain words and phrases can land you in hot water. In marketing properties, agents can run into trouble by using terms or descriptive language that violates the code of conduct implemented by their local real estate regulatory body. You need to familiarise yourself with the clauses relating to misleading or deceptive advertising, because the fines can be severe and may cause you to forfeit your commission. In Australia, go to `www.reia.com.au` for details for the relevant institute in your area; in New Zealand, check out the Real Estate Agents Authority (`www.reaa.govt.nz`).

Government provisions of anti-discrimination legislation in Australia and New Zealand apply to all public communications, including advertising. All of the text on websites, in newspaper and magazine ads, on flyers, and in other printed materials must adhere to these guidelines.

Following are a few words and phrases, perhaps still used in everyday conversations and considered normal real estate jargon, that can't be used in print advertising. These are just a few examples — there are many more.

The moment these terms appear in printed marketing materials, the ad is potentially violating anti-discrimination legislation:

- Able bodied
- Adult community — no children allowed?
- Bachelor pad — what about the female buyers?
- Couples only — why not singles?
- Ethnic references
- No single mothers

When in doubt, the safest advice is to restrict ad copy to a description of the property for sale, while steering far clear of any descriptions of the type of people you think would be good buyers.

Discrimination in housing because of race or colour, national origin, religion, sex, family status or handicap is illegal for both real estate agents and sellers and carries stiff penalties and fines. If you think a seller is discriminating, run, don't walk, away. For complete information, visit the website for the Australian Human Rights Commission (`www.humanrights.gov.au`), where you can access a guide to Australia's anti-discrimination laws. In New Zealand, go to the Human Rights Commission (`www.hrc.co.nz`).

Choosing the right media outlets

You can create the most extraordinary marketing possible, but if it reaches the eyes or ears of people who aren't interested in or capable of buying your offering, your efforts are wasted. That's why media selection is so essential to effective real estate marketing.

For example, suppose you have a listing for a home that has specially built wheelchair access and an elevator and is on a golf course. You'll find very few people out there who are golfers, who have the need for wheelchair accessibility, and who have the assets required to buy a home with an elevator. If you place your marketing through media outlets that predominantly reach 20-somethings who are starting new families, you can bank on little to no response to your efforts.

On the other hand, if you place your marketing in golf publications, or if the golf course is private and you advertise in the monthly newsletter or send direct mailers to the membership list, your marketing messages immediately reach the prospects in your target audience. You can buy a list of golf enthusiasts in your area . . . in our information age, you can find lists for everything and everyone. (If you can't find what you need, virtual assistants and professionals are available for hire and can do almost everything you need for a small fee.) Even better, if you discover a magazine with a good many golfers with disabilities among its subscribers, you can safely bet your advertising dollars on the publication to serve as an ideal vehicle for sharing the targeted benefits of your listed property with the perfect target audience for this home.

The key to effective media placements is knowing the following:

- **The profile of the target prospect you're trying to reach.** Including the prospect's geographic location, demographic facts (which includes age, gender, ethnicity, income level, education level, marital status, household size and other facts), and lifestyle characteristics, which includes personal interests and activities, behavioural patterns and beliefs.
- **How well the media vehicle you're considering reaches your target audience.** If you're targeting families with young children and income levels of $75,000 or more, ask the media representative what percentage of the publication's audience matches that description. The answer can help you determine whether an ad in that publication will be effective.

Converting ad interest to action

Your marketing needs to include a *response mechanism*, which is a fancy way of saying that you need to tell people what to do next and how to do it. Every single communication — whether through a pay-per-click campaign, brochure, website contact, open house or any other outreach effort — needs to include a call to action that motivates prospects to take the next step. One call to action is having prospects provide you with contact information.

To generate responses and harvest prospect information, consider the following ideas:

- **Invite ad respondents to call or go online to request free reports.** These can be on such attention-getting topics as 'Ten Mistakes Sellers Make When Selling a Home' or 'Ten Tips for Buying Property under Market Value'. You'll gain names and mailing addresses as a result.
- **Hold an information seminar for potential investors.** You could organise guest speakers like mortgage brokers, conveyancing solicitors, tax accountants and quantity surveyors. This will give you a pool of prospects to whom you can market suitable properties.

Promoting Properties by Using Flyers

Agents have made promotional flyers a marketing staple for years and years. Even though technology has come ahead in leaps and bounds, marketing flyers still have their place in your marketing portfolio.

Flyers advertising specific properties for sale can be smaller than A4 in size — even down to postcard size — but they must be in colour and include multiple pictures. They must be visually appealing and include the scheduled inspection times. Also keep the following in mind:

- Include property basics, such as the age of the home, square footage, and number of bedrooms and bathrooms.

- List a few amenities that make the home special, but don't divulge all the details. Remember, the purpose of the flyer is to entice prospects to either call you for a showing appointment or come along to the next open house showing. You want your phone to ring. The more information you share, the greater the chance that prospects will cross the home off their consideration list before they ever call you to get inside.
- Include the address of the property and a picture of the home's exterior. This way, when prospects get home after looking at a half dozen or so properties, they can keep your listing straight from the others they may be considering.
- Include your contact information, company information, web and email addresses, and a picture of yourself (if your agency allows this) to advance your brand and drive traffic to your business.

What about including the price?

Whether to include the listing price on the home flyer (or on any other advertising for the property, including its web page) is an issue that raises a heated debate in the agent community. Agents who advocate including the dollar figure say that if you don't include the price, you'll upset some prospects by providing everything but the number they most want to know. However, you'll receive more calls, and the chance to develop more leads, if you leave the price off the flyer. You're in the business of selling real estate. If you state the price and it causes prospects to cross the home off their list without ever calling you for more information, you won't have a chance to sell anything. Neither you nor your seller benefits if prospects take a flyer and never call you.

- Consider using the back of the flyer to present one small paragraph each on five or six other properties listed by you or others in your office that are similar to the home featured on the flyer front. These profiles won't be as extensive or descriptive as the information presented on the featured home, but they'll give prospects a line-up of reasons to call you for additional information. Your objective is to increase the odds of receiving a call or a number of calls for each flyer that you hand out. If sellers are resistant to the idea of listing 'competing' homes on their flyer, remind them that information about their home will appear on flyers for other properties.

Creating inside-the-home brochures

The flyers and brochures that you hand out inside the home at open houses or individual buyer inspections are similar to the smaller flyers, but with these variations:

- Include a full description of the home's amenities rather than a partial list of amenity highlights.
- Include more photos so that prospects can recall their favourite features after the home tour or open house.
- Print the flyer in colour on good quality paper.
- Put a floor plan on the reverse of the flyer or back of the brochure.
- Include at least one testimonial for prospective sellers.
- Feature the price.

Most buyers tour a number of homes in a short period of time. The purpose of the more substantial flyer or brochure is to provide complete information that jogs memories after prospects leave a showing.

Using software to simplify the process

Creating flyers from scratch each time you have a listing is far too consuming of an agent's time. To save hours while also creating better materials, use flyer templates to speed up the process. You can use ready-made templates, or you can create your own personalised templates to use over and over again.

Many real estate-specific customer relationship management (CRM) programs, such as Top Producer, LockedOn, My Desktop in Australia and GoldMine in New Zealand, include templates to create customised flyers as part of their software packages. So, before buying new programs, check to see what functions are included in the software you already own.

Moving to a technology-based method of client contact and client service was the most valuable thing Terri did to accelerate her results and she has never looked back! One of the most popular CRMs used by agents in Australia and New Zealand is LockedOn, which was created for agents by one of Australia's most successful and high-performing agents, Aaron Shiner. For Terri, not being very technologically smart, this system was the easiest and most user-friendly she had ever come across.

LockedOn is a complete real estate database and CRM solution — it manages your client's details, buyer criteria, previous sales, your property area, tasks, appointments, templates, reports, marketing and much more. It's a fully loaded CRM with all the features you need to run your agency. And being cloud-based, all upgrades and new features are rolled out instantly to your account. LockedOn offers free trials and the constant backend support is a huge bonus to anyone wanting to move forward fast. Check out `www.lockedon.com` for more information.

Enhancing Exposure via Virtual Tours

The term *virtual tour* applies to either a video presentation or a series of digital pictures 'stitched' together to create a 360-degree panoramic view of the living space of a home.

When the idea of virtual tours was introduced about a decade ago, it was billed as the home-buying approach of the future. Technology forecasters said prospects would use virtual-tour capabilities to view their selected home and then simply click to make the purchase. Obviously, the sales predictions were wildly off course, but the popularity of virtual tours as a marketing device took off nonetheless.

At a time when consumers are demanding more information, more pictures and greater ease of access, virtual tours are the fastest-growing innovation in real estate marketing. Studies of online home shoppers show that homes accompanied by virtual tours receive more hits, higher page views and longer view times per page than homes featured in only a few grainy pictures. Virtual tours help your property get noticed. Some agents now will not take a listing that doesn't include video in the marketing package.

Be sure your listing is ready to show and that it competes well in its competitive environment before posting a virtual tour, or the tour can backfire on you and drive interest away. If your listing pales in comparison to competitive offerings, you won't get anyone into the home. Flip to Chapter 10 for advice on how to get a listing ready for showing.

Producing a virtual tour

Whether your tour takes the form of video or stitched-together digital photos, our advice is 'don't try this at home' unless you're willing to invest in some sophisticated equipment and training. But keep in mind your primary role is 'agent' — in terms of investment versus reward, you may be best leaving this to the expert.

If in any doubt, use the services of a professional for your property videos — the marketing investment should be returned many times over with the additional interest and inspections the videos generate.

Whether you're using a professional to create your virtual tour or doing it yourself, consider this advice:

- **Be prepared to invest some money.** To produce a true virtual tour with a 360-degree visual presentation, you need to spend at least several hundred dollars per tour.
- **Make sure you, or your professional, has the right equipment.** Good quality video equipment and virtual tour software is a must.

After the virtual tour is completed, put it to work. Feature it online, show it in your CMA presentations, use it when working with out-of-area buyers, and include it in the portfolio you use to present yourself to prospects and for-sale-by-owner sellers.

Important questions to ask

Some agents are quick to spend money, even if they don't have a plan or set of objectives in place. Along the same lines, if not approached properly, virtual tours can cause agents to spend hundreds of dollars, without much return, for each of their listings. Each time you're considering a virtual tour, begin by answering these questions:

- **What is your objective for the tour?** Will you use it to generate leads, close appointments, build your image as a real estate agent, or some other purpose?

- **Who is your target audience?** Will the tour be shown primarily to low-end, mid-range or high-end home buyers? The answer helps you match the presentation to audience expectations and arrive at your budget.
- **What type of tour do you want to produce?** Choose either 360-degree video or digital photos.
- **Will you hire a professional company?** If so, be prepared to interview firms and compare resources based on company costs, the calibre of solutions the company provides, the way its services match your needs and expectations, and how easy the employees are to work with.

Mistakes to avoid

The biggest mistake you can make is to try to create virtual tours on the cheap.

If you attempt to create your own virtual tours, chances are good that they, and by association you, will look cheap. They'll look cheap to potential buyers, potential sellers, and potential leads and prospects who see your work online from around the world.

The quality of the production is interpreted as an indication of the quality of your character and your service. Aim high.

If you don't have a specific virtual tour professional in mind, just do an online search for providers of virtual real estate tours in your area. When you contact possible options, ask to see examples of their work before you commit.

Leading prospects to your virtual tour

To drive prospects to your virtual tour, use these promotional channels:

- When you produce outside-the-home flyers, include your web address and virtual tour information.
- Feature the site address for your virtual tour in your print ads. Some agents choose not to reveal the address because they hope to generate interest so that prospects call for additional information and home access. However, more and more agents are happy to reveal website addresses, hoping that the videos generate enough interest for the buyer to come along to inspect personally.

- Use postcards as direct mailers to promote both the property and the virtual tour. Don't send a letter that may or may not be opened. Send a postcard that automatically makes an immediate visual impression.

Putting Pictures to Work for Your Listing

Thank goodness for digital technology that enables you to email pictures of homes to prospects far and wide with the simple click of a mouse. The right picture can heighten interest, prompt purchase decisions and deliver thousands of dollars in commission income. For that reason, a digital camera and photography expertise are necessary in your business.

If photography isn't your skill, build a strong relationship with a local professional in this vital area. It can make a huge difference to the number of inspections for your property and to the final sale price.

Choosing your camera

If you make the decision to do your own photography, select a digital camera for taking pictures inside and outside the homes you're representing. If you're on a tight budget, you can find a solid camera for around $200. Just be sure it includes the following features:

- **Point and shoot.** Cameras with this function focus and adjust for available lighting. They're easy to use, meaning you're likely to use them often.
- **A reasonable number of megapixels.** Megapixels determine photo resolution, which is essentially image quality. The bad news is that the more megapixels you get, the more money you'll spend. The good news is that you don't want to go overboard because, with megapixels, you can actually have too much of a good thing. They use storage space in your camera and in your computer. They also result in larger files that take longer to email.
- **Easy transfer and storage capability.** Select a camera with an easy-to-use function for transferring and uploading photos. You can also select one that automatically uploads photos to your cloud storage.

Taking digital photos

The key to success in taking digital pictures is to take a lot of them. With digital cameras, you're not spending money on film and development, so each photo is basically free. When you're at a property, snap freely. You can always edit, resize, crop, rotate and enhance your photos with special effects when you're back at your computer.

Capturing the best images

For exterior photos:

- **Photograph when natural light is abundant.** If you live in a climate with long, dreary winters, you may have to take a first round of photos on a grey day just to capture an image to use when you announce the listing. Plan to go back on a brighter day (as soon as possible) to take a second shot that will replace the original one. Or take the photo at night, with outside lights on and the front door open and inviting.

- **Position yourself so that the sun is directly behind, or at an angle behind, your back.** Otherwise your photo will have a glare that you may have to remove during editing.

For interior photos:

- **Create shots that give the illusion of spaciousness.** Do so by incorporating transitional areas, such as hallways or entryways, in with rooms in the same photo.
- **Take lots and lots of shots.** Don't edit on the spot or become paralysed by second-guessing. Don't use the camera's viewing screen to evaluate the pictures at length. Capture as many images as possible, and then wait until you download them into your computer to analyse, cull, select and edit.

Choosing the best shots

The whole point of featuring photos is to entice prospects to come see the real thing. So select and use only those images that convey comfort, warmth and unique quality, and that are capable of evoking a 'wow' response.

Use a photo to show a unique aspect of a bedroom, like an angled nook or architecturally unique wall. If the master bath — always a selling feature — is well beyond plain Jane in its look, show it. When selecting shots, choose quality over quantity.

Creating and organising photo files

Set up a system so you can store and access the images you may need in the future. Following each photo shoot, first delete the pictures you don't want to use, and then store the rest. When storing your pictures, your camera automatically suggests a file name. Rename each picture by choosing a name that describes the home or its address. Then move the images into folders that are labelled by property address.

How to trash your business card, fast

To rev up referrals, stop handing out your business cards.

Before you write us off as crazy, let us clarify. Don't *completely* stop using your business cards. Keep using them to share your contact information following personal encounters. But stop asking others to hand them out on your behalf to those who might be good prospects for your business. Understand this truth: Putting a business card into someone else's hands with the hope it'll get passed along is *not* the route to a new business relationship. It's the beginning of a quick trip to the wastepaper basket.

Many salespeople are taught to hand five business cards to clients with the request that they pass them out to friends who want to buy or sell real estate. Tracking studies have delivered the verdict on this approach: It doesn't work. Even if (a big if) your client passes your cards out to others, the recipients will rarely call you, and sales never follow. This low return (and high trash rate) makes this practice worthless.

Rather than papering the world with business cards in a futile effort to get your contact information into the hands of those considering moves, turn your thinking upside down. Quit worrying about *distributing* contact information and start worrying about *collecting* contact information.

Chapter 12

Negotiating the Contract and Closing the Deal

In This Chapter

- Getting your buyers and sellers ready for negotiations
- Handling each step of the negotiation process
- Advancing offers and avoiding choke points

This is such an important chapter for you — the points we make here are the secrets that we truly believe will create true value for your clients. Most sellers think an agent's real work involves finding the right buyer, and most buyers think an agent's real work involves finding the right house to buy. In fact, the real work involves bringing the deal to a successful close, and that's what this chapter is all about.

Real estate consumers' wants are beginning to shift. Buyers now say that 'help finding the right home to purchase' is way down the list of what they want from an agent. With the advent of technology and unlimited 24/7 access to the internet, buyers can search for properties any time they want. They can look at great photos — internal as well as external — and can access video for many properties as well. They can narrow down their list with no need to contact an agent. Most properties have scheduled open house times listed, so buyers have no need to even involve the agent at this stage. But don't worry — real estate agents aren't becoming redundant! Far from it.

Many buyers instead want the following: Help with price negotiations and help with 'terms and conditions' negotiations. *Terms* include all other options besides the sale price, such as early possession, repairs and the inclusion of personal property. Many buyers cite negotiating skills or services as the top thing they want from real estate agents. However, here lies the problem — unless you have been contracted to the buyer as a buyer's agent, the listing agent has a *fiduciary* (primary) duty to the seller. A real estate agent works for the seller and can't be seen to be negotiating on the buyers behalf. For many agents, this presents a problem, and more and more buyers are choosing to engage a dedicated buyer's agent to represent their interests and negotiate on their behalf.

The public doesn't see the gyrations that go into reaching a contract agreement and closing a deal, but if the negotiation step goes awry, no other step in the real estate sales process matters. Buyers and sellers may feel the emotions during the negotiations, but everything else happens behind the curtain.

The process of negotiating a deal involves fiduciary responsibility, market knowledge, client relations, and enormous skill and tact. Sometimes success means your client's property is the one selected over other considered options. Sometimes success results in a negotiated reduction in a home's sale price. Always, success reflects the realities of the market and the best terms and conditions the buyers and sellers can achieve.

This chapter lays out the rules of negotiating, starting with knowing all there is to know about the market environment so you can convince your client to accept terms and conditions you believe are the best to be had at the present time, based on current market conditions. Often that persuasion needs to be administered to a less-than-enthusiastic client who is hoping for a better outcome. The following pages help you prepare for the task.

Preparing for the Task Ahead

At the listing presentation or buyer interview consultation, after you've gained commitment from the client through a signature on the contract, take a few minutes to outline the next steps. Cover the following two points:

- Briefly describe how you'll work to represent your clients' interests when it comes to negotiating and closing their transaction. Here are three ways you can conduct the meeting:
  - Face-to-face meetings have advantages. They enable you to read the parties' full body language and notice a disconnect between what the parties say and what their body language says.
  - As an alternative, you can provide documents to each party prior to an online meeting, during which you both review the documents. Online meeting platforms are a key tool the real estate industry needs to use more. Skype and Google+ are two options for online meeting

platforms, but you could also use a GoToMeeting type of platform because you can control what each party is looking at. Keep in mind, however, this sort of technology still has its problems, and meeting this way shouldn't be your preferred option.

- You can use a phone approach if necessary, scanning and emailing the documents for parties to read before the phone conversation. If you are working by phone, put down all your points, feedback, campaign history and so on in written form so all parties have time to study this in depth before your call.

The question of which strategy to use is about efficiency versus effectiveness. While the technology creates significant efficiency for you and your clients, you lose a great deal of the effectiveness that comes from face-to-face meetings. Reaching agreement via phone or online meetings is much harder — sometimes a negotiation meeting can take hours, and this is not possible on the phone!

- Advise your seller clients to expect that most initial offers will come in below the asking price. You should always warn your clients that they should expect a below-list price offer, and that rarely will their sales transaction not require a counteroffer. If they express concern about this, just ask them to think about when they're buying something. Do they always offer their highest price first, or do they want a bargain the same as everyone else? This adjusts expectations and averts disappointment.

Your objective is to set the stage for the negotiations that lie ahead. Preparing your client for what's in store is an imperative step that saves you time, emotion and energy in the future.

The right tone

Great real estate agents set an optimistic tone and create an expectation that all parties will work together to achieve a negotiated win–win outcome. This means that the sellers and buyers both need to feel as if they won in the final transaction. The agents for both parties need to feel they won, as well, not just in terms of commissions earned but also in terms of earning the satisfaction of their clients.

When a marketplace becomes unbalanced, it's harder for all parties to feel satisfied. In a buyer's market (with more listings than sales) sellers very often feel that they're at a disadvantage in sales transactions. They're likely to be upset and angry that they are the ones having to make concessions and drop their price to get the sale across the line. Sellers may have to make even more concessions in a market where their home values have dropped dramatically — sometimes to below the price they purchased the property for. When buyers get a hint of seller desperation, it's like blood in the water for sharks. Fortunately, the Australian and New Zealand sales environment is one where win–win outcomes are possible and probable.

One of your jobs throughout the transaction is to serve as a calming influence. When emotions run high — as they are sure to do — be the one to remain focused on the outcome and settle down the buyer, seller and other real estate agents.

Take the approach followed by the best emergency-room doctors and nurses. They serve as a calming influence by displaying confidence and skill while reassuring their patients and other medical staff that everything is under good control. If emergency room doctors or nurses fly into a frenzy, the entire clinical setting is likely to spin out of control on the tide of the unchecked emotion. The same is true in the final throes of a real estate transaction. Commit to yourself that you'll serve as the calming influence throughout the deal.

Keys to representing a seller

Sellers have plenty of reasons to be emotional during the final negotiation. They're undergoing change, making huge decisions, and dealing with a transaction that probably involves the largest investment they own. Your role in this environment, and the key to your success, is twofold: Be prepared and, if you are the seller's agent, protect your client at every step along the way.

Be prepared

By carefully preparing before you present a buyer's offer to your clients, you can shorten the meeting, craft a better counteroffer, keep sellers' emotions in check and focus your clients on the next important steps. Follow this advice:

- First and foremost, remain calm, no matter how high or low the initial offer.
- Highlight the fact that you have an offer on paper, accompanied by a deposit. If the initial offer is below your seller's expectations, don't dwell on this. Instead, acknowledge that this is only the starting point for the real work of negotiation to begin.
- Go through the buyers' offer carefully and note any key issues that need to be addressed.

- Flag any contract points that merit your sellers' attention so you can easily reference them during the meeting. If you're emailing the document, also summarise the key points in the top of the email to which you attach the offer. This way your seller won't have to dig through every line of the contract. That's *your* job!
- If your meeting will take place by online meeting or phone rather than in person, email the offer to the seller within minutes of your conversation. If your phone conference is set for 2 pm, have the documents sent sometime between 1:30 and 1:45 pm. You don't want the sellers to spend hours brooding if the price is low, and you certainly don't want them to call you with questions, concerns and panic attacks half a dozen times prior to the scheduled phone conference. That can blow a hole a mile wide in your time-management strategy for the day.

Protect the sellers at all times

The worst thing that can happen to sellers is to have the transaction fall apart a few days before it becomes unconditional. By then, they're emotionally invested in another property. They've already made plans to move. They're excited about the future and then, wham, everything falls apart, and everyone — including you — loses market time, marketing momentum, and a considerable investment of time and money.

Even the most thorough approach results in a broken deal once in a while. But by taking these precautions, you can keep disasters to a bare minimum:

- Require prospective buyers to deposit enough money to secure your clients' position. Common practice is to ask for at least $1,000 on signing the offer with the balance of 5 to 10 per cent of purchase price on unconditional status. In markets where the contracts aren't exchanged until after finance is approved and other conditions met, common practice is to ask for a 10 per cent non-refundable deposit at this time. The deposit should be high enough to make it difficult for the buyers to purchase another home if they walk away from the deal after all contingent conditions are satisfied. You may be thinking that this advice conflicts with your objective to achieve a win–win outcome. In fact, it simply requires buyers to uphold their end of the deal or sacrifice their deposit. Remember, you're representing the sellers, and protecting your clients' interests is your fiduciary duty.

  Not many buyers will walk away from a deal if an amount like $5,000 is at stake. Yet many agents allow initial deposits of as little as $1,000 or $2,000 with nothing further paid until settlement. The rationale is that buyers won't have the cash available to make a higher deposit, but if buyers need $15,000 to settle in 30 days, depositing $5,000 upfront won't kill them.

- If necessary, consider accepting part of the deposit in the form of a bank guarantee or deposit bond. Only do this if the buyers have no other way to increase the deposit. If available cash is an issue, at least get a few thousand dollars deposited immediately and make arrangements to receive the balance within a few weeks, and note this on the contract. Most contracts have a 'time is of the essence' clause, meaning that if the buyer doesn't live up to the specified time frames for deposit, conditional clauses or settlement, the seller is entitled to terminate the contract with all penalties borne by the buyer.

Don't accept deposits which say on the contract that they will be paid at settlement. If the settlement never happens, your seller won't receive anything, and nor are you likely to ever see your commission. Even legal action won't fix this agent mistake.

- Another area of caution is financing. Require the buyers to provide proof of loan approval in writing. You want proof-positive that the buyers can and will perform, normally within two to four weeks of acceptance of the offer.

The prevailing rule in seller protection is to tighten the language every step of the way. Get legal advice if you're unsure of any part of this, or check with your principal. Remember at all times that your job is to protect and secure the interests of your clients, the sellers. The broader the language of the contract, the greater the number of interpretable clauses — commonly known as *weasel* clauses — that make it into the transaction, each one endangering the level of security you provide your clients. Risk management for you as the agent representing the seller is to have all contract special conditions written by a solicitor.

Keys to representing a buyer

The buyer's agent is responsible for crafting, presenting, writing a proper contract for and prompting acceptance of a good offer. Follow these steps:

- Your first step is to guide your clients toward a competitive offer. Perform at least a quick comparative market analysis, or CMA, to determine the value of the property. Among the factors you want to weigh are the home's current value based on the value of comparable properties, regional housing inventory levels and the competitive nature of the current marketplace. Your findings help your clients arrive at a reasonable price decision and help you counsel them as they make a competitive offer.

- After your clients have arrived at a competitive price to offer, your primary job as their representative, depending on where you are located, is to either properly prepare the contract you present on their behalf to the sellers or send the details to the solicitor for preparation. Your goal must be to protect your clients by writing terms and conditions that convey their intentions and meet their goals.

  For most people, a home purchase represents the largest investment they make, the biggest purchase in their lives, and the greatest and longest lasting debt they assume. The purchase agreement you write must protect them by addressing every issue — the price being offered, the items to be included in the purchase price, the amount to be deposited, the settlement date, the date the offer becomes null and void, and any condition that accompanies the offer, including contingencies based on the outcome of inspections such as building and pest inspections, approval of financing and personal property transferring with the sale.

  Work with your clients to understand all the terms and conditions that must be covered in the contract.

- When you're ready to present to the sellers, present the offer and your buyers as the best in the marketplace. Usually the offer will be presented to the sellers by the seller's agent, so make sure that you keep this agent onside — you want them to present the offer favourably. This can mean the difference between your clients or someone else buying the house. The more strongly you position your buyers by presenting their financial capacity, superior commitment, motivation and even a human connection, the more you swing the negotiation in favour of your clients. The stronger the loan-commitment documents provided by the lender — preferably showing a valid loan approval and a commitment with no conditions — the more cash-like your buyers' offer will seem.

  For some sellers, a human connection is the tipping point in choosing one set of buyers over another. For example, an offer from a family the sellers imagine will re-create their cherished memories in the home may trump another offer that is absent of the human connection, even if the offer results in equal or even slightly less money. Whatever you do, don't make the buyers out to be bargain hunters because doing so usually means the sellers back off without even entering into negotiations.

Educating buyers on true market conditions

One of the keys to negotiating in the real estate industry is knowing the market and educating the client on its true conditions. Using a market trends report, you can set a reasonable expectation of success. For example, you can convey to buyers that for the home they desire, others like it are selling for 97 per cent of the asking price, and the market has only 2.4 months of inventory. Those numbers indicate a diminished leverage position for buyers. Buyers who think they can 'steal' a home in an environment of low inventory and high list-to-sale price ratios are frustrated easily when sellers yawn at their offers. This can cause frustration that is directed at you, the agent. The buyers may think your negotiating skills have failed, when really the marketplace just isn't in the buyers' favour.

Advice for conjuncting with another agent for the sale

When partnering with another agent, you and the other agent in the transaction are obligated to cooperate with each other; that's why you're called *conjunction* agents. At the same time, you're both obligated to represent the interests of your own clients. Their job is to get the best deal for their client (usually the buyer) and your job is to get the best deal for your client (usually the seller). In some respects you're on opposite sides of the goal post. Buyers want to pay the lowest price and sellers want to receive the highest. Of course, nothing is wrong with this — it's just normal buyer and seller psychology! Nevertheless, this relationship can work wonderfully when you both seek a win–win outcome; however, it can become troublesome when the other agent comes to the deal with a we win–you lose mentality. Both of you need to work to come to an agreement where neither side gets so frustrated that they stop the negotiations.

Some agents or agencies have a policy to never conjunct with other agents, so you need to check with your own agency's policy and procedures before entering into an agreement. For Terri, she had no trouble partnering with other agents because she found it to be mutually beneficial, and it often resulted in a quicker sale for her clients if she didn't have the perfect buyer. However, Terri does have a couple of provisos here: One, always ask for the buyer's name from the conjuncting agent (in case you're already working with this person). Two, always insist that the other agent accompany the buyer to the inspection — don't do all the work and then only receive half the commission! Three, always be the one who talks with the seller and presents the offer — never allow the conjuncting agent to build the relationship with your seller.

When you're ready to talk with the other agent, cover these points:

- Explain your desire to create a win–win transaction. Say that you'll be relying on the other agent to create a win for both the buyers and sellers, and that you intend to do the same. Some agents believe their job is to achieve a win only for their own clients. This discussion helps you spot these people.
- If you're the listing agent, let the other agent know that the home is competitively priced — that it's at fair market value with no padding in the asking price. If your clients then counter a low offer at full price or close to it, the response won't be a surprise to the agent or prospective buyers.
- If you reach a snag, challenge or impasse with the other agent or with the agent's clients, test the situation by asking one of these questions:

  If you were representing my clients, would you advise them to accept this offer?

  If you were in my shoes, would you want your clients to accept these terms and conditions?

  If the answer is yes, then ask 'Why?' or 'How would you sell this to my clients if you were in my shoes?'

  If the agent can't give you an answer, the silence will let you know that they know their offer is unreasonable.

  If they can defend their position with strong arguments, you know you must convince your client of the validity of the buyers' offer.

Become your own 'other agent'

The easiest other agent to work with is yourself. You know you. You know you want win–win outcomes. You know whether your listing price has padding or whether your purchase offer has room for negotiation. You know how you work and that your skills are up to the task. You probably know it's easier for you to work with you than with any other agent.

Make your real estate sales life easier by selling more of your own listings. Represent both the buyers and sellers and avoid the challenges of working with another agent to complete the transaction.

Advancing or Accepting an Offer

When representing sellers, always insist that offers be presented to your client personally by you, not the buyer's agent. If you are the buyer's agent, remember that the other agent is not on the side of your clients (who want you to negotiate the lowest price). Sometimes you won't have the option to personally be there when your offer is presented. However, if you have the option to set up a conference call or online chat with the other agent and sellers, take it.

More than 55 per cent of communication is visual, so it's much harder to communicate when you can't see the agent or sellers in person. Instead, you simply have to be a better writer. When you're acting as the buyer's agent, your case is often made with words on the page. Hopefully you can get the other agent to show these words to the sellers. You may share a little bit of information about the buyers you represent, what they like about the home, and anything that creates a favourable connection between the sellers and your buyer.

You can also express this information with a video that you send to the agent. This establishes you as a cutting edge, professional, knowledgeable agent. It also lets you advocate for your client with more than just words on the page.

Presenting a buyer's low offer

When you extend an offer that is under the asking price, be prepared to present offsetting benefits in an effort to make the offer attractive and valuable to the sellers. Redeeming qualities include buyers with

- A solid 10 per cent deposit
- Finance already pre-approved
- A good, solid employment history
- The flexibility to settle quickly, preferably within 30 to 60 days

When presenting the offer:

- Discuss the overall offer before revealing the price. First work through and find common ground on the other stipulations in the offer. For instance, highlight the fact that the offer comes with a high deposit or the offer is in cash or with finance already approved. This will reassure the seller of the genuineness of your buyers. Then work on the price after you've agreed to or adjusted the other items that aren't related to price.

- When discussing price, identify the difference between the asking and offered prices and focus the discussion only on that number. Ask the sellers or the other agent, 'If the buyers had come in here with cash and settlement was in a couple of weeks, what offer would have been acceptable?' Take that number and subtract it from the asking price. Don't deal with the big numbers, such as a $350,000 asking price and a $335,000 offer. Break it down to a comparison between the $335,000 offer and the $345,000 the sellers would take now if a buyer walked in with cash. The real difference is $10,000. Talk and plan in terms of a $10,000 difference between the sellers and buyers.

- Ask the sellers to consider the actual impact of the difference. Say the difference is $10,000. You could ask: 'Is it worth a bit less to know that your home is sold and that you have the freedom to move on to your next step?' This same technique works well to raise the offer on the buyers' side, or even to reach a mid-point agreement.
- Explain how the buyers arrived at their offer price. If it backs up your case, show current comparatives to validate their thinking. Perhaps the property was listed months ago and the market environment has changed considerably in the meantime. Presenting a current market analysis can help justify and win acceptance of the offer.
- If the offer is the highest one the buyers can make, express that fact, saying something like, 'The buyers would really love the home, but they understand if there isn't an opportunity for a win for everyone.' This kind of statement defuses emotions before they arise.

Above all, when presenting a low price, convey that the offer is based on a realistic assessment of the market environment or the buyers' capability, not a personal reaction to the sellers or their home. Sometimes it may be that the sellers don't care one whit about the buyer's situation, so be prepared for them not to budge on this just to accommodate the buyer's budget!

Receiving a buyer's low offer

As the seller's agent, if you did your job way back when you first listed the property, your sellers will be well aware of the likelihood of a low offer. When one comes in, call the buyers or the buyer's agent to learn more about the buyers. Ask whether they have the funds to buy the property and whether they have finance pre-approval. Learn whether they're just starting and haven't even met with a lender yet, or whether they have loan pre-approval and are just working to find the right house.

Taking the insult out of an insulting offer

When you're representing the sellers in a transaction, the first step toward taking the sting out of a low offer is assuring your clients that the offer is not personal. Most likely the prospective buyers don't know your sellers or your sellers' family. They may not even know the rationale behind the number they presented. They may have relied on poor advice, too much advice, an unskilled agent or poor research skills — in which case a well-presented counteroffer is in order.

On the flip side, the sellers' property may indeed be overpriced, either because the sellers insisted on a high price or because the market environment changed between when the home was listed and when the offer arrived. If a home is radically overpriced, a fair offer can look insulting when it really isn't. This is why you must work hard to list the property well at the beginning. In addition, you need to give detailed feedback on price after every inspection so sellers are prepared if an offer comes in lower than their initial expectations.

If your sellers' home is overpriced, you must get them to focus on the gap between the low offer and fair market value, not the difference between fair market value and their inflated listing price. In a situation like this, usually the listing agent is at fault for allowing this circumstance to continue and not being experienced enough to advise the seller better or know the market conditions better themselves.

Presenting low offers

Presenting low offers can be tricky — perhaps you don't want to insult your sellers with an offer that's way below their expectations and way below market value. However, checking the legislation covering this in your area is vital. In many areas, legislation clearly states that *all* offers, whether verbal or written, need to be presented to sellers.

You can prepare your sellers for this in a couple of ways. The first and most important is to establish with your sellers at the initial listing presentation that you will only present written offers as being serious. If a buyer wants you to present a low verbal offer, you can then pass on your seller's instructions, saying something like 'I am really sorry but my instructions are to only present offers in writing accompanied by a deposit.' This shifts the responsibility to the seller, defuses an angry buyer and sorts out the serious buyers.

For Terri, deciding whether or not to present a buyer's low offer in writing to a seller isn't a real estate agent's role. Terri remembers receiving an offer for one of her own properties in Coffs Harbour that was $35,000 below the asking price. At the time it was presented, she had an opportunity to buy exceptionally well elsewhere so she took the offer quickly! She doesn't like to think about what may have happened if the agent had taken it on himself not to tell her because he'd decided the offer was too low. It is always the seller's responsibility and the seller's right to accept or to refuse any offer, not the agent's.

Getting beyond emotion

People get emotional during the negotiating stage for a number of reasons. For one thing, a lot of money is at stake. For another, both parties are anxious to get the deal done, and time is ticking away. Third, home inspections and low-price offers reveal opinions about a home's value that can feel jarring to sellers who have viewed the home with pride and joy for a number of years.

The only antidote to an emotional uprising is a pragmatic focus on the goals the parties are trying to achieve and a renewed commitment to finding common ground and getting the deal done. As the agent, you must be very clear on the motivation of your seller — what do they want to do when the property is sold and will this offer enable them to do this? This is the main question to be considered.

Terri once had a negotiation where the seller and the buyer were $70,000 apart on price. The seller had dug his heels in but so had the buyer. The seller had his head in the sand price-wise, and the buyer's price was actually reasonable considering the market was dropping. Terri also knew that the seller wanted to invest in a big commercial development in the CBD. After many meetings (and lots of coffee), the parties seemed to have reached an impasse. So Terri changed tack and asked the seller, hypothetically, what he was expecting to make with the commercial development he was planning and what would happen if he couldn't free up the capital to invest in this project. He thought for a while, then smiled and said, 'You're right, you know — I should just get this one over and done with and move on to make a fortune with the next one!' Negotiations closed!

When you hit a buyer–seller impasse, find a way to ask: Is this about ego or income? Do they want the satisfaction that comes with a high price, or do they need the money? Usually, you'll bring your client back down to earth in a hurry. You're asking, in essence, what are you really fighting for?

Turning concessions into victories

Buyer offers are usually accompanied by home-inspection conditions that require sellers to make concessions before the deal becomes unconditional. Often these concessions take the form of repairs that the sellers need to make before the buyers take possession. The presentation of repair concessions is one of the toughest steps in the negotiation process. Buyers often use the home-inspection step to make a lower offer. Sellers, who feel they already gave enough at the office when they accepted the price offer, aren't in the mood to give more.

Explain the benefit to the seller of having a professional building and pest inspection done prior to any buyer inspections. If minor problems exist, these can be addressed; if major problems are found, sellers can organise quotes for repair that can be presented to calm anxious buyers.

No matter whether you're representing the buyers or sellers, bring the focus down to the value of the requests. By itemising the concessions and assigning value in terms of dollars, hassle factor and time invested, you can manoeuver a transaction to the end. Follow these steps:

- If the list has ten items, select the six or seven easiest, least-expensive issues to act upon. By dealing with more than half the requested items, you demonstrate your clients' goodwill effort to meet the other party more than halfway.
- Call the other agent and say, 'I doubt I can be persuasive enough to get the sellers to handle all ten requests. If your clients had to have a few of these concessions to keep the deal together, which ones would they be?' This strategy enables you to know which requests represent potential deal-killers.
- Explain to the other agent that while you can't guarantee you'll get your sellers to agree, you'll see what you can do.
- Focus the sellers on what they're gaining out of the deal. If they're pocketing an equity increase and the opportunity to open a new chapter in their lives, focus them on those facts. Urge them not to let $1,500 worth of repairs stand in the way of $300,000 cash in their pockets. Or, if the buyers are moving to a terrific home in the perfect neighbourhood for their family, focus them on that. Use a script like this:

  Mr and Mrs Buyer, you spent days and looked at more than 40 homes to find this one that you described as perfect. Do you really want to start that process over again?

To turn concessions into victories, focus your clients on what they're gaining rather than on what they're giving up.

Dealing with I win–you lose clients

Some clients, and some agents for that matter, only feel satisfied when they win and someone else loses.

The best way to handle I win–you lose situations is to avoid them. If you can't, then deal with them professionally, powerfully and from a position of control. No matter what, don't back down. Most I win–you lose clients are perpetually testing the waters to see how much they can get away with.

During your career, you're bound to meet sellers who have an I win–you lose mentality — and they often emerge during negotiations about paying for their marketing. They may assume that you will be so desperate, or so grateful, to secure their listing that you will agree to any of their conditions. So they offer you the listing on the condition that you reduce your commission and also pay for their marketing! Don't fall into this trap. Stay firm. Terri has found that even though she had to walk away from some listings, the ones she did secure were with reasonably minded sellers who respected her expertise and the service she gave to achieve their results.

Closing the Deal

Most sellers and buyers think of agreeing to the offer as the tricky part of the transaction and that they can take the rest pretty much for granted. Agents know otherwise. As an agent, your work isn't done and your commission teeters in the balance until you successfully complete this final, challenging part of the real estate transaction.

This phase can involve an army of people. Using a different analogy, you're like the conductor of an orchestra; control the instruments well and no wrong note will creep in.

Make it your objective to direct whatever business you can to companies and individuals you know will perform in a timely, professional manner. If you're referring tradespeople, solicitors and so on, give details of people you know personally to be efficient and reliable — otherwise, you could be accused of conflict of interest. To help in this way also assures your clients of good service and fewer surprises, and reduces the time you and your staff invest in taking the transaction to a successful conclusion.

Forming a closing team and working with the players

A good closing team can help you increase your prosperity by letting you efficiently wind up one deal and move on to the next. Following is the line-up of key players who make the closing a smooth process.

The mortgage broker

The mortgage broker completes the loan package for the buyers within a few days of contract acceptance.

Many agencies and franchises have a dedicated loans department with qualified mortgage brokers on board. Make sure the mortgage broker on your team is a great salesperson backed by a team that is highly organised and able to push transactions through to a seamless close. A good mortgage broker can smooth out problems before you even hear about them, averting landmines and sparing you significant and time-consuming challenges.

Mortgage brokers can add considerable value to your business even beyond the sales closing. If you don't have one attached to your office, forming a relationship with a mortgage broker outside your business makes a lot of sense. This relationship can be mutually beneficial because you can work together to prospect clients, follow up on leads and keep deals together.

The building and/or pest inspector

These professionals are hired to evaluate the condition of the property, spot current or potential defects, and give guidance regarding the proper remedies.

You want to work hard to identify and recommend home inspectors who are thorough and who fully disclose all defects and items in need of repair without throwing gasoline on potential problems. Beware of the home inspector who is an alarmist. Look instead for someone who resembles Joe Friday with his 'just the facts, ma'am' approach.

You also want a home inspector who can quickly produce an easy-to-read report written in everyday, commonly understood language. If technical jargon is necessary, insist on plain-English translations. Nothing concerns buyers more than a problem they don't understand. Inspectors may also be able to provide quotes to fix any problems they might encounter, which is a benefit to both sellers and buyers.

The valuer

Because lending institutions often have the largest stake in a home — greater even than that of the borrowers — they employ a panel of valuers to determine the value of the property.

Banks and lending companies can select the appraiser they want to use. However, sometimes appraisers are randomly assigned or put in rotation, so you may get assigned a valuer who doesn't know the area well.

You need to prepare for the possibility of an unfavourable valuation figure. Some valuers arrive at a figure with a quick drive-by glance — if this happens, or if you believe the figure is under value, you or your client have a right to ask for a second opinion and an interior inspection.

Avoiding derailment

Like a train, a transaction can get derailed at any point on the track. A settlement can be hit by a title that's not cleared with the titles office, a home not valuing to the loan figure, structural issues, or one of countless other unanticipated problems.

Choke points cause delays, and delays cause all kinds of problems for buyers, sellers and agents. Moving plans get thrown into disarray. Interim housing or early-settlement requests become necessary. Contingency plans need to be thrown together. Nerves get jangled. The resulting situation can be a nightmare and a productivity killer, even for the most seasoned agent.

Most of the problems in completing transactions fall into three basic areas. Stay on the lookout for these problems and solutions to steer your transactions clear of as much trouble as possible:

1. **Documentation and verification:**

   Lenders need to assemble considerable paperwork and complete dozens of documents based on information submitted by the loan applicants. Then they need to verify all information for accuracy by checking the applicants' employment status, funds on deposit and income level. The document preparation and information verification process takes time. Advise your buyers that if they or their lender fail to submit the required information on a timely basis, or if they turn it in piecemeal, delays are certain to result.

2. **Repairs, repairs, repairs:**

   This is a choke point that good planning can avert. When you're representing the sellers, state clearly in writing that only structural issues will be considered grounds for terminating a contract — cosmetic issues such as cracked tiles won't be enough to kill a contract. If you don't, you leave the sellers open to the risk that the buyers will come back with a laundry list of items, and threaten to terminate if these aren't repaired.

   Required repairs are usually limited to structural, mechanical, or health and safety issues — with not a word about nicks in walls or non-matching doorknobs.

Part IV

Running a Successful Real Estate Business

Five Things to Remember when Running a Real Estate Business

- **Know your big 'why'.** It's okay to set goals and targets but you must know *why* you want to achieve these specific goals, and how you'll feel if you don't achieve them. These goals will result in success only if they are important enough to push you every single day.
- **Take time to plan.** Remember 'busy-ness' is not 'business'! Set weekly Key Performance Indicators and plan your days and your weeks in advance — allow for interruptions but don't just wing it each day.
- **Focus on what your clients want.** There is an old saying (but a true one), 'If you give your clients what they want, then inevitably you will get what you want.'
- **Keep your eye on your bottom line.** Sometimes we can work so hard but forget to focus on the bottom line. Know what you need to survive and budget for this. Track your income and expenses and do your Profit & Loss statement every month. This will help you catch things before it's too late to change course if necessary.
- **Be open to new strategies, new technology, and never stop learning.** Standing still is the prelude to going backwards. Learn, grow and thrive.

Find out more tips for running a successful real estate business with a free article online at `www.dummies.com/extras/successrealestateagentau`.

In this part ...

- We give you tools, systems, strategies and techniques to understand your marketplace, define where you stand in it and stake your own competitive position, whether you actually own the agency or you're a salesperson running your own real estate business under someone else's banner.
- We share advice and tips for building relationships, developing client loyalty, delivering unbeatable service and winning client relationships that last a lifetime.
- We show you how to find great techniques and advice to stop spinning your wheels on unproductive activities and start generating the greatest return on the time you invest in your real estate career.

Chapter 13

Staking Your Competitive Position

In This Chapter

- Understanding your marketplace
- Knowing what statistics to calculate and monitor
- Determining and conveying your competitive advantage

Ask most agents how they're different or better than their agent colleagues or competitors and get ready to hear either a whole lot of ums and ahs, or a line-up of platitudes about how they care more, work harder, make clients happier, are honest and trustworthy or whatever.

This might sound good but every agent probably says the same! What you'll rarely hear is a summary of how one agent is statistically more effective than other agents, or how that statistical advantage translates into a strong position in the overall market and a dominant position in a particular market niche.

Your clients want an expert, someone who knows the marketplace well, and can market property to attract good buyers. They want an agent who can negotiate the highest possible price (or, if you are a buyer's agent, the lowest possible price). If you're struggling to create clear differences between you and other agents, read on. This chapter gives you a clear advantage by showing you how to analyse your marketplace, calculate your performance statistics, compare your statistics with market norms and stake out your own competitive territory by knowing — based on clear calculations — exactly how you excel and what market territory you control better than anyone else.

Defining Competitive Positioning

If you don't know how you stack up against your competitors or how your performance is different or better than average, take comfort in the fact that you're certainly not alone. It amazes us how even very successful agents often can't define their competitive positions.

In a sentence, your competitive position defines how your real estate practice is better than all others in some unique and meaningful way. It may be that you're dominant when it comes to selling properties on the river, or in the heart of the city. It may be that you excel in high-end or low-end properties, or properties in a certain neighbourhood or design category.

In all cases, your competitive position must be real and defensible, which means it must be based on statistics, and that's what the following sections of this chapter explain.

The best agents — the most powerful, experienced, high-volume agents — share a single advantage: They know the statistics of their market, their own performance statistics, and their statistical position in the overall marketplace or in a particular niche market area. They also know how they compare to marketplace averages of other agents or against other competing agents when they go head to head.

Recently Dirk was on a coaching call with a powerful agent. Her business was going great, but she was looking to the future and planning how to grow to an even higher level. She had compiled her sales statistics, and she and Dirk took some time to analyse her performance, define her position, and create a marketing strategy to build upon her competitive advantage:

- **Performance:** Last year, 56 homes were listed and sold in one of her market niches. Of those, 17 (or more than 30 per cent) were her listings; her nearest competitor listed two. By listings alone she was 8.5 times more successful than any other agent in her competitive sphere. She also sold more homes in her niche than anyone else. Her closest competitor was a large company of many agents that listed and sold five homes.
- **Position:** It didn't take long for the numbers to prove that she owns a dominant position in her market niche. She knew she was strong, but until she did the maths she didn't realise just how strong a position she'd staked out. By the end of our call, she had the facts she needed to position herself as the real estate expert in her market niche area.

- **Marketing strategy:** Dirk's coaching client plans to grow her slice of the pie (which is called *market share* and is explained later in this chapter) by taking listings and sales from other agents. By presenting herself as the regional expert — with the indisputable statistics to back the claim — she's ready to attract an even greater number of qualified leads and convince an ever-growing number of clients in her niche area to select her services based upon the proven advantage she offers.

You can employ a couple of strategies to use available statistics to increase your market share and get called in for more appraisals. First, in your marketing to a targeted area, announce the success of yourself (or your team if you're a new agent) and your positioning against other agents and companies. Don't name names but use the numbers of the top agents in the marketplace to truly show your dominance through using stats and bar graphs.

Secondly, and this will work particularly well if you don't have the stats to demonstrate market dominance, you can focus on the message of 'don't list before you get a second opinion or evaluation'. In other words, position potential sellers to interview more than one agent. If you can get on the sellers' shopping list, you obviously have opportunities to secure more than your fair share of listings.

If you're a newer agent, likely you don't yet have the stats to stake your competitive position. However, if you selected your real estate company well (see more on this topic in Chapter 2), your company likely does. Talk with your principal to learn how your company excels in the marketplace and present your company's advantages while you build your own success story.

Calculating and Analysing Real Estate's Big Three Statistics

Three key statistics reflect real estate sales success better than any other indicators. These statistics are: Average list price compared to average sale price, average number of days on the market and average number of listings sold versus listings taken. The following sections look at the value and power of each calculation. If figures are not your strong point, work with your principal or your sales manager to get a better handle on the statistics covered in the following sections, so that you can use these facts to demonstrate expertise and market knowledge.

Average list price to sale price

This ratio quantifies your skill and success in achieving the result you and your client expect when you place a home on the market. By presenting a strong list-price-to-sale-price ratio, you clearly illustrate your effectiveness for your sellers.

Doing the maths

To calculate your average list price to sale price, follow these steps:

1. **Make a list of all your listed homes that sold and settled over a specific period of time, but not less than three months (one quarter).**
2. **Add up the list prices of all the homes.**

   Let's say you listed three homes that sold in the last quarter. If those listings were priced at $259,000, $349,000 and $429,000, you had a total listed inventory of $1,037,000.
3. **Add up the sale prices of all the homes.**

   If your listed homes that sold last quarter closed at $245,000, $337,000, and $405,000, your total sold inventory was $987,000.
4. **Calculate your average list price to sale price by dividing your total sold inventory by your total listed inventory.**

   Using the above example, divide $987,000 by $1,037,000. The calculation results in a list-to-sold ratio of 95 per cent. Based on your recent performance, a seller who lists with you can expect to get an average of 95 per cent of the list price.

Your *list-to-sold* ratio is

Total sold inventory ÷ Total listed inventory

If you choose to sell via the auction process — track these results also! Use the reserve price as your listed price and note the difference between reserve figure and the sale price under the hammer (or price negotiated after auction).

The list-to-sold ratio proclaims from the mountaintops an agents' level of success. It establishes a clear benchmark of how the agent is doing at pricing and negotiating, and it provides a clear indicator of their skills, abilities, knowledge and systems.

Using your ratio

Regardless of the nature of your marketplace, the list-to-sold ratio for all good agents varies only by a few percentage points.

A ratio of 95 per cent is usually at the bottom of the good range. An agent with a list-to-sold ratio of 95 per cent loses $5,000 for every $100,000 in sale price. If you're selling a $600,000 home and settle for 95 per cent of the list price, the resulting reduction is $30,000! Aim for a ratio of 98 per cent or above. A high list-to-sale ratio proves that your marketing plan or strategy is effective. It reduces the perception of risk on the part of the seller.

Beyond achieving a list-to-sold ratio of 95 per cent or higher, aim for a ratio that places your performance in the top tier of all agents in your marketplace. When you can prove to prospective sellers that you consistently achieve a higher-than-average percentage of list price for your clients, their decision to entrust their home sale to your expertise becomes vastly easier.

To determine how your list-to-sold ratio compares in your marketplace, follow these steps:

1. **Learn the average list-to-sold ratio for all agents in your marketplace.**

   Whether you are an agent from Australia or New Zealand, you are able to access this information from websites like `www.rpdata.com.au`, `www.pricefinder.com.au`, `www.realestate.co.nz` or `www.reinz .co.nz`. If still in doubt, check with your agency principal how you can find out this information in your area.

2. **Compare your ratio with the market average.**

3. **Use your outstanding performance to prove numerically that clients will net more money working with you than with other agents.**

   If your average is 98 per cent and your market average is 91 per cent, sellers working with you are likely to put 7 per cent more in their pockets by listing with you.

If you're a new agent with few listed properties, rely on your company's list-to-sold stats while developing your individual performance. Whether you're presenting your own or your company's stats, however, you'll want to present numbers that are higher than market averages; otherwise, they indicate serious problems with your business.

Improving your ratio

Your list-to-sold price discloses your skill in pricing a home properly. Obviously, if you take vastly overpriced listings and deal with the consequences later, your list-to-sold ratio will suffer accordingly.

The list-to-sold ratio is also a strong reflection of your skill in negotiating on behalf of a seller. In a neutral market, most initial offers come in at less than 95 per cent of the list price. For instance, a home listed at $259,000 might generate an initial offer in the low $230,000s. Whether it sells at that price or higher depends on the listing agent's ability to demonstrate to the buyer and buyer's agent the value of the property, with the aim of bringing the offer up to $250,000 or even $255,000, at which point the list-to-sold ratio climbs back to 98 per cent.

Finally, the list-to-sold ratio is affected by your marketing, staging and exposure of the property. Chapter 8 helps you plan successful open houses, Chapter 10 is full of staging advice, and Chapter 11 is all about marketing the properties list.

Average days on the market

Your ability to sell a home, on average, in fewer than 45 days clearly conveys to potential sellers your skill and success level. It further indicates your knowledge of competitive pricing. There is a fine balance here, as well. If you're working with sellers and the days-on-market average is less than two weeks, they may think you're under-pricing homes. You probably aren't, but perception is reality.

To allay your sellers' fears that you may undersell their property in too short a time, make sure all your post-sale marketing emphasises the terrific sale price as well as the time frame.

An agent with a strong track record for quickly moving homes presents a clear competitive advantage to sellers for several reasons:

- Agents who move properties quickly generally achieve higher sale prices and put more money in their sellers' pockets. Buyers in today's marketplace are extremely sophisticated. They have access to a volume of information; however, most public search sites don't disclose days on the market. One of the first questions buyers ask an agent is, 'How long has the house been on the market?' Buyers realise that the best homes sell quickly. If they find out a home has been slow to sell, they adjust their initial offer downward accordingly. Urgency is always a factor in real estate sales. The fear of loss is a powerful motivator to cause someone to move off the fence into action.

- Sellers with newly listed properties have a stronger negotiation position when an offer comes in. If the home has only been on the market a few days, buyers realise that the seller is less likely to offer price concessions.

- Sellers with slow-to-sell homes sacrifice dollars two ways: One, through a lower sale price and, two, through ongoing expenses for a home they no longer want to own. This two-edged sword is the one agents need to point out in order to shorten the time a home languishes on the market. Sellers often want to hold out for a higher offer, but as time goes by that higher offer becomes less likely to arrive. Contrary to the beliefs of many clients, sellers don't make more money by waiting, say, 120 days rather than accepting an offer in the first 45 days from listing. In fact, studies show that they receive less and less over time. And while they wait, they need to make additional mortgage payments that do little to reduce their debt or increase their equity.

By showing that your listings have lower-than-average days on the market, you'll present proof that prospective sellers gain a significant competitive edge and financial advantage when they choose to work with you.

Doing the maths

To calculate the average number of days your listings are on the market, follow these steps:

1. **Make a list of all your listings that sold over a recent period of not less than three months.**

   Alongside each listing, note the number of days that passed between when the home was listed and when a sale contract was signed.

2. **Add up the days on the market for all homes on your list.**

   For example, if you had five sold listings, one that sold after 33 days on the market and others after 45, 62, 21 and 84 days, your total is 245 days.

3. **Divide the total number of days on the market by the number of listings sold.**

   If you had five sold listings last quarter that were on the market a total of 245 days, your average days on the market per property during that period is 49.

Your *average days-on-the-market* ratio is

Total number of days that all your sold listings were on the market ÷ Number of sold listings

Working the numbers

When comparing your days-on-the-market averages with market-wide real estate averages, take into account the following considerations:

- After calculating the average number of days your own listings were on the market, conduct the same calculation for your competitors' listings. If you don't yet have a significant number of listings, obtain the average number of days that your agency's listings were on the market and present that figure while you're building your own business.

- Be aware that the price range you sell in can affect the average number of days on the market. In general, homes in a higher price range result in a higher average number of days on the market.

  If you have a high number of listings, consider creating average calculations for various price ranges or geographic market areas. This will enable you to create apples-to-apples comparisons with other agents by analysing performance in specific segments of the market.

- When comparing your performance with market-wide averages, strengthen your competitive position by including in your calculation homes that failed to sell. When doing so, be careful to disclose that expired listings are included in your calculation. By factoring in expired listings, you reflect the most comprehensive view of how many days homes sat on the market, whether they ultimately sold or not.

  By including expired listings in your average calculation, the market average will go up sharply. The vast majority of expired listings will have been on the market 120 days or more. Therefore, if your overall market saw a number of expired listings and you personally had none, the gap between you and your competitors will stretch considerably and to your great advantage.

Average listings taken versus listings sold

This competitive number demonstrates to the world how well you do your job of selling homes. When you can say to a seller that you sell more than 98 per cent of all the homes that sellers list with you, you present strong evidence that your clients will assume a greatly lowered risk when working with you.

Wanting to achieve a competitive listings-taken-versus-listings-sold number highlights the importance of qualifying your sellers and only taking on work from motivated sellers who aren't set on listing their properties at much more than market value.

One of the greatest fears a seller experiences stems from the concern, 'What if I pick the wrong agent? What if I'm hearing fast talk from a salesperson who wants to pound a for-sale sign in my yard without the experience to get the job done?' By presenting your track record in the form of a high percentage of listings taken versus listings sold, you quickly erase concerns and provide comfort and relief to prospects.

In a neutral marketplace with good sale activity, the average listings-taken-versus-listings-sold ratio historically hovers around 50 per cent to 60 per cent. In a sellers' market, the number is higher, but on average when you look at the number of sales against the number of expired listings and properties withdrawn from the marketplace, the average is in that range. Think about it: That means that more than one-third of homes that are listed fail to sell for some reason. When the market shifts to a more buyer-controlled market, the listings-taken-versus-listings-sold numbers can go below 50 per cent. This is an astonishing figure that escapes the awareness of average agents and most sellers, and it's a nugget you can use to your competitive advantage.

To calculate your listings-taken-versus-listings-sold ratio, follow these steps:

1. **Add up the total of all properties you listed over a recent period of not less than three months.**
2. **Of all properties listed over the recent period, add up how many you sold.**
3. **Divide the number of sold listings by the total number of listings to arrive at your listings-taken-versus-listings-sold average.**

Your *average listings-taken-versus-listings-sold* ratio is

Number of all listings sold ÷ Number of all properties listed

When working at an inner-city agency, Terri used to set her KPIs at signing 10 to 12 qualified listings each month and selling at least 6 to 8. This consistent turnover kept her income high and was impressive when speaking with prospective sellers, creating a strong competitive advantage.

Agents are paid to achieve results. Truth is, you can be the nicest person in the world. You can call your sellers weekly, send them stuff in the mail, share marketing reports and hand out gift vouchers. You can pour love on them as much as anyone can. However, if you don't sell the home within the listing period, in their view you didn't do your job and you're incompetent. If you fail to sell their house, not only will you not get paid, but also you'll lose future sales from all the friends they would have otherwise referred to you.

Sellers base their assessment of an agent's service on results, and results only. Did the home sell? Did they achieve the expected sale price? Did it move in a reasonable time frame? Were they able to move when they wanted to?

Obviously, during a listing presentation, sellers can't know what their experience with you will be. But the statistics and competitive positions you present give them a pretty clear idea of what they can expect. Performance ratios tell your story in numbers and give prospects the facts they need to make good decisions.

Sellers want to know their odds of success. Use your stats to show them the proven competitive advantage you bring to the table.

Interpreting the Findings

Be ready and willing to invest time to analyse and interpret your own and your company's competitive position in the marketplace. Your principal may have useful stats to contribute, but likely you'll need to do additional work to calculate the Big Three ratios described in the preceding section of this chapter and to apply the stats to various segments of your marketplace, including geographic areas and specific price ranges.

Without solid facts, you can't possibly know, define or describe your competitive advantage.

Jack Welch, in one of his six famous rules for business, says, 'If you don't have a competitive advantage, don't compete.' Without stats, you have nothing to compete with. So begin right now to compile the data, slice and dice it in every ethical way possible to find your edge, and then present that edge as your proven competitive advantage to prospects.

Finding your edge

Maybe your edge is that you move the most units, or that you have the highest sales volume, or that your Big Three stats top the charts in a specific geographic region or price range. When you know your edge, you can market and leverage your point of difference to expand your business.

For instance, you may find that you rank in the top five for properties sold in your area. You can leverage that strength as you expand into a nearby geographic marketplace with similar homes. Instead of starting from zero in the new market area, you can use your current dominant stats as a bridge. Instead of ranking in the top five for sales in your current concise market area, spread your numbers over your current and future market areas, and you'll probably rank in the top ten for the combined area. Then you can work from that respectable statistical position to gain more market share in your new and currently weaker area.

When you know your numbers, you can put them to work strategically and tactically as you devise a plan to expand your market share. The key is to start with the facts, dig to find your edge, interpret your edge and exploit it to your advantage. No-one is going to hand over listings and sales; you're going to have to win them over.

Positioning yourself against other agents

Knowing how your competition is performing and how you rank in the field is paramount to your success. Follow these steps:

- Learn the Big Three stats — average list price to sale price, average days on the market, and average listings taken versus listings sold — for other companies and agents. These numbers provide you with a basis for comparison and help you begin the process of positioning yourself and your company to the consumer.

- Define your competitive advantage. Keep in mind that how you state your advantage is often as important as what you have to say. How you present your argument and the level of confidence and conviction you have in your beliefs can make the difference between a listing and a futile effort.
- Convince your prospect of your advantage.

- Use numbers to demonstrate the clear advantage you present to clients. Realise that if prospects can't see a clear difference between you and other agents, they will gravitate to the easy choice, which is to select the agent offering the lowest commission rate or highest initial list price.

Believing in your own advantage

When Dirk was a new real estate agent, the reasons he could present for why sellers should list with him certainly numbered fewer than later in his career, but that didn't stop him from securing listings — largely because his conviction about the advantage he offered sellers was so strong.

Dirk told prospects that selling their home required a partnership with a focused, passionate, successful, sales-oriented agent. He explained that personal service, attention to detail, and creation and conversion of leads would sell their home, and that he was the agent for the job. He contrasted himself positively with other, more-established agents by explaining that sellers hardly benefit from working with an agent who passes them off to interact with a series of assistants who handle the paperwork, marketing strategy, ad calls, sign calls and open houses.

'Do you see the benefit of working with a person rather than this laundry list of underlings?' he would ask, before adding, 'Isn't this type of intimate relationship what you're looking for?'

Interestingly enough, Dirk's conviction regarding the advantage he offered sellers changed dramatically after a few years in the business. By then he had assembled a service team and developed an excellent system for serving the client through others. His argument changed, as well. He now explained to clients that one person couldn't possibly do with skill and precision all the activities that a seller needs and should demand from an agent. With so many hats to wear, a lone ranger agent can't possibly provide the level of exposure, communication, customer service and expertise that the team of experts he represented could deliver.

Both positions were truthful. Both had merit. The difference stemmed from his position at the time and the way Dirk felt and articulated how that position benefited his prospects.

Terri's experiences with building her client base and achieving great success are remarkably similar to Dirk's! Prior to building a strong, loyal client base, Terri's approach was always to emphasise the focused attention that her sellers would receive. At every appraisal and listing presentation, she told the prospective seller that her career was based on having made a conscious choice to work with fewer listings with the intention of giving each client the one-on-one attention not possible if she had taken on too many clients. She followed through and gave each seller service well above their expectations, and produced results that led to many referrals and repeat business.

Once Terri took on a personal assistant and buyer's agent, she could obviously handle more listings. But she always stayed true to the personal service that earned her repeated sales success and many franchise awards.

Creating sales and sales volume comparisons

Evaluating your performance against the statistics of other agents or companies in your market segment is a great starting point, but it's rarely enough to uncover your unique edge or point of difference.

When you compare your own numbers to your competitors' stats for the number of properties sold, number of listings taken, number of listings sold, and total sales volume in your market area, you arrive at a picture of how you did compared to the market at large. However, chances are good that your business is focused on certain segments of the total market — likely you specialise in certain neighbourhoods, certain price ranges, and even certain types of residences. To uncover your edge, you need to *segment*, or slice and dice, the market-wide numbers.

If you're new to the real estate sales business, you can substitute your own stats with your team stats until you have more substantial stats for yourself.

For example:

- You can shrink the geographic area down to a concise neighbourhood or region in order to compare your own performance with market performance in that niche region.
- You can expand the geographic area to include several neighbourhoods or even towns in which you operate.
- You can analyse real estate activity only in a certain price range.
- You can focus on a segment that includes a particular property type, such as apartments, or waterfront homes.

Calculating per agent productivity

Often, the largest company in a market will account for the largest sales volume and sales numbers, creating a strong market presence that eclipses the performance of small companies and individual agents. If you face a David and Goliath situation, reach down and pick up the stone of per agent productivity to put in your slingshot.

Calculate per agent productivity by dividing a company's total performance by the number of agents working at the firm. You can use this calculation to bring listings taken, listings sold, total unit volume, sales volume, or buyer-represented sales down to a per agent basis. Suddenly, Goliath won't look quite so dominant.

Using market-area statistics to set your goals

Always know the average agent success numbers for your marketplace. These are the numbers you want to eclipse by the end of your first six months in the business — at least.

Know the Big Three statistics (if you're not crystal clear about what these are and how to calculate them, turn to the first pages of this chapter for definitions and formulas) and know exactly how your own performance stacks up against market averages. Then, when the numbers are in front of you, compare your performance to the market area average. Ask:

- What doesn't look good at first glance?
- Where are you falling behind?
- If you broaden or shrink the criteria, does your positioning improve?
- How can you craft a position from which to sell if you're stuck with these stats?

Use the first two questions to set improvement goals. Use the third question to determine a segment in which you excel. Use the fourth question to package the facts, whatever they are, into a position that you can present with confidence and conviction.

Increasing Your Slice of the Market

Nothing attracts business more easily than dominant market share. When you increase your slice of the pie to the point that it dwarfs your competition, the prospects begin to seek you out.

How to define market share

Market share is the percentage of sales that you control in your marketplace. Market share can be based on listings taken, listings sold, buyer sales, sales volume or sales by units. In any case, your share reflects the portion of total market activity that is represented by you or your agency.

How to calculate market share

To calculate your market share, simply divide your or your company's production against the overall production of your marketplace. For example, if 575 homes sold last year in your market area, and if your company sold 215 of those 575, your company handled 37 per cent of all transactions and controls 37 per cent of the market activity (215 ÷ 575 = 0.37).

Also calculate market share in various market segments, following the 'slice and dice' advice described earlier in this chapter. You may find that your overall market share is low but that you have a commanding market share in a certain neighbourhood or price category.

How to increase market penetration

Market penetration is another way to describe market share. If you command a large share of your market, you've achieved significant market penetration. If your market share is minimal, your penetration is minimal, as well.

Focusing on a niche market

A niche is a segment of the overall market. Niche marketers serve a select group of consumers whose interests and needs are distinctly different from the needs of the market in general. Think of niche marketers as big fish in small ponds.

You can create a market niche by serving consumers in a particular geographic area, consumers seeking a certain property type, a certain type of buyer or seller, a certain income category — the list goes on and on. You can create a niche by focusing your efforts and increasing your penetration of for-sale-by-owner properties, expireds or withdrawns, non-owner occupied properties, or residential homes.

Creating niche penetration

The key to gaining penetration in a niche is focus. You have to decide which smaller section of the marketplace you want to work and quit trying to be all things to all people. Then, when you identify your niche, you need to create presence, penetration and dominance, following these steps:

- Make contact with prospects in your niche not just once but repeatedly over a compact period of time.

Studies show that it takes six impressions for a consumer simply to recognise or retain who you are. By increasing both the number and frequency of contacts with prospects, you can increase your market awareness, which is a first step in achieving market penetration.

- Make personal contact. For most agents, the preferred method of contact with people located in a geographic segment is mail. They mail and mail and mail their prospects to death. They send refrigerator magnets, notepads featuring the agent's name and face, local football or cricket game schedules, calendars and more. Guess what? That's not enough to achieve market penetration.

When Terri relocated to a new inner-city agency, she had trouble getting traction and, during the first couple of months, almost gave up with frustration. Then she decided to focus her efforts and stop trying to prospect everywhere. She chose a small part of her area, which offered many character homes close to a major hospital and to a university. She drove this area every day, getting to know it like the back of her hand, and quickly became the area expert on what was for sale, what was sold and what prices were achieved. She started a newsletter that she circulated in the area, offering local news and even vouchers from local businesses. It wasn't long before the phone started ringing with prospective sellers, and she was off and running again!

How to achieve market dominance

To become a dominant market force, you need to take market share from someone else. Dominance involves growing your percentage of the overall marketplace until you control a greater share of market business than any competitor. In markets that are shared by a great number of competitors, a 10 per cent share might be dominant. In situations where fewer competitors exist, you might need 30 per cent or even a higher share in order to be the dominant player.

To gain market share and dominance, first you need to gain recognition, which results almost automatically from simply doing more than you're expected to do:

- Do more personal prospecting.
- Create more useable market and industry information.
- Have more communication with your clients.
- Do more for your community by sponsoring picnics, football or cricket teams, or community events and festivals, as a few examples.

Doing more than is expected will earn you recognition and create a buzz about how you're different. Your reputation will be enhanced. Suddenly, rather than being an unknown agent you'll be a 'name', a known entity.

Then, with the confidence you build through your awareness-development efforts, go one step further. What about a local newsletter for your area, promoting local businesses (which will often contribute with free vouchers or discounted offers)? Be sure to include your new listings and sales (even those from your whole team because this shows you're active in the area). Go that step further and dare to do things that no-one else is willing to do.

By taking each of the preceding steps — choosing a market segment, establishing contact, gaining awareness, establishing personal rapport, going beyond the expected and daring to be different in your communication approaches — over a period of 18 to 24 months, you will penetrate your target market niche and be well on your way to achieving market dominance.

Conveying Your Competitive Advantage in Prospect Presentations

Let's start with the bottom line first: The whole purpose of a prospect presentation is to establish your competitive advantage. In the least time possible, you want to communicate what makes you different from the rest. You want your prospects to see exactly why they should hire you, what's in it for them and why they should proceed with confidence to sign your listing agreement.

Most agents spend the presentation explaining what they will *do* for the client rather than focusing on the *results* the client can expect the agent to deliver. Website pages, home magazines, dazzling flyers, and a line-up of other marketing items are tactics that, in truth, nearly all agents use in the normal course of business. They're not competitive advantages. In fact, you must assume before a listing presentation that every agent will promise a near-identical marketing plan.

So why will they hire you over the others? They'll hire you because they see what's in it for them. And what's in it for them is the set of benefits they receive as a result of your proven competitive position.

To differentiate yourself in the field of real estate sales you need to create, define and consistently convey a competitive position that positively distinguishes you from your competition.

By knowing and exploiting the difference between your products and services and those of your competitors, you'll attract more prospects, win more clients, grow your market share, increase your revenue, expand your profits and, eventually, weaken your competitors.

To pinpoint your unique competitive position, answer these questions:

- Are there key statistics that set you apart from your competitors and provide you with a clear point of difference?
- Do any of your Big Three statistics create a unique competitive position?
  1. Average list price to sale price
  2. Days on the market
  3. Listings taken versus listings sold
- What benefits or values do consumers receive only when they deal with you?
- Do you have dominant or strong market share in a geographic region?
- Do you specialise in a particular property type?
- Is your market share success tied to a particular price point?
- When representing sellers, do you achieve quantifiably higher sale prices?
- When representing buyers, do you achieve quantifiable savings in sale price?

Your answers don't need to lead to 20 unique competitive positions. You only need half a dozen reasons the consumer — whether you're presenting to a buyer or a seller — should choose you over everyone else. Focus only on advantages that matter to your prospect. Keep in mind the old sales adage: 'It's easier to sell to someone what they want to buy, than what you have to sell them.'

Chapter 14

Keeping Clients for Life

In This Chapter

- Realising your clients' lifetime value
- Creating lasting, loyal client relationships
- Winning client loyalty with amazing after-the-sale service

Every businessperson wants to win clients for life — and there's good reason for that. It costs energy, time and money to gain awareness in your chosen marketplace, gain attention when every other agent is trying to do the very same thing, convince potential clients of the benefits of doing business with you, and invite them into your trusted business circle through an initial listing, sale or property management transaction. If that first sale is the only sale you ever make to that client, your sales investment has only a one-time payoff. But if that client keeps listing, selling or buying from you on a repeated basis — and refers others to you, as well — your investment is exponentially increased over numerous transactions and money-making opportunities. Not only this, but you will also enjoy your work so much more than if you were out there hassling for new business every day.

The trick is to make yourself indispensable. Today's consumer has access to a broad array of real estate information. From an almost unlimited ability to search properties on websites such as agent sites, company sites, `www.realestate.com.au`, `www.domain.com.au`, `www.realestate.co.nz` and others, the public has gained a do-it-yourself mentality when it comes to real estate information. The traditional idea of using a real estate agent to 'find our dream home' has shifted. Many sellers no longer call agents in for an interview, preferring to attend open houses and the like, conducting their own research on many agents and, when required, finally choosing one based on their experience when dealing with each agent.

The do-it-yourself mentality has created a shift in referrals and repeat clients. Other factors contributing to that decline in referral-based business include economic shifts, job relocations and a market change that has resulted in many experiencing a lack of equity in their properties — which could now be worth less than what owners paid in the first place. This lack of equity has caused many homeowners to get stuck with houses they must rent out rather than sell. More than ever, your past clients need the long-term service and value transfer that you can offer.

Some businesses have an easier time keeping clients in their business circles, simply because they have more opportunities to see and serve their customers. For instance, a car dealership sells a car and then, even if the buyer doesn't purchase another car for a decade, the dealership often has the opportunity to see the customer face to face every time the vehicle is due for service, oil changes or tyre rotations.

A real estate agent also makes big sales on an infrequent basis to clients. The difference is that in real estate, after-the-sale service isn't automatic. You have to create strategies to keep in contact with your clients and continually remind them of the value you deliver. That's what this chapter is all about.

Achieving Relationship Excellence

As a real estate agent, your success depends on the quality and durability of the relationships you build with your clients, and the one and only way to build solid, enduring relationships is to deliver excellent, unrivalled service. To be an outstanding agent, you need to lavish your clients with service that exceeds their expectations — from the get-go and throughout a long business relationship.

The key to winning clients for life is to avoid defections. When a former customer decides to buy or sell with another agent, you have a defection. When a client doesn't join your referral team, that's a defection as well. Don't waste your time complaining about it — for some reason, your client has decided to go elsewhere, and you must critically examine the level of after-sale service you have given.

The challenge is that not all clients expect or want the same kind of service. What constitutes excellent service to one client may seem inadequate or even like overkill to another.

It seems hard to imagine, but an agent can sell a client's home in less than a week, at full price, and still have a dissatisfied customer because of some action or oversight during the negotiation, inspection or closing that simply didn't match with the client's service expectations. Perhaps the speed of the sale has made them unhappy with the price (at full listing price!) and worry that you should have listed higher and they have been 'robbed'. In this situation, you are the one in the firing line — most sellers don't accept responsibility for these kinds of decisions, believing if something appears to have gone wrong, it is almost always the agent's fault!

To avoid service mismatches, learn each person's service expectations by doing something that few agents take time to do: Ask. Then put your findings to work, following these steps:

- **Learn each person's service expectations.** Before you enter a new prospect presentation, make it a rule to learn everything you can about what your prospects are looking for in an agent and how they define excellent service. If you're not sure how to do this, have a quick look at Chapter 9 — we provide heaps of tips there for you.
- **Customise and personalise your service delivery.** In your initial presentation and in subsequent contacts — whether you're working to make the sale, service the client, build an after-the-sale relationship, or request a referral — refer to your initial research and highlight the service aspects that each client finds important. Weave in the words you heard them use to define great service. Highlight the communication points they described as essential service attributes. Let them know that you understand their needs and are focused on exceeding their expectations.

- **Never get complacent.** Don't assume that if your service falls a bit short your best clients will simply turn a blind eye. And by all means, don't think that if your clients want more or better service they will say something to you. They won't, because they don't want the confrontation. They'd rather just go away quietly and never come back. As the saying goes, 'people vote with their feet'.

Of course, we've both seen agents who are successful in spite of their 'my way or the highway' approach to service delivery, and you'll likely come across these agents too. Rather than focusing on customised service and long-term relationships, these agents prefer to serve a stream of here-today-gone-tomorrow clients that they acquire through relentless prospecting and high-volume lead development. These agents have a take-it-or-leave-it attitude about service. They practise what we call a fast-food burger-joint philosophy: 'We sell burgers and fries, and if you don't like burgers and fries, pick another restaurant.' The difference, of course, is that the number of people who want burgers and fries is huge and, if the fare is good, most customers automatically come back for more. The same is hardly true when it comes to home buyers and sellers.

As an agent, your prospect universe is limited, and your customers aren't apt to become repeat customers unless they're treated with the kind of unparalleled, consistent and customised service that turns them into clients for life.

Using the internet to generate leads may seem like a good move at first, but it doesn't lead to relationships and referrals. Agents who use internet lead-generation stealth systems such as www.listinginnovations.com.au, the lead generator available through www.agent.realestate.com.au, or similar, usually rely too heavily on these systems and don't develop repeat and referral strategies.

When Terri worked in inner-city suburbs in Brisbane, she used an online lead-generation program that advertised free appraisals to prospective sellers. Interested parties would send an inquiry and then be referred on to Terri as 'the preferred area agent'. While she did get some appraisals, in the end it was the personal contact at her open houses that gave Terri the most listing success.

Defining your service standards

When you deliver excellent service on a consistent and ongoing basis, your current client relationships will lead to repeat business and referrals that draw new clients into your business. As a result, your success will breed yet more success, your business will grow bigger, and you'll need to provide superb service to an ever-growing group of people. At some point you'll face the important but difficult task of transitioning from an individual service provider to a service provider who works with a team to communicate with and serve clients.

If you're just starting out, your main focus should be on carving out your own niche and excelling in the service you provide. When the time comes to expand, you will know it.

Making the shift from do-it-yourself service delivery to delivery that's leveraged through an agent team is an essential turning point in a successful agent's business. It's also a dangerous point, for these reasons:

- Even though you know it's necessary to leverage your service ability by assigning tasks to others on your team, you may find it difficult to release ownership. This inability to let go can result in service lapses and frustration among both staff members and clients.
- Unless you clearly establish and communicate your service philosophy and program to those on your team, you risk delivering an inconsistent or lower level of service to your clients. You can fall into the trap of 'spinning your wheels' as you try to fill the agenda for your team rather than focusing on what you do personally.

The remedy to both of these pitfalls is simple: Your first task is to define and communicate the kind of service that you and your team stand for before you share responsibility for service delivery. Then, be very clear in communicating the job descriptions for each team member.

Choose your team with the objective of combining skills. A common mistake is to choose team members who are 'just like yourself'; doing so means you're likely to all love the same tasks. Who does the ones no-one (including you) wants to do?

To help you to articulate the level of service you want your clients to receive, take some time out from your busy day to answer the following questions:

- **How frequently do you communicate with sellers?**

  The number one complaint consumers have about real estate agents isn't that they charge or make too much money. The number one complaint is that they're bad or infrequent communicators (and unfortunately this is too often the case). Especially if you're representing the seller, understand that your client wants consistent communication. If you're not making a weekly call or a short personal visit to provide an update on the process of the sale, you risk a poor customer relationship. So, you need to outline your client service strategy:

  - How frequently do you make calls, send emails or email written reports?
  - What is your process for sending sellers copies of your marketing pieces for their property?
  - Do you provide sellers with links to virtual tours or websites promoting their property? Do you make it easy for them to see, feel and touch what you're doing?
  - How often do you meet face to face, and do the meetings take place in the sellers' home or in your office?

- **How do you receive and share feedback from showings?**

  - Do you call your seller after every single buyer inspection to give some feedback? They're likely waiting anxiously for this call, so don't disappoint them.
  - Do you have a link to a site or other software that can give the seller feedback from agents in real time, and can you give sellers access to your marketing 24/7 just by going online?

  - Do you relay showing feedback to the seller right away, or do you collect feedback to share in a once-a-week meeting? Feedback after every inspection will win you lots of kudos.

- **What marketing strategy do you employ for each property you list?**
  - Do you work with conjunction agents and, if so, do you send details of newly listed properties in case those agents have the perfect buyer?
  - How do you generate awareness and interest within the pool of real estate buyers?
  - How do you promote the property online? How many sites is the property marketed to, and can you easily create a traffic report to share with the sellers?
  - What marketing techniques and systems do you employ to attract qualified buyers to your seller's property?
  - Do you have a marketing plan that's flexible for the needs of your seller but will result in the very best outcome possible?

Figures 14-1 and 14-2 toward the end of this chapter help you create checklists that everyone on your team can use and follow. When you're clear about what you stand for and how you deliver service to clients, you're in a position to train those on your team to deliver on your behalf and to your standards. At that point, your transition from a one-person service provider to professional service team is complete. Congratulations!

Promising, then flawlessly delivering

It's one thing to have a service delivery plan. It's another thing to implement your plan on a never-fail basis. Anyone can create a super-duper marketing package — the trick is creating one you actually use. Most include 30-point, 50-point, or 100-point service action plans provided by the company the agent works for or created by the agent herself. Ask yourself, 'Will I really do all of these things?' The reality is that you will probably implement fewer than 30 per cent of the service tasks listed on your marketing plan.

Over-promising is easy, but then you lose track of what you said you'd do because you lack a system to follow.

Our advice is this: Go through the multi-point action plan you currently provide to sellers and separate out the highest-value activities that you know you can perform with total consistency. Then commit to always perform those tasks and be ready to execute flawlessly on your commitment.

Be ready to under-promise and over-deliver.

The separation between marginal performance and stellar performance doesn't come from an abundance of magical extras. It's the result of keeping your commitments. For the vast majority of consumers, a professional who keeps commitments is a rarity.

Viewing settlement as a starting point, not a finish line

Great agents know that their job isn't over when the sale settles. After you've negotiated the sale, closed the deal, banked the commission cheque and spent the money, it's time to start fortifying your client relationship. Sure, you need to get on to the next income-producing activity. But as you cultivate your next deal, don't make the mistake of turning your back on the clients you just served.

Your clients may actually need you more after the settlement than at any previous point in your relationship for any of the following reasons:

- After moving into their new home, they may discover repair issues that need attention. They may need the name of someone who can fix their roof, or they may need the names of service providers who are honest, trustworthy and fair and who do quality repair work. Providing your clients with approved suppliers and contractors is an excellent way to add value to your service.
- Your clients' home purchase may have sparked thoughts about building wealth through real estate investments. They may be thinking about how to secure their retirement or how to create a nest egg for their children's further education. If your clients view real estate as a piece in their wealth puzzle, they may seek your advice about how to acquire and retain properties as a key step toward wealth creation.
- Your clients may simply be interested in how the market around them is doing. When you call them to chat, you're likely to get the question, 'How's the market?' or 'What's happening in the marketplace?' Now that they're homeowners, your clients are vested in the local real estate marketplace. Become their resource and you'll be first in line when they're ready to make the next physical or investment move. You may want to provide an ongoing market update to all past clients. This market update should show inventory, supply and demand numbers, and key opportunities in the marketplace. It truly affirms the position that you're a market expert.

After reading through this list, you may wonder why an agent needs to be told that the settlement must be viewed as the first step toward a long client relationship and countless service opportunities. The reason is that research shows this is an area of agent deficiency.

Unfortunately, industry stats reek of poor after-the-sale communication and woefully short relationship development. The only logical conclusion is that, in general, after-the-sale service in the real estate industry is way less than satisfactory. The next section helps you break the stereotype.

Creating After-the-Sale Service

If you don't plan for it, after-the-sale service won't happen. You'll get so consumed with the next deal and with the task of earning the next commission check that you'll overlook the opportunity to create long-term revenue through your past clients.

An after-the-sale service program is like most things in life: People get derailed before they take the first step, and if they don't take the first step — the step that involves establishing the program they commit to follow — they can't begin to meet the objective.

Use the upcoming section to guide you as you create your plan. It helps you define exactly what you need to do in the first 45 days after the sale and on an ongoing basis thereafter.

In it for the long haul

It used to be the case that most property in Australia and New Zealand would turnover every seven years, but this figure is much higher now. The cost of moving and buying again is causing many homeowners to instead consider staying put and perhaps planning extensions or renovations to improve what they already have. This means that you must be in it for the very long term if you're building a referral- and repeat-based business. You must make the effort to be top of mind when the opportunity comes for your past clients to move on. Regular newsletters — that don't apply sales pressure but do allow you to keep in touch and remind them that you're still around and active — are vital or you will be forgotten and passed over.

Laying the groundwork during the transaction period

When working a real estate transaction, you have two prime opportunities to develop interpersonal connections and high-grade referrals. One is during the transaction period when you're working with your client to buy or sell a home and take it to a successful settlement. The second is during the 30 to 45 days that follow the closing. And this is what many agents forget.

If you do a poor job during the transaction, you'll be hard pressed to recover lost ground after the settlement. A barrister who blows a case doesn't get a second chance from the client, and the same holds true for real estate agents. Your service during the transaction must be awesome, or you'll sacrifice the chance for repeat and referral business, which is the easiest and least costly business to acquire. If that isn't bad enough, you'll also lose the opportunity to collect client testimonials and generate positive word of mouth.

During the transaction period you're in frequent contact with your clients and have ample opportunities to provide excellent service, make a strong, positive impression, and develop the basis for a long-term relationship by following these steps:

- When you begin to work with clients to buy or sell a home, their enthusiasm is high. They fully anticipate and expect that they'll be able to either sell their beautiful property at a great price or, alternatively, find the perfect home to purchase, and that you're the ideal agent to accomplish the task. During this initial period, your clients think about little other than their real estate hopes. Your presence becomes woven into the fabric of their lives and their conversations with friends and family members. This is an ideal time to ask for and win referrals.

- If the sale or purchase process drags on, expect your clients' level of excitement and energy to ebb. At the same time, expect their focus on their purchase or sale to intensify. The most important thing you can do during this potentially dangerous time — when your clients are experiencing concern and talking non-stop about their real estate issues with others — is to stay in frequent communication, offer solutions, provide calm, professional advice, and retain the clients' confidence in you and your abilities.

Flip back to the section titled 'Defining your service standards' as you establish a plan that ensures frequent and professional contact throughout the transaction period.

Setting a service agenda for the first 30 to 45 days after settlement

If you did everything right during the transaction (and if you're using this book as a resource, we're going to assume you did), then your clients were totally satisfied with your service when the deal settled. Now you have a decision to make: Do you wish your clients well and walk away, or do you begin an after-the-sale service program that turns them into clients for life? You've seen this chapter's title, so you already know the answer: You begin to turn them into clients for life. Use the following process:

1. **Begin by personally calling your clients at least four times in the 30 to 45 days after settlement.**

   - Call in the first few days after settlement to thank them for the opportunity to have worked with them. Tell them how excited you are for them to be moving into their new home. Share an anecdote about working with them that will make you all laugh and touch their hearts.
   - After the call, send a handwritten thank-you note further expressing your thanks and asking for future business or referrals.
   - By the end of the first week, call again. Once again, express thanks for trusting you. Then ask: How did the move go? Did anything get broken? How do the kids like their new rooms? Have they met any of the neighbourhood kids yet? Did the seller leave the home properly? Is there anything that wasn't right that they need any help with?

   Asking if they need help with anything can open a Pandora's Box of issues, and that's exactly why to ask it. If there are problems you don't know about, you may be blamed for the mishaps without any opportunity to do anything about them. Most will be issues between the seller and the buyer, and the buyer's power over the seller — unless legal action is involved — is gone because the transaction has settled. Sometimes all you can do is provide a listening ear and sympathetic voice. Other times you can make a few phone calls to help right the wrong. The fact that you're willing to listen and see what you can do speaks louder than any demonstrable action. It shows that you care. Some of your most ardent fans will come out of an initial negative situation that you are able to resolve.

   - At the conclusion of the second call, send another handwritten note. Express concern for any unresolved issues and again thank them for their trust and for taking time to talk with you today.

- Call again at the two-week mark. Ask how they are doing getting out of boxes and settling into their new home. Update them if you've made progress on the issue that was concerning them. Ask them about the kids and their transition. Before hanging up, ask if your service is needed. Also, ask them for referrals.
- On their 30-day anniversary in the home, call again. Congratulate them on their great decision in selecting this home. Check on the kids and their progress settling in to the house and neighbourhood. Thank them again for the privilege of working with them.

As simple as this approach sounds, it enables you to lock your clients in for life, plus it opens the door to referral business that flows freely.

2. **While you're at it, call the other party involved in your real estate transaction, as well.**

   Every real estate deal involves a buyer and a seller. In most cases you represent only one of the two parties, but why not call and offer after-sale service to both? Do you think the other agent is doing this? In our experience, fewer than 15 per cent of agents actually call their clients regularly after closing.

   When calling to follow up with the other party in your transaction, be ready for a response of surprise and great appreciation. The fact that you're calling four times in a month, will positively awe most people. You'll be the one receiving their referrals.

3. **Deliver or send a gift to your client.**

   This gift is usually called a settlement gift, but even if you attend settlement at the solicitor's office, don't take the gift with you for two reasons:

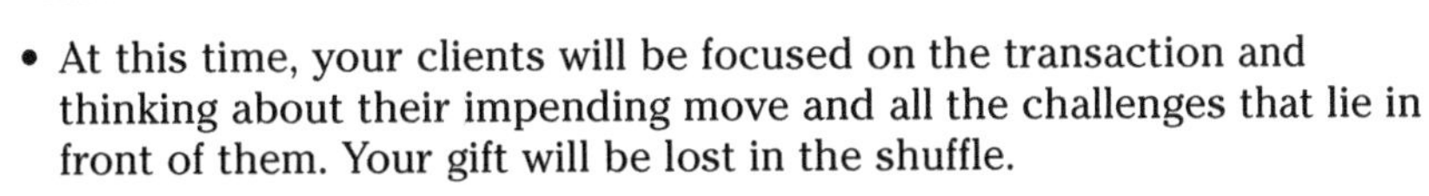

   - At this time, your clients will be focused on the transaction and thinking about their impending move and all the challenges that lie in front of them. Your gift will be lost in the shuffle.

     Normally, you don't need to attend the settlement, so you have a great opportunity to personally deliver your gift afterwards.

   - The papers presented at the settlement put the amount of the real estate commission in writing, causing your clients to focus on exactly how much money you made from the transaction. If you give your gift at the same time, they may make a negative comparison between the value of the gift and the money you received.

   In choosing your gift, don't go overboard. Save any over-the-top gestures you want to extend until after your clients have settled in and after your commission has long-since been paid. The more you deliver after you get paid, the more your gift communicates that you care about your clients, not your commission cheque.

Find a settlement gift that reminds clients of you and your service. Give them something that can be used rather than consumed. A great bottle of wine or gift basket quickly disappears. A customised mailbox, door knocker or yard plant will last almost forever.

By delivering your gift to your clients' new home, you put it in their hands at a time when it can create the most significant feelings of good will and warmth — and the best likelihood of referrals. If you still want to give them something at settlement, hand them a thank-you note instead.

Another nice gesture is to help your clients notify their friends of their move. Offer to create a postcard with a picture of their new home on the front and to print up a few hundred for their use. Then offer to mail them out on your clients' behalf. You'll save them the cost and enlarge your database to boot.

You may even call people on the list to make sure they received the card you sent for your client. You can then ask them if they're committed to another agent. If not, you've opened the door to a new client relationship.

The problem with commissions …

When settlement time arrives, sellers now have to focus on the commission that you are taking for completing the sale. Chances are they've already forgotten the risk you took with your time and money to market their home and the many services you provided. Plus, you made countless efforts they never knew about — such as contact with solicitors, mortgage brokers or financiers, building and pest contractors, other agents, valuers, and all the other people involved to achieve the sale of the home.

Although clients don't understand the hours of work it took to create a smooth transaction, they most certainly understand how much you got paid: The number is presented in black and white at the settlement. They even forget that most of the commission could be going straight to your agency, not into your own pocket. And because most agents do little after the sale, the clients' parting memory is how much you got paid, which isn't exactly a great way to launch a long-term relationship.

The way all agents have to collect their commission makes it more difficult to achieve a high level of warm feelings from clients, and it hardly encourages customer retention. You can't change the industry and the way that commission is paid but you need to be aware of its inherent challenges and to make doubly sure that your last contact with your clients isn't on the day you get paid. After-the-sale service is the best antidote.

Establishing an ongoing communication strategy

After your clients have completed their moves and put their real estate transactions behind them, you still need to be in touch at regular intervals if you want to remain on their radar screens.

Unless you develop a pattern of frequent communication with phone calls, emails, direct mailings and other forms of contact, too many clients (even your best ones) won't remember you at the important moment when they need real estate advice or when their friends need it. You need to remind them that you're still in the business and ready to be of assistance.

Using direct mail

Direct mail is still an effective way to generate business, but only if it gets to the right people and only if it gets opened and read. In fact, direct mail can be even more effective today because of the social-media revolution. Our mailboxes are no longer stuffed with direct mail; it's our email inboxes that are overflowing. Direct mail puts your message in a smaller group where it can have more impact.

Australia Post offers a variety of services for customers sending larger volumes of mail. Usually, if you're sending at least 300 articles at a time, you can qualify for the lower prices available. The postage rate depends on the size of your articles, and the options you choose. A similar service is also available in New Zealand.

Direct mail is also effective with your past clients and sphere of influence. To get your mail to the right people, create a carefully developed list that includes the addresses of past clients and people within your sphere of influence, which basically consists of people you know.

To get your mail opened, make it look personal. People sort their mail with the rubbish bin close by. They rifle through the pile and within seconds put pieces into an A pile that will definitely get attention, a B pile that has a 50/50 chance of getting opened or the bin. Your objective is to get into the A pile.

To get your mail into the A pile, try putting these tips to work:

- Send your correspondence on notecard-sized pieces.
- Handwrite the envelope address. Avoid computer labels or, if you must use labels because your writing resembles hieroglyphs, use clear labels that are almost invisible and at a glance allow your address to appear typed onto the envelope.

- Send special-occasion cards. Use the clients' anniversary, the anniversary of the day they moved into their home, Mother's Day, Father's Day and birthdays to reinforce your connection with the clients and remind them that you care. Also send thank-you or 'just thinking about you' cards.

Don't expect your direct-mail program to just happen spontaneously. Plan it out a year in advance. Select about half a dozen times over the course of the year to send handwritten cards to past clients or people in your sphere. Program the dates and the nature of the mailers into your database to remind you when to do it. And then do it.

Staying in touch via email

Email provides an easy and cost-effective way to deliver your correspondence to your prospects and clients, so long as you create a good list full of recipients who want and have given you permission to send them your mailings.

Establish at least two databases of email addresses:

- One database should include the names and addresses of all prospects who have given you permission to send them email messages. When mailing to these people, you're trying to generate interest and confidence and to coax them into a relationship with you. The text in their messages is sales oriented and articulates reasons they should take action in the real estate market now. Mailers may focus on appreciation rates, listing stock levels, interest rates and projections of future rate increases. Back up any information with solid evidence — don't use the crystal ball. Additionally, each mailer should include a concise statement about the value of doing business with you, why they should hire you and the benefits they will receive from working with you over the competition.
- A second database should include the names and addresses of past clients and those in your sphere of influence, which includes friends, family members and professional associates. When mailing to this group, tone down your sales message. You still want to provide an update on current and emerging market conditions, and most certainly you still want to convey the value you deliver, you just want to do it all with a softer, more personal approach. Your purpose when mailing to this group is to generate referrals. By sharing marketplace facts, you provide them with information they can use in their conversations with friends.

When mailing to your databases, put the following advice to work:

- A newsletter still has value in today's blog-centred world. Send a monthly newsletter. Choose a template from your word-processing program or one of countless third-party resources. Your customer relationship manager (CRM) should also have one of these for you. Then all you have to do is fill in the text area with a customised message.
- Develop content that is solid, helpful, positive and valuable. It doesn't have to be earthshaking in terms of news value. And it doesn't have to be written in award-winning prose. It just needs to be current, customised to your local market conditions, and capable of making a good impression over the few minutes between when it's opened and when it's deleted.

- Avoid email blasts that send identical messages to a long list of addresses. If you're sending without a dedicated email program, be careful to address the main letter to yourself and put the other addresses in the BCC section for privacy. Work to personalise the notes you send. A dedicated email marketing system can address each message by name. Your clients are well versed in email and know exactly how much (or little) time and effort goes into a communication that involves absolutely no personalisation. Subconsciously, they'll translate the mass mailing as a definition of the quality of your relationship with them. For that reason alone, use mass emails sparingly.

A few necessary words about spam

Spam, or unrequested, unwanted email, is the scourge of the online world. In Australia, the *Spam Act 2003* prohibits the sending of any spam with an Australian link. The Act defines spam as unsolicited commercial electronic messages and that message has an Australian link if it originates or was commissioned in Australia, or originates overseas but was sent to an address accessed in Australia.

In New Zealand, the Department of Internal Affairs has an Anti-Spam Compliance Unit, specifically introduced to investigate complaints about unsolicited electronic messages and alleged breaches of the *Unsolicited Electronic Messages Act 2007*.

No matter where you live, the general requirements remain the same. Legislation requires, among other things, that anyone who sends unsolicited email must follow some clearly stated rules. The sender must be clearly identified, the email must include a valid physical postal address, the message must present a means for the recipient to opt out or unsubscribe, and the person or organisation sending the mailer must honour unsubscribe requests within a specific time frame. Be sure your mailings comply.

Picking up the phone

In your effort to stay in touch, add value and generate referrals, you want to pick up the phone and call some of your contacts weekly, some monthly and maybe some only one time each year. To organise the effort, create phone lists that are segmented by the level of connection and frequency of contact you have with each group.

- Your star clients and closest friends and associates deserve star treatment. These people are sold on you and the service you provide. They want to help you advance your career. They're happy to hear from you, and they're likely to send you more referrals than you'll get from any other portion of your contact list. It's okay to treat them differently than everyone else. In fact, it's good business. Call those in this category monthly or at least one time every other month, and weave a referral request into each conversation.
- Past clients and those in your sphere of influence should be called at least once a year. Unless you have an enormous database, anyone you have serviced in your career should hear from you personally at least once every 12 months.

Don't hesitate to pick up the phone and make calls just to thank people for their business, see how they're doing, and ask if there's anything you can do for them. Most consumers, when called by a service provider, are delighted and honoured by the contact. If you got a friendly call out of the blue from your insurance agent, solicitor, accountant or financial advisor, you'd be both surprised and pleased. The same is likely to be the case when you call your clients.

Writing the thank-you note

One of the most powerful forces in the business world is a handwritten thank-you note. That may sound terribly 'old school' to tech-savvy agents, but it's exactly what you need to send if you want to set yourself apart.

Back in the 'olden days' (before email and smart phones), writing thank-you notes was a standard operating procedure. Today, thank-you notes arrive rarely, and as a result they carry far more weight. They convey, in essence, 'You matter so much that I took the time to write a message with my own hand.'

Exceeding expectations

The keys to exceeding expectations are few and pretty obvious: Extend courtesy. Say thanks. Demonstrate appreciation. And always be professional and keep in mind that little gestures go a long way toward building strong relationships.

You don't have to go overboard. Small gifts like ice-cream vouchers for the children, movie tickets for the adults or coffee-shop coupons make the point that you appreciate working with your contacts and receiving their referrals, whether they result in business or not.

Keep your efforts in line with your professional image. Getting groceries for out-of-town clients is thoughtful but inappropriate for a professional; helping arrange for a personal shopper is thoughtful and professional. Mowing the lawn for sellers who live interstate is thoughtful but unprofessional; arranging for a professional yard crew is thoughtful and professional.

Customising your messages

From an early age, every child learns the Golden Rule: Treat others the way you want to be treated. Customer service pros replace the Golden Rule with the Platinum Rule: Treat others the way they *wish* to be treated.

The Platinum Rule was coined by speaker/trainer Tony Alessandra, who explains that a salesperson's job is not to treat and serve clients as *you* want to be treated but as *they* want to be treated.

The only way to know how a person wants to be treated is to ask and observe. Different kinds of customers have different values and service expectations. A one-time client expects a different level of attention than is expected by a long-time client. A busy executive expects more efficiency than is expected or even desired by a person with a fairly empty calendar.

Know yourself. Understanding your natural style and strategy for sales and business is imperative. We all follow some basic individual patterns. If you want to know more about yourself, try a behavioural assessment. (Dirk has one on his website that you can take for free — `www.realestatechampions.com/freeDISC`.) By discovering and recognising your communication style, decision-making style and expectations, you can supercharge your business. You can modify your service and selling style and strategy to better meet the needs of your clients and prospects.

Understanding the difference between unique and one-size-fits-all communications

The difference between junk mail and personal mail boils down to a single question: Is the message targeted and tailored to the interests of the recipient, or could it just as easily be sent out with an address label that reads 'occupant'?

The more you segment your database, the better you'll be able to customise the messages you send. Prospects, clients and those in your sphere have different information needs. Likewise, those with various interests will respond to different kinds of messages.

Segment your mailing list by the nature of your relationship with the contact and also by the recipients' lifestyle facts such as children or no children, age group, special interests and faith, to name a few categories. Then with a few keystrokes you can pull up address lists of people with shared interests and information needs. You can send a great article on golf to all the golfing enthusiasts in your database. You can send an invitation to a family-oriented event to all prospects with children. You can be sure that every mailer that leaves your office conveys that you know and care enough about the recipient's interests to send appropriately tailored information.

Dealing with one-time or transactional clients

A transactional client isn't looking for a long-term relationship with a business or service provider. Transactional clients simply want to complete a deal. Their eye is on the bottom line, and their decisions are based on dollars and cents. When the real estate marketplace is robust, expect to encounter a good many transactional clients.

In his book *Rethinking the Sales Force*, Neil Rackham outlines the key characteristics of transactional clients:

- Transactional clients view service as standard and readily substitutable.
- The transactional buyer's primary concerns are the price and ease of acquisition.
- The timing of a transactional purchase is triggered by a specific event, rather than by a whim.
- The key nature of the relationship is cost-based, and the relationship can be contractual.

In serving transactional clients, ask yourself whether you can turn enough of a profit off this single transaction to make the effort worthwhile, because the chance of repeat business is slim. You may, with your memorable service, turn a transactional client into a relationship client, but the odds are not great. This kind of client is primarily motivated by the cost of your service. If the numbers don't fly, the level of your relationship won't matter.

Dealing with long-term or relationship clients

Relationship clients are clients who give you the opportunity to serve them on a repeated basis. Unlike transactional clients, relationship clients view their contact with you as part of an ongoing relationship. Unlike their transactional brethren, relationship clients expect to do business with you again. You can also expect referrals to their friends.

When dealing with relationship clients, be aware of what matters most:

- They are focused on how your characteristics are different from others and how your services are customised and unique. They want the benefits that you provide to help them solve their problem.
- The price of your service is not their highest concern. The solution you provide carries equal or more weight than the cost.
- They are willing to consider price and performance trade-offs to arrive at a lower-risk, higher-probability outcome.
- They respond favourably to the service and communication aspects of your business.
- They expect and require a high level of customer service.
- They have a cooperative attitude and want to work together with you toward a common goal.

You can wish all you want, but the truth is that not all clients fit into the relationship category. You'll meet agent trainers who tell you to work only with people in this category, but you'd be foolish to limit your business so significantly.

If you place your service emphasis on buyer clients, odds are good that you can win a preponderance of relationship clients. But if you're a listings agent who works primarily with sellers, get ready to deal with a good many transactional clients. The difference: Sellers pay the fees to real estate agents, so they're often more focused on the commission rate than the service. Stay in the business long enough and you'll watch relationship-oriented buyer clients adopt the traits of transactional clients. As your buyer clients become sellers, their purchasing traits shift too.

Establishing Awesome Service

A service encounter happens any time a consumer interacts with a servicing organisation. Every website hit or incoming ad or sign call is a service encounter. When a prospect talks to you, your team, your company receptionist, your principal, your buyer's agent, your PA or anyone on your service team, that person is having a service encounter.

If one person in the long chain of people who help you get your job done says or does anything negative, it affects the impression of the nature of the service you provide. There's no way to separate yourself from your colleagues if they mess up. It's even possible for your service to be tainted by those outside your service team. Your future business and referral opportunities can be affected by the actions of someone entirely outside your influence. You need look no further than the repercussions when an agent is featured negatively in a current affairs television program or in print media — everyone in the industry is labelled with the same negative connotations, especially those under the same franchise brand.

To direct your service encounters toward superb outcomes, follow these steps:

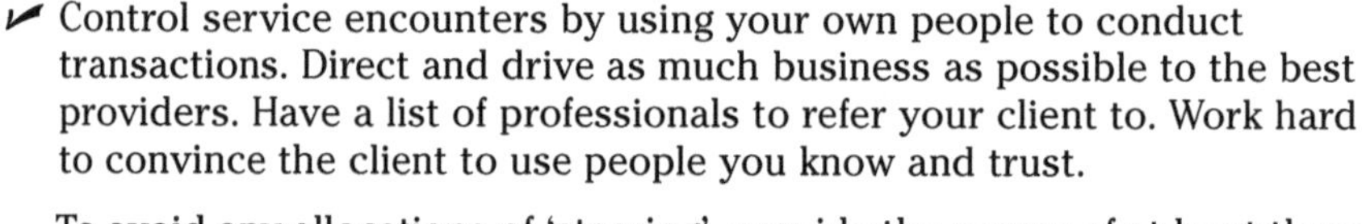

- Control service encounters by using your own people to conduct transactions. Direct and drive as much business as possible to the best providers. Have a list of professionals to refer your client to. Work hard to convince the client to use people you know and trust.

  To avoid any allocations of 'steering', provide the names of at least three individuals or companies you trust in the area required, and declare this interest to your clients on an appropriate form if required.

- If possible, make sure your clients work with lenders who know their stuff and are responsive. Be aware that the lender triggers the choke point in most transactions. Take time to counsel your clients toward a resource you know will perform.
- Have a plan for recovering from service disasters if necessary. If your client is reasonable, no situation is too far gone to salvage. In fact, handle the problem well and you're apt to turn a disgruntled client into one of your most vocal supporters. Take these steps:
  - Do what is necessary to right the wrong.
  - Find out from the client what it will take to turn the unsatisfactory situation into a satisfactory outcome. Ask what it will take for them

to be delighted. Be cautious here. Forgoing a fee or reducing a cost doesn't usually create a more satisfied client. The service and the cost are not linked at this stage of customer satisfaction.

- Avoid the blame game. If you point out that it was the client's decision to use the service provider who caused the problem, you only make the situation worse. Conveying that 'I told you so' is never a way to soothe feelings.
- Follow up. Eventually sore feelings will wane, but the only way to replace the negative impression is to make a better one through continuous and professional contact. In the early stages after the sale mishap, you may not see many referrals, but when they start to come through you'll know that your service recovery plan was a success.
- If you can't turn the situation around, don't concede your profit. In other words, don't take this as a signal to reduce your commission. Some clients only feel placated if they get into your wallet and win cash compensation. If you did something that caused them to be hurt financially, you may have to make this up to them. Most of the time, though, that won't be the case. Before you ever give up your hard-earned money, ask yourself three questions:
  1. Will offering a discounted commission really turn this client into a raving fan?
  2. Is there another way to turn this client into a raving fan?
  3. Is there a reasonable chance that I'll win future business and referrals from this person?

  If your answers don't cause you to feel confident that giving up money will net a future return at a low risk, keep the cash in your pocket.

Dirk is an ardent supporter of Hyatt hotels, and a good part of the reason is that years ago they took a bad situation and turned it around. He'd flown to Tampa, Florida, from Bend, Oregon, which entailed leaving at 6 in the morning and arriving in Tampa sometime after 7 at night. He was tired and hungry and faced a full schedule the next day. From the airport, he called for the shuttle van three times before it showed up 45 minutes later. Dirk's last call had gotten through to the manager on duty. She was sympathetic to his weary travel story, but he expected only a listening ear.

When he arrived at the hotel, which was less than ten minutes from the airport, the manager greeted Dirk as he stepped off the bus. She told him she had already personally checked him in. She walked Dirk to a wonderful room where wine, cheese and fruit were waiting. While walking to the room, she took a genuine interest in his day and travel trials. She later sent up a tray of desserts. She knew how to create a raving fan out of what could have been a lost situation.

Developing a service plan

The best way to provide the level of service you and your client agree upon is to create two checklists — a New Listing checklist that details the steps you will follow when accepting a listing, and a Sale Agreement checklist that details all the steps that happen from contract to close.

Figures 14-1 and 14-2 present samples of each of these checklists to guide you as you develop forms that work for your own business. Although the samples included in this book will be 90 per cent accurate for your situation, you need to customise them to fit the requirements of your country, state, region and industry code of ethics.

NEW LISTING CHECKLIST

Seller ______________________________

Address ______________________________

Within Two Days of Listing

At the House:

☐ Make duplicate key ☐ Take photo

In the Office:

☐ Order sign up
☐ Submit listing to office
☐ Fill in information on listing folder
☐ Log listing in current listing log book with copy of listing
☐ Obtain and keep:
  – Property disclosure/disclaimer
☐ Create flyer
☐ Add property to internet ad
☐ Add client to database or change ID/status to 'Current Listing'
☐ Communicate with sellers
  – Send thank you note
  – include:
    ☐ Copy of all their listing forms ☐ Sellers agency disclosure
    ☐ Listing agreement ☐ Property disclosure or disclaimer
☐ Send 'Just Listed' cards
☐ Place home on Office Tour ___ Confirm ________ Date Toured
☐ Place home on Agents Tour ___ Confirm ________ Date Toured
☐ Include listing on Pre-Scheduled Ad form

In the Future

☐ Keep track of showings ☐ Send copies of ads to clients
☐ Track when and where ads run ☐ Follow up with agents
☐ Keep copies of ads on file ☐ Follow up with clients

Figure 14-1: Customise this checklist to reflect the steps you follow with a new listing.

SALE AGREEMENT CHECKLIST

Close Date ______________________ Sales Price ______________________

Seller ______________________

Buyer ______________________

Property Sold ______________________

- ☐ Complete sales transaction sheet
- ☐ Complete trust monies agreement
  - Submit ☐ Original (listing side) or ☐ Copy (buyer's side) to office administrator
  - ☐ Send originals to listing agent, if applicable
- ☐ Trust monies $__________ Held by: ______________
- ☐ Complete buyer/seller agency disclosure forms. Submit original to administator
- ☐ Submit 'Sale Pending' addendum to the office
- ☐ Send copy of property disclosure to ☐ Seller ☐ Buyer
- ☐ Receive fully signed property disclosure
  - Submit ☐ Original (listing side) or ☐ Copy (buyer's side)
- ☐ Note deadlines for conditional clauses in diary or calendar
- ☐ Record information on agents, lender, settlement and buyers or sellers on file folder
- ☐ Sent settlement letter to clients with copies of their paperwork
- ☐ Send copy of sale agreement and preliminary title report to lender
- ☐ Check internet listing to make sure the property is listed as 'Under Contract'
- ☐ Schedule inspection dates:
  - Building and pest inspection ______________ Completed ______________
  - Finance approval ______________ Completed ______________
  - Other conditions ______________ Completed ______________
- ☐ Put up sold sticker

Sale Closes

- ☐ Deliver keys to buyers
- ☐ Order post sign down
- ☐ Submit 'Sold' addendum to office
- ☐ Update buyers and sellers information in database to 'Past Clients' category
- ☐ Send thank you note to seller and/or buyer

Figure 14-2: Customise this checklist to reflect the steps you follow from contract to closing.

Following Settlement

- ☐ Contact past client one day after settlement to ask for referrals
- ☐ Contact past client three days after settlement to ask for referrals
- ☐ Contact past client seven days after settlement to ask for referrals
- ☐ Prepare closing statement letter
- ☐ Contact past client 30 days after settlement to ask for referrals

Commission Due __________ + __________ (Processing Fee)= ______________

Remember to follow-up weekly with lenders and agents

Extending extra touches that create gold

A whole book could be written on the topic of customer service. One important thing to remember is that a little extra service goes a long way.

Ask the agents in your office what extra touches work for them. Ask your principal what they think falls into this category. Following are two favourites: One that is extended right after settlement and one that works well for long-term clients:

- Right after settlement, arrange for two hours of complimentary small repair work or perhaps gardening or lawn maintenance. The cost of this much-appreciated added value is usually only about $100, and the perceived value is huge. More often than not, clients use more time than the amount covered by your gift, so the service provider acquires new clients and as a result will probably give you a great deal on the time they sell to you.

  Also, by sending in a repairer, you help the clients resolve small issues that weren't handled at settlement — before they fester into something bigger that leads to frustration with the transaction, which leads to frustration with you. This idea is an inexpensive win–win.
- For long-term clients, consider buying four season tickets to an event series you enjoy in your town — perhaps Gold Class movie tickets, the symphony, theatre or sporting matches.

Chapter 15

Maximising Your Time

In This Chapter

- Steering clear of time-wasting activities
- Tracking your time and using time-blocking tools to power through your day
- Putting an end to procrastination
- Generating the greatest return on the time you invest in your business

The most significant challenge in an entrepreneurial business like real estate sales is managing time effectively. The daily battle against procrastination, distractions, interruptions, low-priority activities and ingrained customer expectations of instant accessibility can exhaust even the most energetic agent and can derail the plans of all but the most disciplined time manager. You may be an agent working in someone else's business but, unless you think of your own business as just that — your own — you'll find it impossible to really rise to the heights of success! There is no ceiling on your income as a sales agent, which is pretty exciting! No agency principal will ever put a little on what they want you to earn.

This chapter helps you take control of your calendar, giving you the time you need to build skills, prospect, follow up with leads, plan and make quality presentations, market properties, and position and present yourself successfully. Your ability to manage your days and invest your time for the highest return will separate you from the other agents who are vying for top-producer status and also enable you to earn your desired income.

Spending Less Time to Accomplish More

Many real estate agents invest too much time and too little urgency in their businesses. They commit well over 40 hours a week to the job, and they put themselves on call seven days a week. They spread themselves thin and then, in order to sustain themselves over this endless schedule, they dilute their intensity. No other professional works so many hours. Even doctors have a lighter on-call schedule than most agents choose to accept. This is even truer in today's technology-based world of instant communication.

A real estate agent lives in an over-stimulated world. The sensory overload of smartphones, emails, text messages, websites and social media makes the time-management challenges more acute than ever.

We suggest that you commit right now to become more effective in way less time each week. Consider this advice:

- **Set aside at least one day a week to recharge and refresh yourself.** Before you say you can't afford the day off, realise this truth: Work expands to fill the time you give it. Reduce your work hours and you'll automatically squeeze more productivity into shorter spans of time. The day off should be a true day off. That means you shut down access (your smartphone, email, social media and so on) and enjoy your family and other activities without interruption.

  When taking your day off, set an auto-reply message on your email account and leave a new voice message for any incoming phone calls. The frustration expressed by most buyers and sellers is because they are left in the dark when trying to contact an agent. If your message advises that you will return their email or phone call within 24 hours, the vast majority of people accept this.

- **Increase your productivity by increasing your intensity.** Give yourself deadlines with no procrastination options. If you know you need to accomplish a line-up of goals over the course of a five-day workweek, your focus automatically zooms in, you sweep away distractions and you get the job done in the time allowed. Just think about how much you get done in the week leading up to your holidays — you can apply the very same principle to any deadline you give yourself.

  Early on, Terri decided to stick to a six-day working week. She scheduled Sunday off each week, and only ever violated this day off for emergencies like getting a contract signed. She also clocked off at 7 pm unless she had listing or sale appointments booked. Her self-imposed constraints didn't hurt her productivity or sales results at all. In fact, having to manage her time effectively helped her to separate the serious prospects from the time wasters — a decided bonus! To keep clients in the loop, she always remembered to change her voicemail and auto-reply email message.

- **Take away your time-wasting options.** Commit to time off and force yourself to work during established, reasonable work hours. Automatically, you'll force yourself to eliminate time-wasting activities.

- **Give yourself no option to add hours back to your workweek.** If you allow yourself the option to add time back to your workweek, you leave yourself open to time-wasting choices.

Begin to treat time as your most valuable asset. Real estate agents are often too casual with their time, leading to career, relationship or bank-account casualties that could be avoided by treating time as life's most precious resource.

Applying Pareto's Principle — The 80:20 Rule

In the late 1800s, an Italian economist named Vilfredo Pareto observed that in Italy a small group of people held nearly all the power, influence and money, which they used to create a significant advantage over the rest of the population. He theorised that in most countries about 80 per cent of the wealth and power was controlled by about 20 per cent of the people. He called this a 'predictable imbalance,' which eventually became known as the 80:20 rule.

In the 1900s, researchers realised that the theory of a 'vital few and trivial many' — 20 per cent of the participants accounting for 80 per cent of the results — applies across many fields of expertise. Most certainly, it's true when it comes to time investment, and here's what that means to you:

- Overall, 80 per cent of your results are generated by 20 per cent of your hard-fought efforts. Conversely, 20 per cent of your results are generated by 80 per cent of your mediocre efforts. In other words, one-fifth of your time-consuming activities delivers four-fifths of your gross sales or gross commissions.
- You can increase the productivity that results from your time investment by assessing which activities achieve the highest-quality results. Too many agents allow their time to be consumed by activities that generate a mere 20 per cent of their revenue. The moment they shift their time investment into higher-return activities, they see dramatic income results.

The 80:20 rule holds true across a spectrum of life activities. Whether you're investing in your career, relationships, health, wealth or personal development, 20 per cent of your efforts deliver 80 per cent of the results you seek. The secret is to figure out which activities deliver the highest-quality returns and invest your time accordingly.

Do you make time for the few activities that return the most significant results? Or are you, like most people in the world, giving your time to the time-gobbling 80 per cent of activities that deliver a meagre return?

Top performers in nearly any field quickly identify which actions account for the great majority of results, and they weight their time toward those activities, performing them with great regularity and intensity.

Following is the list of the half-dozen important activities, in order, that you should focus your efforts on:

- Prospecting
- Lead follow-up
- Listing presentations
- Buyer interview presentations
- Showing property to qualified buyers
- Writing and negotiating contracts

If you dedicate yourself to these six activities, you'll see high returns on your time investment. In our experience, on average, real estate agents spend fewer than two hours a day engaged in the activities on this list. Instead, they work long hours, often putting in more than ten hours a day, spending 80 per cent or more of their time on activities that generate less than 20 per cent of their revenue. Flip the principle to your advantage. Begin spending more and more of your time on the activities that are proven to deliver results, and refuse to be crushed by the weight and waste of those that don't.

Making time for the things that impact your success

If controlling time and gaining discipline to invest hours in better, higher-value activities were easy, everyone would be making big money in real estate sales. Facts prove otherwise. On average, newer agents make less than $50,000 a year. Almost certainly the low-income statistics correlate with poor time-allocation choices.

To allocate larger amounts of time to success-generating actions, follow what we call the four Ds:

1. **Decide** that your time-management skills, habits and activities are going to change.

   This is a challenging first step for most people. That's because changing behaviour isn't easy, and time usage is a behaviour. To avoid change, people search for solutions that enable them to keep doing what they've always done. In doing so, they waste yet more time by vacillating between the change they know they must face and the hope that they won't have to face it.

   The biggest waste of time usually occurs between the moment you know you need to do something and when you actually set out to do it. That's why it's so important to make an immediate commitment to change your time-management patterns and habits. Make the decision to change today!

2. **Define** what needs to change. This step involves two phases. First you have to determine the specific activities that are causing you to waste time or sacrifice productivity. Then you have to figure out how you can remedy the situation.

   For example, do you need to get to your office earlier each day? Does that mean you need to go to sleep earlier each night? Do you need more prospecting time or more time for lead follow-up? Does that mean you need to turn off your mobile to minimise distractions when you're trying to undertake these activities?

   What is barring your success?

3. **Design** a time-management plan. Get proactive rather than reactive. Typical day planners and smartphone scheduling apps are reactionary time-management tools. They enable you to schedule time for client needs, appointments and limited activities, but they don't help you take control of time for your own priorities and purposes. You need to do that part on your own.

   To master your time, you need to adopt a time-blocking system that dedicates predetermined periods of time to your most valuable activities. The section 'Time Blocking Your Way to Success', later in this chapter, describes time blocking in detail. The key point is that you can't leave your days vulnerable to the time needs of others. You must block out periods of time for your own priority activities. Otherwise, you risk giving your days away to the appointment or time requests of clients and colleagues, leaving yourself no time for your own needs. No wonder so many agents feel like they're being pulled like taffy.

4. Just **do** it! Nike urged the world to take action now. These words should be your life-success slogan.

   Don't wait to analyse every aspect of every problem and design the absolutely perfect solution before taking action. Waiting promises only unrealised income, unfulfilled potential and limited wealth. Instead, decide what to change, define how to change, design a time-management plan that allows for change and then just do it.

Weighting your time to what matters

In order to achieve success, any newer agent must commit a minimum of 15 hours a week to direct income-producing activities (DIPAs). That means that you need to dedicate 15 hours every single week — three hours every day — to prospecting and lead follow-up. Do that, and you assure your success and income. Fail to do so and your success is in question.

Don't cheat by trying to replace DIPA tasks with what we call IIPA, or indirect income-producing activities. IIPA tasks include things like making client-development marketing pieces, producing direct mailings, creating or fiddling with your website, optimising your search-engine placement, publishing newsletters, and a near-endless list of other efforts that agents invest in to indirectly produce income. These can become great procrastination exercises — they can fool you into thinking you are super busy, when all you're doing is avoiding the productive activities that will actually bring in the money.

Social media can become a trap for all agents. Although social media is valuable to your business, the truth is that far too many agents expect social media to replace all other forms of lead generation. Too often agents think they can sit behind their computers and generate large volumes of quality leads. This easy and often lazy way to work will result in less than great results for you.

Social media is a wonderful way to communicate with, engage and listen to clients, past clients and prospects. But balancing your time is essential. You can spend hours checking posts and private messages, but you're fooling yourself if you think that's a productive use of your time. The key is to invest just 30 to 60 minutes a day in social media and be firm with yourself — don't deviate from your allocated time.

The problem is, IIPA activities are difficult to control in terms of the time, effort, energy and dollars they require, and they're almost impossible to measure in terms of outcome. Often, countless hours of your work result in marketing pieces that go straight to the trash bin, emails that are deleted with a single keystroke, or social-media posts that don't reach the right audience.

Indirect marketing efforts result in a high *quantity* of contacts. Direct marketing efforts result in high-*quality* contacts — and sales success is the result of quality rather than quantity.

Aim to spread your time between DIPA and IIPA tasks on at least a four-to-one ratio: For every hour you spend in IIPA, spend at least four hours in DIPA. Veer from that ratio and you risk dramatic income swings rather than consistent revenue growth.

Keeping PSA time in check

Agents spend an undue amount of time on production-supporting activities, or PSAs. These activities include all the steps necessary to support such direct income-producing activities as prospecting, following up on leads, taking listings and making sales. You can't avoid the administrative functions that support your sales and customer-service efforts, but you can and should handle them in the fewest number of hours possible.

Using your time wisely

PSA functions surrounding sales tend to be recurring — requiring weekly or even daily attention. Here are several ways to keep these supporting tasks on a firm leash:

- **Streamline the process.** Determine whether you can create a system to make the process faster, possibly eliminating some unnecessary steps. Instead of doing a task once for each prospect, can you do several at once, batching the work for greater efficiency? It takes almost as much time to assemble one set of marketing-material packages and brochures as it does ten. Invest the time to create the ten and have nine ready to go out the door.
- **Create templates.** Don't craft a sales or lead follow-up letter from scratch each time. The same goes for proposals. You can take a basic format and customise it for individual use.
- **Batch your work.** Make your PSA calls one after another. Bunch together the PSA actions as much as possible so you can move quickly from one similar call or action to another.

- **Eliminate the step.** Sometimes your examination of process may uncover that a particular function doesn't need to be done at all.
- **Delegate.** Is there administrative help somewhere in your sales department? Can you find someone to lend a hand? Are there TAFE or university programs that might provide some eager business students who want to learn the business from the ground up? A talk with your sales manager may help.
- **Hire help.** If you can't get support within your department, are you willing to pay a few bucks for it? Maybe you can hire a university or high-school student, a stay-at-home parent, or a part-timer who just wants a low-pressure opportunity to earn a little money. For many of the PSA tasks that aren't proprietary, the work can also be done off-site using a VA (virtual assistant). For help finding one, check out sites like `www.odesk.com` or `www.elance.com`.

Asking for referrals to turn PSA into DIPA

When you must turn to PSA work, you can often take the opportunity to get in a little DIPA action at the same time. For instance, customer-service follow-up calls are part of your production-supporting activities. Checking to confirm that the prospect or client has received expected materials or information is a routine task that doesn't relate directly to income generation.

But don't stop there. Get some extra mileage from this PSA effort by turning your customer service call into a prospecting call: Ask for a referral.

It's never too early in a sales relationship to begin building a referral base. A truly qualified referral request, however, takes a little time and attention. Be ready to invest at *least* five minutes in conversation to avoid appearing like a hit-and-run referral driver. You may use a great segue statement like:

> *I have a very important question to ask you.*

This statement forces a pause, builds anticipation, and sets the tone for a meaningful conversation. And it requests permission to explore client or prospect contacts. You may use a script like this to help you:

> *I'm really happy that I've been able to work with you. I was wondering about others you might know who would also benefit from my service. Could we explore for a few minutes others who you think I might be able to help?*

Managing Your Day

How often do you exclaim at the end of the day, 'Where did the day go?' It's as if we've gotten nothing of significance done in the last eight hours on the job. When you feel that way, go back and review the mix of PSA, IIPA and DIPA. How much time was spent in each category?

If you find that your time investment was a little off-balance, accept that today is gone, but tomorrow can be a new opportunity to get it right. Spend a few minutes figuring out where the day *did* go. Did you put off tackling your DIPA tasks until your day was derailed by interruptions? Were you so engrossed in IIPA tracking that you spent more time than you intended in analysing the results? Did you lose momentum by jumping back and forth between prospecting and lead follow-up?

Pinpoint the problems, plan for the next day, and nail down a schedule that ensures maximum productivity and keeps you on the path toward success.

Knowing the power of the 11 am rule

The 11 am rule goes like this: The world around a real estate agent gears up at 11 each morning. Solicitors, conveyancers, loan officers, other agents, valuers, building and pest inspectors, and clients will most likely call you after or close to 11 am.

Because of this, it's imperative that you come into the office early and complete your prospecting and lead follow up before the clock strikes the hour.

You could even adopt the extreme approach of not answering your phone until 11 in order to minimise the chance of being distracted during your most important production hours. Just make sure your voicemail message reflects this.

Tracking your time

Knowing exactly how much time you spend on DIPA, IIPA and PSA functions is hard unless you've tracked your activities over a period of time to determine an average. This is very important, and it supports an undeniable truth in sales: When performance is measured, performance improves. By tracking your time usage, you're guaranteed to increase your time effectiveness.

Figure 15-1 is a form you can use to record and report how you utilise your time in half-hour increments. Most people have between 16 and 20 half-hour increments to invest at work daily. Tracking how you use your increments may very well surprise you!

Here's how this form can help you make the most of those increments:

- Keep the form with you and fill it out as you go. Don't wait until the end of the day to complete it — you're bound to forget something.
- Track yourself for at least a week — longer is better. This allows for daily anomalies and helps create more of an 'average' work flow.

Repeat this tracking process at least every six months. Over time, habits and behaviours may creep into your routine to diminish your time effectiveness. A routine check-up keeps you on track.

You must monitor the mix of total hours in each category. The goal is to spend at least 40 per cent of your hours in DIPA, with more than 50 per cent of those hours spent in prospecting and lead follow-up.

Dealing with time-consuming fires

Time-consuming fires are the hot issues that result from the emotional turmoil involved in many real estate transactions. Sometimes they require calm and caution; other times you need to put on a fireman's hat and start dousing the flames of a delayed closing, emotionally frustrated buyer or seller, problem agent, or slow-moving inspector, appraiser or loan officer. Let the following rules guide your responses:

- **Rule #1: Very few settlement issues can't wait an hour.** Unless it is less than an hour before something like unconditional status, in general, when your transaction hits a snag, you don't need to let it dramatically change your day's schedule. Wait to resolve the issue during the time you've blocked for administrative tasks.
- **Rule #2: A frenzied reaction only adds fuel to the fire.** More often than not, when one closing party gets riled it's because someone else in the transaction is riled — and hysteria is catching. Aim to serve as the calming influence in the transaction. If the problem arises two hours before your predetermined administrative time slot, inform the parties that you have prescheduled appointments that you can't change, but that you'll be able to take action when you get out of the appointments in two hours.
- **Rule #3: Fires often burn themselves out.** Rather than jump into the mess, give the issue a bit of time to simmer down. Remember that your

prospecting and lead follow-up tasks are appointments to which you've committed. Sticking with your daily plan may give the issue time to cool or even resolve itself.

- **Rule #4: Don't wait for a three-alarm fire to call for the pump truck.** If the fire becomes hot, talk with your principal or sales manager right away. Before the transaction flares out of control, ask for help. The longer you delay, the more effort you'll spend getting the situation cooled down.

Activity Tracking by the Half-Hour

7:00-7:30	________	DIPA	IIPA	PSA
7:30-8:00	________	DIPA	IIPA	PSA
8:00-8:30	________	DIPA	IIPA	PSA
8:30-9:00	________	DIPA	IIPA	PSA
9:00-9:30	________	DIPA	IIPA	PSA
9:30-10:00	________	DIPA	IIPA	PSA
10:00-10:30	________	DIPA	IIPA	PSA
10:30-11:00	________	DIPA	IIPA	PSA
11:00-11:30	________	DIPA	IIPA	PSA
11:30-12:00	________	DIPA	IIPA	PSA
12:00-12:30	________	DIPA	IIPA	PSA
12:30-1:00	________	DIPA	IIPA	PSA
1:00-1:30	________	DIPA	IIPA	PSA
2:00-2:30	________	DIPA	IIPA	PSA
2:30-3:00	________	DIPA	IIPA	PSA
3:00-3:30	________	DIPA	IIPA	PSA
3:30-4:00	________	DIPA	IIPA	PSA
4:00-4:30	________	DIPA	IIPA	PSA
4:30-5:00	________	DIPA	IIPA	PSA

DIPA Payoff Hours ________

IIPA Payoff Hours ________

PSA Payoff Hours ________

Total Hours ________

Figure 15-1: Productivity form for recording time spent.

Time Blocking Your Way to Success

A time-blocked schedule reserves and protects slotted time segments for pre-planned, pre-determined activities. The objective of time blocking is to increase the amount of time you can invest in direct income-producing efforts.

Time blocking takes discipline but is probably the most reliable method for seizing control of time and boosting productivity.

Many people have heard of time blocking, but few master its use. The challenge isn't in creating the schedule; that's the easy part. The challenge is keeping on the schedule. That's the hard part, because most people set their time-blocking expectations very high, reserve large portions of time, and then can't maintain the schedule. The good news, though, is that even if you need to compromise your time blocks, you still come out ahead. Even maintaining half of your blocked-out time can produce incredible results.

Setting your schedule in time blocks

Good time blocking starts with a schedule grid. See Figure 15-2 for a good sample to follow. In the beginning, create a grid that breaks your schedule down into 30-minute segments. As your skill progresses, you may shift to a 15-minute grid format.

As you complete the grid, try blocking your entire daily schedule, not just your workday. Follow these steps:

- **Block time for your personal life first.** If you don't, you'll be hard pressed to squeeze in personal time after scheduling everything else.

  Decide which are the most important personal activities in your life and block them out before you allow any other obligations onto your calendar. Set aside a date night with your spouse or significant other. Block time for exercise, quiet time, personal-development time and family time. If your daughter has football games on Tuesday and Thursday evenings, put those in your schedule. If someone wants to see you during those times, say you're booked with a previous appointment.

- **Decide which full day you'll take off each week.** No ifs, ands or buts. You must take at least one day off. The reaction of new agents is, 'Oh! I couldn't do that.' Remember — even God took the seventh day off.

TIME BLOCKING SCHEDULE

	MONDAY	TUESDAY	WEDNESDAY	THURSDAY	FRIDAY	SATURDAY	SUNDAY
6AM	Personal Development	Personal Development	Personal Development	Personal Development	Personal Development		Day Off
6:30	+	+	+	+	+		+
7:00	Workout	Workout	Workout	Workout	Workout		+
7:30	+	+	+	+	+	Breakfast with Family	+
8:00	Breakfast	Breakfast	Breakfast	Breakfast	Breakfast	+	+
8:30	Flexitime	Flexitime	Flexitime	Flexitime	Flexitime	+	+
9:00	Prospect	Sales Meeting	Prospect	Prospect	Prospect	Prospect	+
9:30	+	+	+	+	+	+	+
10:00	Lead Follow-Up	Office Tour	Lead Follow-Up	Lead Follow-Up	Lead Follow-Up	+	+
10:30	+	+	+	+	+	Lead Follow-Up	+
11:00	Flexitime	+	Flexitime	Flexitime	Flexitime	+	+
11:30	Return Phone Calls	Return Phone Calls	Return Phone Calls	Return Phone Calls	Return Phone Calls	Flexitime	+
12PM	+	+	+	+	+	Appointments	+
12:30	Lunch	Lunch	Lunch	Lunch	Lunch	+	+
1:00	+	+	+	+	+	+	+
1:30	Administration	Administration	Administration	Administration	Administration	+	+
2:00	+	+	+	+	+	Flexitime	+
2:30	+	+	+	+	Planning Time	Appointments	+
3:00	Flexitime	Flexitime	Flexitime	Flexitime	+	+	+
3:30	Marketing Activities	Marketing Activities	Marketing Activities	Marketing Activities	+	+	+
4:00	+	+	+	+	Return Phone Calls	+	+
4:30	Return Phone Calls	Return Phone Calls	Return Phone Calls	Return Phone Calls	+	+	+
5:00	+	+	+	+	Evening Off	Evening Off	+
5:30	Appointments/ Prospecting	Appointments	Flexitime	Appointments	+	+	+
6:00	+	+	Evening Off	+	+	+	+
6:30	+	+	+	+	+	+	+
7:00	+	+	+	+	+	+	+
7:30	+	+	+		+	+	+
8:00			+		+	+	+
8:30			+		+	+	+
9:00			+		+	+	+
9:30			+		+	+	+
10:00			+		+	+	+

Figure 15-2: Use a schedule grid such as the one shown in this illustration to block your time and manage your day.

A few words on the definition of a day off: It means no real estate calls, no answering your mobile, no negotiating offers, no taking ad calls, no taking sign calls, and no meeting with clients or prospects. The minute you do any business activity, it's a workday, even if it's just for five minutes. Honour yourself and your family with one day a week away from real estate. The 24/7 approach leads to family frustrations and burnout. It's hard to receive the love you need from a pile of money.

- **Decide which evenings you will and won't work.** Again, set boundaries. Make no more than three or four nights a week available to clients. Designate them during the time-blocking stage and then move prospects only into those evening time slots.
- **Begin blocking time for DIPA,** or direct income-producing activities.
  - Block time for prospecting and lead follow-up first, and preferably early in the day. You're probably thinking: 'Aren't more people home in the afternoon and evening?' Probably so. But will you prospect consistently if you do it in the evening? The fact is the answer is no. More people being home at night doesn't matter if that's not when you're picking up the phone to call them. Schedule calls for morning hours when you can and will make the contacts.
  - Schedule time slots for appointments next. Determine how many appointments you need to hold and how long they need to run. How long do you need for a listing presentation? How much time do you need to show a buyer homes in a specific area?

    When you work with buyers, you need to plan on longer appointments. With sellers, your typical listing presentation should last 30 to 45 minutes. Scheduling appointments in hour blocks gives you at least 15 minutes of drive time to reach your next appointment.

    Schedule appointments at a quarter after the hour. This demonstrates to the prospect that you're exact with your time, you can be relied on and that you respect that both theirs and your time is valuable. Also, it's a unique time, so more memorable, and the prospect was less likely to forget the appointment. (You can also send an SMS to clients around 30 minutes before an appointment to remind them.)

    When you block appointment slots, you know exactly when to ask people to meet with you. You can say, 'I have an opening at 5:15 on Tuesday or 4:15 on Wednesday. Which would be better for you?'
- **Schedule time for administrative tasks.** This includes phone calls, office meetings, company property tours, and the like. Make a list of your regular, necessary activities and then put them into your time-blocked schedule.
- **Finally, block some flexitime.** Flexitime helps you stay on track. It allows you to put out fires, make emergency calls, handle unscheduled but necessary tasks, and still stay on your schedule.

Most agents who are new to time blocking create schedules that are too rigid. The lack of flexibility causes them to be off their schedules before 10:30 in the morning. From that point, they're off schedule for the rest of the day.

As you start out, block about thirty minutes of flexitime for every two hours of scheduled time in your daily grid. You can always reduce or remove the flexitime blocks as your skills and discipline increase.

Avoiding time-blocking mistakes

Sales professionals in the top 10 per cent of their industries share a common trait: They control, use and invest their time more wisely and effectively than their lower-performing associates. Among sales professionals, time usage determines income.

The most significant challenge for most sales professionals is time control. Through years of study and coaching sales professionals, we've discovered common challenges that most salespeople experience when trying to master their time-block schedule:

Mistake #1: Making yourself too available. The biggest error that salespeople make is getting sucked into the interruption game. You need times in your schedule that are free of interruptions, during which you bar access to all but those to whom you grant exceptions. Follow this advice:

- If possible, use an effective gatekeeper (usually the office receptionist if you don't have a personal assistant) to screen your calls, redirecting all minor issues, problems, challenges and interruptions that can be handled by an assistant or some other person.
- Use your voicemail to screen and inform. Record a new voicemail greeting daily. Tell the listener when you're in appointments and when you'll be returning calls. This sets the standard that you're busy and valuable but also available.
- Limit the number of people who have unfiltered access to you. Create a short list of the important few people who can interrupt your schedule at any time of the day, and don't let anyone else in during time blocked for interruption-free activities. As you make your list, include only those who are extremely important to your personal life. Very few clients find their way onto the short lists of truly successful people.

Mistake #2: Choosing the wrong office location and set up. The nature of your physical office has a dramatic effect on your time management and productivity. Give serious consideration to the following two issues:

- The size of your work environment. Make sure the size matches the size of your practice. If you don't have enough space for yourself and your staff, your production will be stunted.

  Don't let your physical space limit your growth opportunities. If you're crowded by your staff, you're in the wrong physical location.

- Your personal office's accessibility. Your office must be private. Top-producing agents have too many focused activities to be in the bullpen of activity. If you're surrounded by the buzz of staff, inbound phone calls, problems and challenges, it's too easy to be tempted to jump in and help, tackling the issues of servicing at the expense of new business creation. The only way to control your planning and prospecting environment is to locate your practice in a private office away from distractions and staff.

Mistake #3: Failing to operate on an appointment-only basis. Too many agents are willing to meet at all hours of the day and night and on a moment's notice. By time blocking, you can create appointment slots and drive prospects into those slots, just as your doctor, dentist or solicitor does.

Studies show that 80 per cent of all prospects are willing to fit into the schedules of their professional advisors. But when they aren't alerted to a schedule, they take control on their own, dictating the appointment time and leaving an agent like you juggling your schedule to adapt to their needs. Sadly, agents accept this knee-jerk scheduling approach as a necessary aspect of a 'service-oriented' business, as if total availability equals service.

Operate as a professional on an appointment-only basis, with all appointments scheduled during time-blocked periods when you know you'll be available, focused and uninterrupted by any issue other than the one your client is sharing.

Mistake #4: Bowing to distractions. Real estate sales is among the most interrupted and distracted professions on the face of the planet. Agents are distracted by the constant jangle of desk phones, home phones and mobiles.

If the phone isn't ringing, you have the distraction of email, usually interrupting you with some unsolicited miracle offer or, less often, with a new lead opportunity. Here's a tip: Don't derail your day just because your computer tells you that you've got mail. Turn off your email notifications and discipline yourself to check only at scheduled times.

Control distractions following this advice:

- Block time in your day for the distractions you know you'll encounter. If you want to socialise with other agents, plan a set time to do that. Just remember to keep it short and limit the coffee break to the time you allocated for it.

- Create a list of no more than five people who are granted instant access during your workday. Have your assistant memorise the names. If you don't have an assistant, work with your receptionist so that only those few people are granted unfiltered access.

Position yourself as an agent-in-command versus an agent-on-demand. Block your time and maintain your schedule. Rather than putting yourself at the beck and call of others during all hours of the day and night, work on an appointment basis, eliminate distractions and take control of your days, your business, your income and your life.

Killing the Time Killer Called Procrastination

The number-one obstacle between real estate agents and higher production is interruptions. A close second is procrastination.

Procrastination is the direct result of a lack of urgency to do what needs to be done and to do it *now*. Urgency is directly linked to success. You can increase your output by 30 per cent if you work with urgency in mind.

The top sales trainer Brian Tracy talks about the *law of forced efficiency*. This idea is based on the premise that you'll never have enough time to do everything you want or need to do, but that in every day you'll always have enough time to accomplish the most important tasks. Obviously, you won't get to the most important tasks if you're bogged down with tasks of low importance that can easily wait until later. Nor will you get to the most important tasks if you procrastinate.

An upcoming section in this chapter helps you set priorities. After you set your priorities, take action without procrastination by following these two pieces of advice:

- Limit the time in which you can get the job done. Too much time to work can lower urgency and lead to procrastination. By identifying days off and time off, you raise the efficiency and effectiveness of your production on the days you're working.
- Give yourself deadlines. Have you ever noticed how much gets done when you're leaving on vacation in a day or so? Most likely, you've seen yourself or others double or triple their work output in the days leading up to a vacation. What if you operated every day at that pace and urgency? Your income and quality of life would explode to heights you never imagined.

Moving forward with a clear vision

A good deal of procrastination results directly from the lack of a clear vision or clarity about what to do. If you don't know what you want, you can't possibly achieve it. You can hardly hit a target you can't see.

Clarity of purpose kills procrastination, yet fewer than 3 per cent of all people define and write down their goals.

Answer these questions:

- What do you want to be?
- What do you want to do with your life?
- What do you want to have?
- Where do you want to go?

Of course, you want to be financially independent. Otherwise, you wouldn't be in real estate sales. But what does financial independence mean to you? How much money do you need to live the lifestyle you dream about? The famous success motivator Napoleon Hill explains the importance of identifying your goal when he says, 'There is one quality that one must possess to win, and that is definiteness of purpose . . . the knowledge of what one wants and a burning desire to achieve it.'

Clarify your desires. When you're certain about what you want to achieve, you'll find it far easier to set and follow an action plan that isn't hindered by the problem of procrastination.

Knowing your objectives

You'll set annual goals, of course. But also view each day that you work or play in terms of daily objectives. What do you want to accomplish today? What result do you want to effect by day's end?

Setting your priorities

Your priorities are the most important actions or steps you must take in order to achieve your objectives for the day. Objectives and priorities aren't one and the same. Objectives are results you intend to achieve. Priorities are steps you take to achieve success.

By prioritising the importance or value of the tasks on your to-do list, you greatly increase the probability that you'll be motivated to overcome procrastination and get the job done.

Most people go about creating task lists in the wrong way. They write down all of the things they must do each day and then go to work, proudly ticking off items as they are completed and equating their level of success with the number of items they check off the list. Success, though, doesn't result from how many things you get done. It results from getting the *right* things done. In other words, you need to know your priorities.

Following is an outline for a simple, and successful, prioritisation system:

1. **Create your daily task list as you normally would.**

   You can do this before you leave the office each day, or you may prefer to get in half an hour early each day and do it then. When creating your list, don't think at all about what is most important. Just think about what needs to get done over the course of the day. Put yourself in brainstorming mode and get your thoughts down on paper.

2. **When you have your list, create task categories.**

   You're not prioritising during this step. This isn't about what to do first, second or third. All you're doing is sorting tasks into these categories:

   A. You'll suffer a significant consequence if you don't complete these tasks today. If it means you have to work all day and all night, these items must get done.

   B. These tasks trigger a mild consequence if they aren't completed today. You probably wouldn't stay late to finish them.

   C. These tasks have no penalty at all if they aren't done today.

   D. These tasks can be delegated. They involve low-value activities that should be performed by someone who has a lower hourly dollar value than you.

   E. These tasks can and should be eliminated. They probably made their way onto your list out of tradition or habit. They aren't necessary, so you need to figure out a way to get them off the list. We call this *pruning*.

Dirk's friend Zig Ziglar used to tell a story of a little boy who asks his mother as they are preparing a holiday meal why she cuts the ends off the ham. She says, 'I don't know. My mother always did it this way.' Now this four-year-old says, 'Let's call Grandma right now and find out.' So they call Grandma and ask why she always cuts the ends off the ham. Her reply: Her roaster is too small for the whole ham! Break out of the habit of doing things a certain way because you have always done it that way. You need to be constantly looking to eliminate non-productive activities.

3. **When your list is categorised, prioritise the tasks.**

   Begin with your A category and determine which item deserves A-1 status. Follow by designating A-2, A-3, A-4, A-5 and so on. Then repeat the process for the B, C and D categories. Go to work in the order of these priorities, and you'll be amazed at how you can accomplish more in less time without falling into the procrastination trap.

As you master the art of prioritising, expect to see fewer cross-offs or checkmarks on your task list. By undertaking your most important tasks first, you'll complete fewer but more important activities.

Consider every day that you achieve closure on all your A category items a terrific success. If you complete your A items on every single one of the days you work this year, you'll see your production and income explode.

Giving yourself deadlines and rewards

Moving away from pain and toward the pleasures of life is human instinct. That's why you have to link deadlines with rewards if you want to keep yourself motivated to complete your work in a sustained way. Without a reward, it's darned hard to face the rigour of a difficult task.

Each day when you set your objectives and priorities, set deadlines as well. Then link completion of your tasks with a clearly defined reward.

For example, set a deadline to get all of your prospecting and lead follow-up calls done by 10:30 am, and then reward yourself with a trip to your favourite coffee shop or lunch restaurant. Beyond that, promise yourself that if you meet your deadlines and complete all of your priorities for a full week, you'll reward yourself with a massage, facial or special evening out.

Realise these two truths about rewards:

- You have to give them to yourself. Don't expect to receive them from your principal, clients, prospects, staff or even family.
- You have to set interim goals to keep you moving forward on a consistent basis. If your reward is financial independence, your pay-off may not arrive for 10 or 20 years. That's way too long to wait for a pat on the back.

Sales involves high pay, for sure, but also a fair amount of rejection and discouragement in between. Rewards encourage you to do the things you know you should do even when you don't feel like doing them.

Carpe Diem: Seizing Your Day

One of the most identifiable characteristics of high performers is that they're action-oriented. They don't wait around to see what will happen or how things will turn out. They seize each day, wringing all the possibilities, performance and profit out of every encounter. They treat each moment as a gift. As the saying goes, that's why we call today the present!

Stop wasting time

To quote Napoleon Hill again: 'Do not wait; the time will never be 'just right.' Start where you stand and work with whatever tools you may have at your command, and better tools will be found as you go along.' In other words: Get to work!

If you're a newer agent, don't waste time fretting over the fact that your skills or tools aren't at the level of other agents. Work with what you've got and know that your abilities will improve with use. At the worst, you'll make a mistake from which you'll learn a good lesson. Finding out early in your career what *not* to do delivers value that pays off again and again in your future.

Stop letting others waste your time

Too many consumers feel no loyalty or obligation to agents. They have the idea that agents are well paid through commissions, but they don't seem to acknowledge that we're not paid at all if no sale occurs.

Because you only get paid if a sale occurs, it's very important that you work with clients who are serious about buying or selling and who agree to work exclusively with you to accomplish their real estate objectives. Otherwise, you're letting real estate shoppers waste your time.

The biggest loss that most agents experience is lost opportunity. Each time you invest in helping a prospect who fails to take action or, worse yet, leaves you for another agent, your investment results in absolutely no financial compensation. That's like a personal injury lawyer losing all his cases. He will be out of business soon.

Manage interruptions

The best way to handle interruptions is to stop them from happening in the first place.

Especially when you're conducting direct income-producing activities — when you're prospecting or doing lead follow-up — turn off your mobile. Tell the receptionist to hold your calls and take messages instead. Turn off your email program so the email alert icon doesn't blink onto your computer screen. Sign out of your online instant-message program. Put a sign on your office door or on your desk advising that you aren't to be interrupted. Perhaps even invest in a set of headphones so that others will presume you're on a call and not interrupt.

Follow the same rules when you're with a client. Nothing is more impolite than an agent who handles phone calls while driving around showing clients property. At the very least, set your phone to vibrate rather than ring when you're doing buyer interviews, showing properties or attending listing appointments.

Eliminate distractions for your own good and for the good of the relationship with the client you're trying to serve.

Handle intrusive clients

In real estate, we're in a customer-service business. We place a high level of value on our customers. But the thought of 'the customer is always right' can be taken too far.

You know that in order to provide the best service to each customer, you have to seek some balance. If the 'squeaky-wheel' clients take up more than their share of your time and resources, you won't be able to give the attention to other deserving customers.

Educating customers about your availability is important. Let new customers know your schedule and the best times to reach you — as well as how to leave a message when you can't be reached. As part of this education, you also want to establish how quickly they can expect a response from you after they leave a message: 24 hours? The same business day?

As for existing clients and customers, be sure to update them whenever your availability circumstances change. If you make changes to your schedule, notify them of the schedule revisions and your new availability. Depending upon the importance of the client and the immediacy of the situations you deal with, you may even want to let customers know when you're on vacation or on a business trip so they know your response time will be longer.

Creating reasonable expectations is key in good customer relations. It may not be unreasonable to take 24 hours to return a client's call — but not if the client is used to and expects to hear from you within an hour.

You can also reinforce your response time through your voicemail message. When you leave your availability and response details as part of your message, callers are more likely to recall and retain. For example:

> *You've reached Jan Brown. I'm out of the office today, Tuesday, 2 September. Please leave a message, and I will return your call by end-of-day Wednesday, 3 September. If you need immediate assistance, please call ____. Until then, have a great day!*

You've now set the scenario: The caller should not expect a return call from you today. And, in fact, because you'll be returning to an inbox filled with calls, emails and correspondence, you may not be able to get back until as late as the end of the day. However, you've offered a back-up plan if the situation is more urgent. This should satisfy virtually anyone who calls.

Don't be tempted to include, as many agents do, 'If it's an emergency, call me on my mobile (or office number),' unless you're prepared for lots of interruptions. After all, isn't *interruption* exactly what you're trying to avoid?

Keep phone calls short

Especially when you're making or taking transaction-servicing calls or production-support calls, you need to conduct business in the shortest time period possible. Otherwise you'll erode the time you need for high-value income-producing activities. To keep calls short, employ these techniques:

- Establish an indication of the time available as you begin the call. For example, say something like, 'I have an appointment in 15 minutes, but your call was an important one, and I wanted to get back to you as quickly as I could.' This technique alerts the call recipient to your time limitation. It says, nicely, 'Get to the point quickly.' It underscores that you value the caller and made a special effort to make time for the conversation.

If you're on a time-blocked schedule, everything is treated as an appointment, including times for returning phone calls, so you'll be speaking the truth. You *do* have another appointment in 15 minutes. This technique is particularly appropriate for prospect or client calls.

- Offer an alternative to a short phone call. If you think your client or prospect wants or needs more than a short return phone call, follow the above technique but then go one step further: Assure the other person that 15 minutes should be more than enough time, but if it's not you can schedule a phone conference when you'll be available for an appointment later in the day.
- When possible, handle production-support calls with voicemail messages. You don't want to rely on voicemail with prospects, because you want to establish personal relationships that lead to face-to-face meetings. But when you're handling service calls, voicemail is a time-effective option for both you and the other party. Make a call, leave a message, and offer the option to call you back with the assurance that if your message resolves the issue then there is no need for a return call. Follow a script such as this one:

  Bob, I know that you're busy. I believe that this resolves the issue. If you agree, there is no need for you to call me back. If you do need to speak with me, I'll be available later today between 3:30 and 4:15. Please call me then.

Use your car to gain efficiency and career advancement

One of your greatest assets in your career is your car. You know why? Because you can turn it into your personal skills-development classroom. You should never turn on the engine without listening to something that will teach you something (except when you have clients with you, of course).

You have a large learning curve ahead and plenty of drive time during which you can 'go to school' with downloads and podcasts that help you improve your business, sales and personal skills. Connecting your iPod or MP3 player to your car to engage in auto university will explode your income.

Use your drive time as educational time. You're success-oriented or you wouldn't have invested in this book and read thus far. Keep acquiring new ideas by turning your commute into skills-development time, and get ready to watch your career take off.

Part V
The Part of Tens

Check out www.dummies.com/extras/successrealestateagentau for a bonus (free!) Part of Tens chapter.

In this part . . .

- Gain access to a treasure trove of tools that are essential for any real estate agent's success.
- We give out the top keys to making great listing presentations.
- Get the lowdown on handling distressed sales professionally, effectively and efficiently.

Chapter 16

Ten (Almost!) Must-Haves for a Successful Real Estate Agent

In This Chapter

- Choosing the right tools
- Establishing your professional image

To be a successful agent, you need to be focused, determined and organised. You also need a few items to keep you on the path to success. Keep the following things in your agent toolbox and you'll be well on your way to achieving your goals.

Good Contact Management System

As a salesperson, you have to be able to keep in touch with prospects and clients easily and effectively. You must be able to put your hands on names, addresses, phone numbers and email addresses in an instant.

You can track people and prospects the old-fashioned way, on 4 × 6 note cards, but you'll soon outgrow that method.

If you're not the least bit 'techno', don't despair! When Terri came into the industry in the early 1990s, the only computer in the office belonged to the admin person. Salespeople were not allowed access to this computer, so agent databases were entirely in a box of cards. Terri managed to make lots of sales and secure many listings, working her way to the top of her real estate group, using only her 4 × 6 cards. However, to keep up now and be a top-performing agent, you will, at some stage, need to acquire computer skills or employ an assistant to do this for you.

Our advice is to get a customer relationship management (CRM) software package as soon as you possibly can. Many, such as GoldMine and Salesforce, are generic products designed for salespeople. These programs automate your client database, sales and more.

Another option is to buy something that is specific to the real estate industry. Many franchises subscribe to CRMs specifically designed for their own teams— just check with your colleagues or your principal. The programs that are specific to real estate agents hold many advantages over general sales programs. They're usually programmed with letters and correspondence an agent can use. They also have pre-created lead follow-up and client follow-up plans already built in. Most have plans to apply when marketing a property. They also have plans you can launch after you've secured a buyer for a listing. You will find incredible time savings when you utilise these features instead of inventing your own.

Most agents now are choosing to use web-based programs like LockedOn Cloud, Port Plus, My DeskTop or similar. These CRMs are suitable for both Australian and New Zealand agents and can be accessed from anywhere or from any tool, such as a computer, laptop, tablet or smartphone. To help your budget, most charge a monthly fee. This allows you to pay as you go rather than budgeting for a large upfront cost, and you get the updates for free. If you do an online search for cloud-based CRMs, you can find lots of options for both Australia and New Zealand and most of these have free trial periods for you to test each one.

A good contact management system is a must for any serious agent. Most agents attempt to use Outlook . . . mistake! In our opinion, Outlook doesn't have the necessary power and lacks the 'cascading action plans'. You need to be able to set a lead follow-up or contact sequence and automate the process of reaching out to clients and prospects.

Tablet Computer

To keep up in the real estate market, you need to be technologically driven. One essential tool is a tablet computer, such as an iPad, the Samsung Galaxy or the Toshiba Envy.

A tablet is critical because of the mobile environment in which real estate agents now work. The sleek design and portability of the tablet is perfect for the real estate industry.

You must have a tablet with both WiFi and 4G capabilities. Being able to show clients real-time property listings, including videos and pictures, can make a big impact. Use a tablet for open houses, listing presentations and buyer consultations, whether at your office, at a client's home or at the local coffee shop. This will impress your clients and give you credibility as an agent ahead of the game.

Showing such information to prospective clients who walk into your open houses expands their options, enhances their knowledge base and creates an opportunity for them to linger at the open house longer — and get to know you better.

Tablet computers also create opportunities for a paperless process, which is an attractive option in the real estate industry. Just a word of warning though: Be careful to keep hard copies of any documents required for your property file — for example, your CMAs (comparative market analyses) — in case you're asked for evidence as to why you advised a certain listing price to your client. (You must be able to prove that your appraisal was backed up with market evidence.)

Smartphone

Although mobile phones can become a curse for some agents, making them think they need to be contactable 24 hours a day and distracting them from their main business of lead-generation and selling, a smartphone such as a Samsung Galaxy or iPhone is an essential technological requirement for real estate agents hoping to keep up with today's fast-moving markets.

A smartphone allows you to be contactable when you're on the move — and using voicemail and a well-phrased message, which covers when you'll get back to people who leave a message, can save you from being too contactable. With a smartphone, you can also keep up to date with properties listed in your area, and monitor email inquiries and respond to people when you're out of the office (perhaps while waiting for a client).

You can also use your smartphone to read the QR codes on signs and marketing materials for other properties. This allows to you read the information provided for that property and get a good grasp of how QR codes work — and how to make them work for you.

Facebook Business Page

Facebook has become an effective tool for service-based businesses, such as real estate agents. The balance between your personal Facebook page and a business Facebook page is delicate. Both need to be used to communicate with your sphere of influence. Use your personal page for commentary, sharing funny or inspirational stories, quotes or videos and very occasionally work-related posts.

Agents can make the mistake of posting too many listings and other business topics on their personal pages. This makes you appear as less than professional, using your page only to drum up sales. The sooner you can establish a business presence on Facebook, the more muted you can be on your personal page.

The goal is to establish yourself as an expert and a portal of key real estate information for your area. You can use your business Facebook page to highlight market trends, share national and local real estate articles, and even promote real estate best buys and opportunities.

Personal Website

With the majority of serious buyers using the internet to search for properties, your website can be a powerful tool for generating leads and promoting your sellers' homes.

However, if you're a new agent, it is important not to get caught up in this to the extent that you're neglecting the actual work of face-to-face contact with your prospects. Hiding behind 'busyness' is easy, and can give you an excuse not to be working on your more dollar-productive activities. You don't need the fanciest, most expensive website you can find. A lot of companies make solid template-based websites. These sites are extremely economical, considering the low initial investment and monthly hosting fees. Many of these companies build cost-effective sites and earn most of their income when they charge monthly fees for hosting your site.

For more information about WordPress, a popular and free blogging platform, see *WordPress For Dummies*, 5th Edition, by Lisa Sabin-Wilson (Wiley).

You want to work with an IT company that builds template sites as well as custom sites. Most new agents start on a budget, so you may start with

Keeping low-cost contact with 'iffy' prospects

Sometimes you want to maintain relationships with moderately motivated prospects, in hopes that they choose to work with you when they're finally ready to buy or sell.

A good, low-cost way to stay in touch with these contacts is to send an email version of your real estate newsletter or some other form of cyber-correspondence that costs you nothing for delivery or printing. (Refer to Chapter 6 for advice on staying in touch with moderately motivated prospects.)

Don't expect a high percentage of these long-term prospects to convert into listings or sales based on this contact technique, but your cost is almost non-existent, so any success is nearly pure profit. However, be reasonable with your expectations. If you achieve a 3 per cent return, consider yourself fortunate.

a template site and then, as your business grows, move to a custom site. You also want a company that has the ability to place you higher in search-engine rankings. This is how you'll generate traffic and leads.

Professional Stationery

Letterhead paper, personalised note cards and business cards (preferably with your picture on them) are all essential tools for a successful agent, even in today's technology-based world. You want business cards with your picture on them to help create a quicker connection and recognition. Our caution with a picture is to make sure it's current. We've seen too many agent business cards that caused us to look three times at the card and person to detect any resemblance. Also avoid the soft-focus glamour shot. If you don't look like your photo when you first meet a prospective client, you lose credibility straightaway.

Having note cards, letterhead paper and envelopes that identify you is also a good idea. You need to ensure that your professional image is carried through with every contact and piece of correspondence with clients and prospects. Keep the same photo for all your branding.

Although our technology-driven world is powered by email, Facebook and instant messaging, you still have a large opportunity in personal, lasting correspondence. A handwritten thank-you note is more powerful and meaningful today than ever before. Few people take the time to do this extra step, so you really stand out when you do.

A Phone Headset

As we cover throughout this book, prospecting should be the cornerstone of your business, and a headset makes it much easier for you to prospect effectively. It enables you to stand while you're making phone calls and keeps your hands free. That way, you can engage your whole body in your communication or type notes directly into your CRM while talking. A headset improves your posture, position, energy and enthusiasm. It's the only way to do it.

A word of caution: Don't go the cheap route. You can get cheap headsets for $50, but they sound like cheap headsets. Make the investment of a couple of hundred dollars and get a good one. Wireless headsets are more expensive at the start but will pay off big time for you.

A Numbers-Based Business Plan

Too few salespeople have a business plan that encompasses the sales ratios and numbers of this business. These ratios and numbers are usually called your *key performance indicators* or *KPIs*. Agents often don't know the number of contacts needed to generate a lead, the number of leads needed to generate an appointment, the number of appointments needed to create a committed client or the number of committed clients needed to generate a commission cheque. When you know those numbers, you can easily calculate how to make any amount of money you desire to earn (refer to Chapter 4 for guidelines).

Sales Scripts

Knowing clearly what to say in every situation really separates the high earners from the low earners in real estate sales. Our best advice is to find scripts that have worked for others. Invest several hours each week practising those scripts to perfection, preferably with a role-playing partner. A word of caution: Practice does *not* make perfect, as the old saying goes. Practice makes *permanent*. Only perfect practice makes perfect. To achieve perfect delivery, be sure to have the right attitude, an expectation of success, appropriate pauses and enough repetition to master each script.

Find a role-playing partner who is as committed to your success as you are. You may both benefit and can laugh at each other when you make a mess of it. Better to practise with a friend or partner than with a real-life client!

Chapter 17

Ten Bulletproof Tips for Listing Presentations

In This Chapter

- Preparing for an outstanding listing presentation
- Swaying prospects with technology and benefits
- Closing the deal — and knowing when to walk away
- Prepping your clients for the next steps

Representing sellers and securing exclusive listings is the best way to leverage your business and create future business. A listing creates more leads and opportunities for any agent. Although an agent's marketing ability and online presence can somewhat make up for a lack of listing inventory, the bottom line is that listings are always king! This chapter helps you nail your listing presentations and win more clients.

Winning the Seller with Preparation

What you do before you arrive at the listing presentation sets the tone for your engagement with the sellers. What you ask before you meet them can be the difference between success and failure.

When you are first in touch with a prospective seller, your aim is to build rapport, to show genuine interest in their needs and ask questions that will help to focus your research before the actual appointment. This is why it is so important not to rush straight out if a prospective seller phones to ask for an appraisal.

Your first task is to qualify your prospect — you need to discover whether they're actually thinking of selling or just wanting an appraisal (an opinion of market value). Start a conversation and ask relevant questions — for example, have they done any renovations since their property was purchased, or have there been any extensions or landscape work? You can of course look up this property online, but the view you access may not be the most recent and will not include any interior work that has been completed. Answers to these questions will guide your estimate of appraisal price.

You can also tell sellers that you will bring detailed market information when you come to the first appointment and that it would help considerably to focus your research if they could give you a general idea of price range so you're not wasting their time.

Then it's time to view the property in person! Your conversation here should be focused on your sellers and their needs — for example, what's important to them in service and outcome? Have they bought or sold properties before and what was their experience? Are they interviewing other agents? Do they have a time frame for the sale? Obviously, you shouldn't fire these questions at your seller — instead, try to weave them into the conversation, taking careful note of the answers. The agent who has the most information about the sellers and their thought processes has a huge competitive advantage. It enables you to adjust your listing presentation to fit their needs, wants and desires.

Asking specific questions about the sellers' wants and expectations is best left to your first face-to-face meeting. What Terri has found is that these sorts of questions come across as a bit intrusive if asked before you've actually met in person. Instead, she always prefers to ask these important questions in a conversational tone when sitting at the table with sellers.

Knowing Your Competition

(Almost) gone are the days of asking a friend for a referral for a real estate agent or just interviewing a couple of agents and selecting one. Technology has given consumers the ability to search multiple real estate companies and read through numerous online reviews about agents. Competition is increased, and referrals are decreased. Many sellers now do their own 'secret shopping' of agents by attending lots of open homes and observing how the agents work. Sellers look at whether agents are professional, how they dress, what their marketing material is like, how they talk to buyers, and how regular and professional their buyer follow-up is. These and other aspects are considered before sellers even choose which agent to interview for the business of selling their home.

When you access a prospect, it's just as important to gather information about your competition as it is to find out the prospect's buying or selling needs. Ask what other companies and agents they're interviewing. This way you can do some research and find out how to plan your presentation based on your competitive points of difference, including how your background and services differ from those of the competition.

Knowing Your Strategy and Not Deviating

Some flexibility is essential during a listing presentation. However, a wholesale strategy change usually doesn't end well.

When preparing for a listing presentation, choose either a one-step or two-step strategy. Here are some details on the two processes:

- A one-step process has you go to the home or meet with the seller once. You don't go out in advance to see the home and connect with the seller. You prepare your CMA (comparative market analysis) in advance and deliver your sales presentation at the one visit. The goal is to walk out after this meeting with a signed listing agreement in hand.
- A two-step process has you meet the prospect and see the home. Then you complete your appraisal or CMA. You then have a second meeting to deliver your findings and convince the seller of why you're the best agent for the job. Remember, your first and most important sale is of yourself!

When you are very experienced with your listing presentation or when you have repeat clients, you can probably deviate from your initial plan. However, until then, the important thing is keeping your flow consistent — stick with your agenda, or you may well go off topic and find you have run out of time and haven't discussed everything you need to.

Forgetting about a 'Be Back' Listing

A 'be back' listing is when the seller gives you stalls, objections and brush-offs, and doesn't sign the listing agreement before you leave the presentation. When you walk out the door after your presentation, the odds that you'll actually secure this listing have dropped considerably. You haven't sold yourself or your sale strategy convincingly enough.

If you're in competition with other agents, the seller probably won't remember all or even most of the differences between the agents. She is more likely to select the agent who gives the highest list price or lowest commission fee. All the presentations start to run together in sellers' minds after a few days of decision delay. If you don't get a signed agreement at your listing presentation, you need to act fast to stay in your client's mind.

What you do after the presentation is vital to the seller's decision. Be sure to assertively follow up after your presentation; call, email, text and send handwritten notes.

Some sellers experience 'seller remorse'. Once you have left the house and the sellers have time to chat, often they will start to doubt their decision to give you the listing. You need to allay their concerns. What Terri always did was to email or call within the first 24 hours, thanking the sellers again for entrusting her with the sale and telling them what she had already started to do for them. Taking the time to do this reassured her sellers that they had indeed chosen the right agent for the job.

Using Technology to Impress a Prospect

In today's technological world, a flip chart or a presentation without visuals may not cut it — especially with the younger generation, who will expect you to use a tablet or laptop computer to make your presentation sleek, tech-savvy and visually stimulating. However, your older prospects will likely still prefer you to talk, show pictures and even draw out your strategy on paper for them to follow more easily. You must 'read' your prospects. Some are more auditory (they like to hear your strategy), whereas others are more visual (they like to see your strategy) — and some are kinaesthetic (they like to be involved hands-on, so you need to hand them marketing material, CMA printouts and so on).

To discover which style to use, watch your sellers' body language as you go through your listing presentation — if their eyes glaze over as you're talking, they're not really auditory and you need to involve them more.

You may like to impress your seller by demonstrating the use of *QR codes*. These are coded symbols on signs and marketing materials that enable prospective customers to access complete property information on their smartphones phones, simply by scanning the QR code. Another use of technology is to demonstrate how buyers can enter the dedicated mobile webpage address on their mobile web browser — for example, `www.24brownstmiddlepark.com.au` (refer to Chapter 11 for more on property information websites). When buyers enter this URL, listing information and pictures are sent directly to a buyer's smartphone. Your phone then receives a text showing that a potential buyer sought information about that listing, allowing you to contact the prospect within seconds. Demonstrating this technology at a listing presentation is sure to impress your seller prospects. Any technology you can demonstrate that captures buyer leads aligns with the sellers' need to get people into their home to buy it.

Understanding and Conveying Your Benefits Clearly

Too many agents sell features instead of benefits. A seller buys benefits but yawns at features. Your presentation has power and punch when you showcase benefits that answer the question, 'Why should I hire you? What's in it for me?'

If you can connect your company, your technology, your personal service and whatever you're selling to a specific set of benefits, the seller will take notice and clearly see how you're different from other agents.

If you're a newer agent, sell your agency's benefits more than your own. For example, if you're with a team that has large market share, that is a feature of the company's service. The benefit is lower risk in working with you and your company because you produce more leads, which increases showings, increases urgency with more buyers creating competition, and leads to higher, speedier initial offers. Additionally, you reduce the risk of the home not selling. All of these are key benefits that you can sell as a result of being with a strong company.

If you're with a smaller boutique agency, sell the benefits of the focus that is possible with a smaller inventory. You're able to concentrate on the sale of their property rather than spreading yourself too thin looking after a huge number of clients at the one time.

Inserting Trial Closes Strategically

Most agents go through their listing presentation without doing any trial closes at all, so they arrive at the end of their presentation uncertain about whether the seller is tracking with them or leaning their way. Because of the potential rejection, they frequently fail to close at the end of their presentation — they fail to actually ask for the business. Sometimes this is nerves, but most likely it is because they're avoiding possible rejection if the seller says no. Instead of being clear with their question, they're likely to say something like 'So, what do you think?' That is clearly not professional, but it's used more often than not. And, more often than not, the seller will say 'Let me think about it and get back to you.' Recipe for disaster — this usually means the agent has lost the listing. They were not decisive or convincing enough. If you sense this could be you, ask for help — role play with a colleague, a coach or your principal and practice on them first rather than on your prospect. Failing to close effectively with sellers is too expensive in terms of lost listings and sales.

You want to place trial closes after every few benefits and services you highlight for the seller. Use powerful statements like 'Do you see how this creates an advantage for our sellers?' or 'Is this the type of service you're looking for?' These statements lead the seller to confirm with you that you're heading in the right direction — that your service and value is aligned with what they expect.

Talking about Value Rather than Price

The real purpose of a CMA is to research the value of the home based on today's market conditions. It's not to determine the price — this is the job of a registered valuer, not the agent. The sale price of the home will be determined by how many people will be interested and what the market says. The value doesn't change just because your sellers want to overprice their home.

If you focus on the word 'value' rather than 'price', you can shift the discussion to how the value is determined by the marketplace, and competition from other similar homes on the market, rather than what the sellers want or hope to get. Everyone always wants to price their home higher than the actual value of the property. Your goal is to delay the discussion on price until you gain agreement on the value of the home. The truth is that homes can be priced at any price, but it will not change the value.

Not Being Afraid to Walk Away

If a seller is demanding, confrontational and unrealistic in her expectations of your service and the value of the home, it's probably better to walk away from the listing. One of the biggest and most soul-destroying mistakes you can make is working with people you should have passed on. The amount of emotional energy you invest to service an overly demanding and unrealistic seller isn't worth the commission or aggravation. The empowerment you receive by saying no is unmatched. And the look on most sellers' faces when you turn down the business is priceless.

When the philosophy gap can't be bridged

Sometimes, a prospective client relationship just doesn't feel right. That doesn't mean the prospect is a bad client. It means the prospect is a bad client for you. The only way you'll know is to do your homework.

Enter the listing appointment with a clear understanding of your own service approach and philosophy and use that as the basis for determining whether the prospective client is a good match for your business. You can then follow one of three paths:

- If your minds meet easily, proceed full steam ahead.
- If you uncover philosophical differences, work to iron them out by presenting the benefits of your approach and seeking agreement to proceed along the path you know will result in success.
- If you can't find common ground, walk away from the opportunity if it doesn't feel right. You probably should walk away from a bad client match at least one time to see how it feels to take control of your life and career. Sadly, most agents are too scared to do so. Instead they plough ahead through nightmarish situations with toxic clients — this is soul destroying and costly.

Clarifying Service and Next Steps

After being at the listing presentation for 45 minutes or more, the typical agent wants out of there as quickly as possible. But when you complete the signing of the listing agreement, disclosure forms and other documents, you need to pause to debrief sellers about the next steps.

Spend even just five to ten minutes sharing the following information:

- What your service steps will be in the first 14 days
- When the listing will go live
- When to expect showings
- How communication and feedback systems work
- What happens if you haven't secured a buyer in a specified time frame

When you invest five to ten minutes to go through these steps, you'll have clients who are less stressed out and more satisfied. They'll be less likely to call you or feel that you're not calling, texting or emailing enough. You'll reassure them that they have indeed chosen the right agent — you!

Chapter 18

Ten Tips for Navigating Distressed Sales

In This Chapter

- Guiding sellers through the distressed sale process
- Making sure the buyer is committed and qualified
- Working closely with lenders to keep the deal moving
- Winning referrals to other distressed sale prospects

The distressed sale has actually been around as long as mortgages have been, but it hasn't been as well known until recently. This kind of sale occurs when a property owner owes more to the bank than the property is currently worth. The owner can't afford the payments, so the property will eventually be returned to the bank's ownership — known as *repossession or receivership*. Sometimes the only way for the property owner to stop the bank foreclosure is a distressed sale. Here, the owner tries to find a buyer for the property before the bank takes it.

Banks are increasingly likely to allow homeowners to remain in the home so vandalism of the property doesn't occur. Owners are anxious to sell the home and move on with their lives. When dealing with this kind of sale, an agent must have sensitivity and stamina to get the process done.

Dominique Grusbic is one of Australia's most reputable real estate mentors. She is an experienced and successful property investor and a qualified barrister, and is an expert in teaching her clients the process of purchasing distressed properties. If this avenue interests you, we strongly suggest that you check out her website — `www.dominiquegrubisa.com.au`.

This chapter covers ten things an agent must do when working a distressed sale.

Ensuring the Seller is Cooperative and Committed

The distressed-sale process is a long process. It can take months, even years, to get to the finish line. You have to be very patient and very tenacious. The process produces massive documentation and paperwork. Paperwork is easier in our electronic world, but it's still voluminous.

A distressed seller must be in it for the long haul with you. Flurries of activity are followed by long waiting periods of quiet from the bank. Your client will live in uncertainty for a long time. You need to be empathetic, because it's tough living with that cloud over your head — month after month of not knowing what's going to happen or when it will happen.

There is a benefit to this process, the largest coming from sellers in a recourse state. In a recourse state, banks have the right to come after the deficiency between the loan amount and the sale price and fees. The majority of home loans in Australia and New Zealand are recourse loans, so owners can't just say to the bank, 'See you later, I'm leaving — you cop any loss.' Owners are still on the hook for whatever's remaining on the loan. So that's a very big incentive for Australians to keep paying their mortgage. Sadly many homeowners put their heads in the sand until it is too late and the bank has to move in, take possession of the property and sell it — often at a very low price — to repay the debt.

Bank policies on calling in debts can vary, so never assume the type of loan an owner holds or advise a distressed property owner without being very sure of your facts. Often, lenders are very reticent to give out information to agents so it's important to have your sellers on side to pass on key information.

Your job is to convince a distressed property owner that you will be doing your best to find a buyer who will pay more than the lender can achieve if the property is repossessed.

Finding Out Whether the Seller Has a Legitimate Hardship

Here in Australia and New Zealand when the real estate market collapsed from 2008 to 2012, home values in some markets fell 50 per cent from their peak, particularly in the luxury market. Many people felt frustrated and discouraged about losing their hard-earned payments and much of their equity. In some areas, homes decreased in value by hundreds of thousands of dollars. The distressed-sale process came into being to deal with homeowners with legitimate financial difficulties. When news got out about this selling option, banks were inundated with people who wanted out of homes that were worth less than the mortgage amounts. Banks today are looking for buyers with true hardship, not just people who don't want to pay more on their loan than the home is worth. Because you'll have to do a lot of work to get a distressed sale approved, only work with clients who have legitimate hardships.

A true hardship is something like the loss of a job or a major medical issue that incurs high debt. It involves having an unsustainable debt structure in monthly payments and overall debt. It's not, 'I make a reasonable income, but I just don't want to pay anymore.'

Selecting the Right Buyer

The right buyer in a distressed-sale transaction is essential to success. The buyer has to be willing to wait in the same limbo as the seller. The buyer needs to understand and accept that it could be at least 90 to 120 days before the sellers will hear anything back from the bank.

When you're representing a seller, selecting the right buyer is essential. If the buyer withdraws his offer before the bank approves the price, you go all the way back to Go, but you don't get $200 like in Monopoly. You just get to start over. If you're not the patient type, this is not the avenue for you.

When the bank has approved the sale price, however, the buyer is a little bit easier to replace. A new buyer knows what the bank is willing to take, so the risk is decreased and the process can move more quickly.

Try to gain commitment from any distressed-sale buyer of their willingness to stick with the bank process as long as it takes. You can do months' worth of work only to have it blow up in the end because the buyer gets cold feet or becomes impatient.

Making Sure the Buyer is Lender Approved

The buyer must be able to perform (settle on the property) immediately should their offer be accepted. Although the distressed-sale process is long, buyers can't delay getting their financial ducks in a row. Look for buyers who are pre-approved or working toward pre-approval, just as they would for a regular sale. They should have a pre-approval letter for at least the amount stated in the purchase agreement. Often banks will submit a counteroffer for a higher sale price. If the buyer has already offered as much as the pre-approval letter allows, that can spell trouble. The bank may come back with a higher counteroffer, and you are now sunk with this buyer.

If you don't know the lender, call to set up an interview with the buyers' loan officer about where they are in the loan process. Some lenders may cite privacy rules, but keep pressing for information. You owe it to your seller. When will the buyers have loan approval? What else does the lender need before approving the loan? The last thing you want is a problem with financing at the 11th hour. It's important to note that a distressed-sale approval can expire or even be revoked at any time by the lender who owns the mortgage.

Pricing the Property Correctly

In a distressed sale, the pricing game is all about balance. The lender wants to see you make every effort to maximise the value of the property. But most buyers won't pay fair market value for this kind of sale because of the extra work, risk and delay. They want a better deal than they could get from an equity seller. On the other hand, if you vastly under-price the property, the bank will reject any offers you get and tell you to start over. All of your work, and the work of the buyer, seller and other agent, gets thrown out the window.

Your best strategy is to price the property at fair market value or slightly above. Then make solid and consistent price reductions until you get the property positioned in the right zone to generate activity and offers. Don't forget that market activity drops dramatically for properties that have been on the market more than six weeks. You need to reposition the price before that time elapses.

Doing an Outstanding Job

This might sound trite, but many agents pound a sign into the ground and forget about the distressed-sale home. Your job is to market this sale as robustly as you do an equity sale. When you receive an offer, craft the right counteroffer. Your job is to fight for your seller to get the highest possible price, the best terms and the best buyer.

Although at this stage most sellers will sign anything to get the millstone from around their necks, they may just be delaying challenges they'll encounter later. If it's not a reasonable deal, the bank probably won't approve it.

Do your due diligence in regards to the buyer. Some buyers make a large number of offers, tie up a large volume of properties, and then pick and choose when the banks respond. They select only the very best deals and leave the other sellers in the lurch. Check out whether your buyers have other properties tied up in pending deals. Can they actually afford to close all the transactions that are pending?

Finding Out Exactly What the Lender Needs

Each lender needs different information packaged in a different way. Some of the delays in distressed sales are caused by getting documentation to the lender in the form requested. This problem increases exponentially if the seller has both a first and second mortgage. Each lender will operate differently. Whatever is requested in whatever format, give the lenders exactly what they need. An incomplete package of information about your seller's financial situation will go nowhere.

Following Up Tenaciously

Have you heard the saying, 'The squeaky wheel gets the grease'? That is so true in distressed sales. You have to be that squeaky wheel in the lender's ear. Use phone calls and emails in combination to continually follow up on the progress of the file.

You'll encounter obstacles, but you must push through them. At this stage, you need two things: Tenacity and problem-solving skills. Don't let your sellers get squirrelly. They can easily lose faith and give up hope in the process. They may say to you, 'I'm not giving that lender one more document.' You can respond with, 'I understand that they're asking for everything and the kitchen sink, but you have to be patient and not get frustrated. In the end, this is your way out, and we need to make this work.' The distressed sale is akin to a financial colonoscopy; it's not pleasant . . . and not meant to be.

Being Knowledgeable about the Seller's Liability after the Sale

In terms of the liability that a seller has after the sale if the full mortgage amount isn't paid off, conditions may differ depending on which area you are in. In most regions, first and second mortgages are treated differently. The second mortgage is often treated as a consumer loan, so it may follow the seller after the distressed sale unless the lender signs a document releasing the seller from liability. Most consumers are unaware of this issue, so it is up to you to do your homework thoroughly to understand all the possible ramifications.

Be sure your sellers read all the terms and conditions of the distressed-sale documents. They need to read, sign and accept them. If they have questions, direct them to their solicitor to answer questions specific to the fine print. Don't answer those questions yourself; you'll assume too much liability — this is too risky an area for you to venture into.

Staying in Touch after the Distressed Sale is Complete

Real estate is a referral-based business. If you want to build your business, others must recommend you to their friends, neighbours and relatives. If one of your clients is in a distressed-sale situation, he may know other people who are contemplating the same thing. Although it's hard to tactfully ask whether sellers have other friends in financial trouble, you can present yourself as a person who is willing to help them. The key is to connect the discussion with how difficult navigating the distressed sale has been for this seller, just as it is for many people. This will open the door for sellers to talk about people who may be in a similar situation.

Don't forget about your sellers. Keep in touch, because if they work at it they may be able to re-enter the real estate market in two to three years. If they begin to save money right away and re-establish a solid payment history on their debts, they'll be credit-worthy buyers more quickly than if they had gone through foreclosure.

Appendix

Useful Resources and Websites

When you're starting out in real estate sales or perhaps looking to move to the next level, it can be confusing as to who and what are the best options to turn to. For this reason, we've provided here some really useful resources and websites to access for your ongoing career success.

Customer Relationship Management Systems (CRMs)

These days you can access CRMs to help you manage your database, plan for prospecting and generating leads, create letters, flyers and templates for buyers and sellers, enter goal setting and key performance indicators, record marketing ideas and much more.

CRM options for real estate agents include the following:

- LockedOn `www.lockedon.com`
- My Desktop `www.mydesktop.com.au`
- Property Suite `www.propertysuite.co.nz`

Real Estate Sales Trainers and Coaches

A god real estate trainer, and one that fits in with your sales approach, can really help you achieve your life goals and maximise sales.

Options include the following:

- Glenn Twiddle, founder of Glenn Twiddle Real Estate Training. Glenn is a trainer, coach and mentor — `www.glenntwiddle.com.au/blog`.
- Aaron Shiner and Ray Wood, providing sales training, coaching and mentoring programs — `www.bestagentshq.com`.

- Tom Panos, Real Estate Advertising Director for News Limited. Tom is a trainer, auctioneer and speaker — www.tompanos.com.au.
- Peter Hutton, co-founder of Brand You. Peter is a branding and marketing expert, coach and author — www.brandyoublog.com.au.
- Peter Brewer, founder of REBarcamp Australia and consultant at Inlinemediabiz. Peter provides real estate management and sales coaching — www.thatpeterbrewer.com.
- Mark Dwyer, founder of Sales Trainer Active. Mark is a trainer, author and coach — www.salestrainer.com.au.
- Mat Steinwede, award-winning real estate agent, author and speaker — matsteinwede.com.
- Jet Xavier, peak performance mindset coach, NLP practitioner and leadership coach — www.jetxavier.com.
- John Abbott, provides sales and auctioneer training for Australasia — www.johnabbott.co.nz.
- Ian Keightley, provides specialist sales training and real estate services — www.salescoach.co.nz.

Index

• A •

• B •

• C •

• D •

• M •

• Q •

• R •

• S •

• T •

• U •

• V •

• W, Y •

Notes

Notes

About the Authors

Terri M. Cooper entered the real estate industry in the early 1990s after a professional background in the fields of psychology, coaching and training. She was a hugely successful agent for over 12 years, with many industry awards putting her firmly into the upper echelons of real estate sales in Australia. She was awarded membership of the REMAX Gold Club for high performing agents from 2002 to 2004 and was among the top twenty REMAX sales agents throughout Australia in November 2005.

Terri's extremely successful background in real estate sales, her extensive training and coaching credentials, and her qualifications in the field of psychology and communications combine to give her a unique position among real estate trainers. She is also a qualified Master NLP coach, which gives her training a further, powerful edge. Participants not only gain industry skills but are also given powerful insights and strategies to eliminate personal roadblocks to success.

Under the banner of Real Estate Mastery, Terri and her team of trainers have been offering coaching and training to the real estate industry since 2005. Her training business now is almost 100 per cent referral-based, testifying to the personal commitment she has to each and every student, and the massive improvements in sales results for participants and sales teams. A by-product of this has been incredible personal growth for graduates of her trainings.

In addition to her trainings, Terri has co-authored *Women on Top — Against the Odds*, a popular and well-received book profiling the journeys of many women who overcame huge personal and professional challenges to succeed. She is in the process of authoring further books in this series, focusing on specific industries and giving support and inspiration to others. The next one in the pipeline will profile exceptional women in the real estate field.

Terri is in high demand as a speaker at numerous industry seminars, a regular guest on real estate radio, and a regular contributor to industry magazines with her insightful articles.

She lives in Brisbane, Australia, with her partner, Dennis. They love to travel overseas, to the heartland of the beautiful Aussie outback and to the beautiful North and South Islands of New Zealand, meeting people from all walks of life, and experiencing the best of what this life has to offer.

Dirk Zeller has been a licensed realtor, speaker, coach, investor and real estate industry expert for more than 20 years. As an agent he quickly rose to the top of the real estate field. Throughout his sales career, Dirk was recognised numerous times as one of the leading agents in North America. He has been described by industry insiders as the most successful agent in terms of high production with life balance. His ability to sell more than 150 homes annually while only working Monday through Thursday is legendary in the real estate field.

Dirk turned his selling success into coaching significance through founding Real Estate Champions. Real Estate Champions is the premier coaching company in the real estate industry, with clients worldwide. Dirk has created custom performance-improvement programs for Century 21, Coldwell Banker, and ERA Real Estate that are taught worldwide. These programs and others like them have changed the lives of hundreds of thousands of real estate agents across the globe.

Dirk is one of the most published authors in the areas of success, life balance, sales training, and business development in the real estate field. He has more than 500 published articles to his credit. His blog and newsletter, *Coaches Corner,* is read by more than 200,000 subscribers. He has authored ten books, including a number of *For Dummies* titles:

Your First Year in Real Estate
Success as a Real Estate Agent For Dummies
Telephone Sales For Dummies
The Champion Real Estate Agent
The Champion Real Estate Team
Successful Time Management For Dummies
Thriving in the Marketplace For Dummies
Selling All in One For Dummies
Effective Time Management For Dummies
Running a Great Meeting in a Day For Dummies

Dirk is also one of the most sought-after speakers in the real estate arena. He has been the keynote speaker for real estate and sales conferences on five continents.

Besides contributing to the real estate agent community, Dirk and his wife of 23 years, Joan, are very active in their church. They live with their 11-year-old son, Wesley, and 8-year-old daughter, Annabelle, in Bend, Oregon.

Dedication

From Terri: I would like to dedicate this book to every agent who has a passionate desire to do whatever it takes to succeed in the world of real estate sales. The skills, strategies, tips, anecdotes and insights within these pages have been gleaned over many years in the trenches, and my hope is that you use this book as your personal mentor. Let the words support and guide you through the exciting journey you are on.

From Dirk: So many people have contributed to my success in life, from my parents to my two brothers, my mentors and coaches, and now my two children, Wesley and Annabelle. No one, however, has contributed to my success in the real estate field more than my wife, Joan. I dedicate this book to her: My supporter, encourager, coach, role-play partner, accountability partner, and best friend. The success that has been achieved in real estate sales, writing, speaking, training and coaching was achieved only through our partnership. We did it together! Some 23 years later, I'm still amazed at God's grace in giving me a wife without compare.

Authors' Acknowledgements

From Terri: Firstly I give every credit to the amazing For Dummies team at Wiley — from the first contact with Clare Dowdell, who first approached me to co-author this book, to her colleagues Kerry Laundon, acquisitions editor, Dani Karvess, project editor and Charlotte Duff, copy editor. Your advice and help has been invaluable.

And how could I not mention Dirk Zeller, without whom this book would not have existed? Dirk authored the US version of this book, and his incredible research and original content amazes me in every page. He is a true industry professional and my own contribution owes an incredible vote of thanks to him. Every sales agent in Australia and New Zealand now has the benefit of his vast experience.

My partner, Dennis, and my beautiful family and friends have always supported, encouraged and believed in me and for their support I will always be grateful.

And, last but not least, I would like to acknowledge the countless industry professionals who have made my career the exciting journey that it has been. Many wonderful agents and coaches have walked with me on my journey — too many to name — but I will never forget the transformation that resulted from your presence in my life. You congratulate me in good times and support me when things sometimes go awry. Thank you all and my very best wishes go with you!

From Dirk: Just as a successful business is always a collaborative effort, so is a book. Although I receive the unfair lion's share of the credit, countless others are behind the scenes making me look good.

To the team at Real Estate Champions, an incredible group of people who change people's lives each day, you are the best. Thank you to our support staff of Julie Porfirio, whose loyalty all these years means so much to me. To Wende Fletcher, who has also been with me for a couple of tours of duty between family responsibilities. You two ladies are unmatched in your value . . . Thanks.

To our coaches and salespeople who really change the lives of everyone they touch; to Al Mayer, who for years has been an outstanding mentor and coach for Real Estate Champions; and to Caryn Yates, who is the best Virtual Training Coach in the sales industry.

I also need to thank the team at Wiley: Tracy Boggier, acquisitions editor, and Linda Brandon, project editor. You are truly pros at what you do.

Lastly, I must thank my personal clients and our Real Estate Champions clients. With you constantly challenging us and passionately wanting to improve, you drive us to work so hard to stay ahead and to build new programs and intellectual property to enhance your business and lives. It would be easy to become complacent, but you don't let us. Thanks!

Publisher's Acknowledgements

We're proud of this book; please send us your comments through our online registration form located at `dummies.custhelp.com`.

Some of the people who helped bring this book to market include the following:

Acquisitions, Editorial and Media Development

Project Editor: Charlotte Duff

Acquisitions Editor: Clare Dowdell

Editorial Manager: Dani Karvess

Production

Graphics: diacriTech

Technical Reviewer: Peter Ford, Raymond D. Modglin

Proofreader: Kerry Laundon

Indexer: Don Jordan

The author and publisher would like to thank the following copyright holders, organisations and individuals for their permission to reproduce copyright material in this book:

- **Cover image:** © iStockphoto.com/MarsBars
- **Chapter 11, p. 220, sidebar 'Using technology to market yourself and your properties':** Agent Brand Co. Peter Hutton is the CEO of Agent Brand Co. Peter is known for creating 'Locally-Famous' Real Estate Agencies. He works exclusively with owners of small independent agencies.

Every effort has been made to trace the ownership of copyright material. Information that enables the publisher to rectify any error or omission in subsequent editions is welcome. In such cases, please contact the Legal Services section of John Wiley & Sons Australia, Ltd.

Business & Investing

978-1-74216-998-9
$45.00

978-1-118-22280-5
$39.95

978-1-118-39670-4
$39.95

978-0-73030-584-2
$24.95

978-1-74216-971-2
$39.95

978-1-11864-122-4
$39.95

978-1-11857-255-9
$34.95

978-0-73037-807-5
$29.95

Reference

978-1-118-49327-4
$34.95

978-1-118-30525-6
$19.95

978-1-118-30521-8
$12.95

978-0-7303-0442-5
$24.95

Order today! Contact your Wiley sales representative.

Available in print and e-book formats.

Business

Bookkeeping For Dummies, Australian & New Zealand Edition
978-1-74216-971-2

Business Planning Essentials For Dummies
978-1-11864-126-2

Creating a Business Plan For Dummies
978-1-118-64122-4

Getting Started in Book-keeping For Dummies, Australian Edition
978-1-74246-874-7

Getting Started in Small Business For Dummies, 2nd Australian & New Zealand Edition
978-1-11822-284-3

Getting Started in Small Business IT For Dummies, Australian & New Zealand Edition
978-0-7303-7668-2

Leadership For Dummies, Australian & New Zealand Edition
978-0-7314-0787-3

Making Money on eBay For Dummies
978-1-74216-977-4

MYOB Software For Dummies, 7th Australian Edition
978-1-74216-998-9

QuickBooks For Dummies, 2nd Australian Edition
978-1-74246-896-9

Small Business For Dummies, 4th Australian & New Zealand Edition
978-1-118-22280-5

Success as a Real Estate Agent For Dummies, Australian & New Zealand Edition
978-0-73030-911-6

Successful Job Interviews For Dummies, Australian & New Zealand Edition
978-0-730-30805-8

Successful Online Start-Ups For Dummies, Australian & New Zealand Edition
978-1-118-30270-5

Writing Resumes and Cover Letters For Dummies, 2nd Australian & New Zealand Edition
978-0-730-30780-8

Xero For Dummies
978-1-118-57255-9

Finance & Investing

Buying Property For Dummies, 2nd Australian Edition
978-0-7303-7556-2

CFDs For Dummies, Australian Edition
978-1-74216-939-2

Charting For Dummies, Australian Edition
978-0-7314-0710-1

DIY Super For Dummies, 2nd Australian Edition
978-0-7303-7807-5

Exchange-Traded Funds For Dummies, Australian & New Zealand Edition
978-0-7303-7695-8

Getting Started in Property Investing For Dummies, Australian Edition
978-1-183-9674-2

Getting Started in Shares For Dummies, 2nd Australian Edition
978-1-74246-885-3

Investing For Dummies, 2nd Australian Edition
978-1-74216-851-7

Making the Most of Retirement For Dummies
978-0-7314-0939-6

Managed Funds For Dummies, Australian Edition
978-1-74216-942-2

Online Share Investing For Dummies, Australian Edition
978-0-7314-0940-2

Property Investing For Dummies, 2nd Australian Edition
978-1-1183-9670-4

Share Investing For Dummies, 3rd Australian Edition
978-1-74246-889-1

Sorting Out Your Finances For Dummies, Australian Edition
978-0-7314-0746-0

Superannuation For Dummies, 2nd Edition
978-0-7314-0715-6

Superannuation: Planning Your Retirement For Dummies
978-0-7314-0982-2

Tax for Australians For Dummies, 2013–14 Edition
978-0-730-30584-2

Order today! Contact your Wiley sales representative.

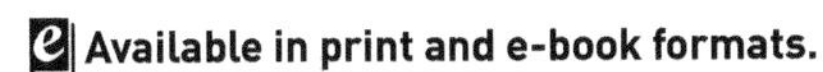

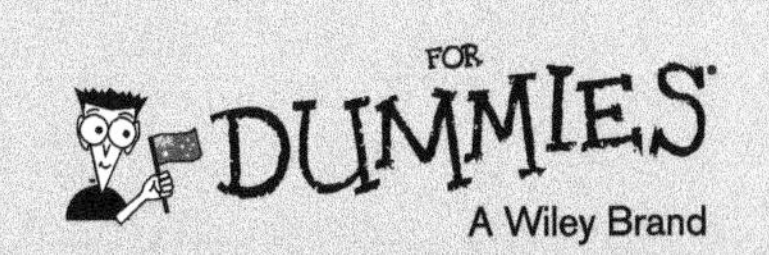

Fitness

Aussie Rules For Dummies, 2nd Edition
978-0-7314-0595-4

Cycling For Dummies, Australian & New Zealand Edition
978-0-7303-7664-4

Fishing For Dummies, 2nd Australian & New Zealand Edition
978-1-74216-984-2

Fitness For Dummies, Australian & New Zealand Edition
978-1-74031-009-3

Pilates For Dummies, Australian Edition
978-1-74031-074-1

Rugby Union For Dummies, 2nd Australian & New Zealand Edition
978-0-7303-7656-9

Weight Training For Dummies, 2nd Australian & New Zealand Edition
978-1-74031-044-4

Yoga For Dummies, Australian & New Zealand Edition
978-1-74031-059-8

History

Australian History For Dummies
978-1-74216-999-6

Australian Politics For Dummies
978-1-74216-982-8

Indigenous Australia For Dummies
978-1-742-16963-7

Kokoda For Dummies, Australian Edition
978-0-7303-7699-6

Tracing Your Family History Online For Dummies, Australian Edition
978-1-74031-071-0

Health & Health Care

Beating Sugar Addiction For Dummies, Australian & New Zealand Edition
978-1-118-64118-7

Being a Great Dad For Dummies
978-1-742-16972-9

Breast Cancer For Dummies, Australian Edition
978-1-74031-143-4

Dad's Guide to Pregnancy For Dummies, Australian & New Zealand Edition
978-0-7303-7735-1

Food & Nutrition For Dummies,Australian & New Zealand Edition
978-0-7314-0596-1

IVF & Beyond For Dummies, Australian Edition
978-1-74216-946-0

Kids' Food Allergies For Dummies, Australian & New Zealand Edition
978-1-74246-844-0

Living Gluten-Free For Dummies, Australian Edition, 2nd Edition
978-0-730-30484-5

Menopause For Dummies, Australian Edition
978-1-740-31140-3

Pregnancy For Dummies, 3rd Australian & New Zealand Edition
978-0-7303-7739-9

Type 2 Diabetes For Dummies, Australian Edition
978-1-118-30362-7

Reference

Cryptic Crosswords For Dummies
978-1-118-30521-8

English Grammar For Dummies, 2nd Australian Edition
978-1-118-49327-4

English Grammar Essentials For Dummies, Australian Edition
978-1-118-49331-1

Freelancing for Australians For Dummies
978-0-7314-0762-0

Passing Exams For Dummies, 2nd Edition
978-0-730-30442-5

Solving Cryptic Crosswords For Dummies
978-1-118-30525-6

Writing Essays For Dummies
978-0-470-74290-7

Order today! Contact your Wiley sales representative.

Available in print and e-book formats.

FOR DUMMIES
A Wiley Brand

CPSIA information can be obtained
at www.ICGtesting.com
Printed in the USA
LVHW110003241221
707030LV00006B/445